# FROM THE VAULT

# London Free Press
# FROM THE VAULT

A Photo-History of London to 1950

FROM THE COLLECTION OF THE WESTERN UNIVERSITY ARCHIVE

JENNIFER GRAINGER

With forewords by *London Free Press*
Editor-in-Chief Joe Ruscitti
and Western University Archivist Robin Keirstead

BIBLIOASIS
WINDSOR, ONTARIO

FIRST EDITION

Library and Archives Canada Cataloguing in Publication

Grainger, Jennifer, author
London free press : from the vault / Jennifer Grainger.

Includes bibliographical references and index.
ISBN 978-1-77196-182-0 (hardcover)

1. London (Ont.)--History. 2. London (Ont.)--History--Pictorial works. I. Title.

FC3099.L65G736 2017 971.3'26 C2017-901965-1

Edited by Sharon Hanna
Copy-edited by Allana Amlin
Typeset and designed by Chris Andrechek and Ellie Hastings

Published with the generous assistance of the Canada Council for the Arts, which last year invested $153 million to bring the arts to Canadians throughout the country, and the financial support of the Government of Canada. Biblioasis also acknowledges the support of the Ontario Arts Council (OAC), an agency of the Government of Ontario, which last year funded 1,709 individual artists and 1,078 organizations in 204 communities across Ontario, for a total of $52.1 million, and the contribution of the Government of Ontario through the Ontario Book Publishing Tax Credit and the Ontario Media Development Corporation.

PRINTED AND BOUND IN CANADA

# Contents

# FOREWORD
## by *London Free Press* Editor-in-Chief Joe Ruscitti

On a wall in a corridor in the *Free Press* building hang 25 elegantly-framed photos. Almost all were taken before 1930. Some also appear in this equally elegant book you hold in your hands.

Read as a group, they tell a pretty detailed story about what it took to put out a newspaper about 100 years ago, give or take a few years.

Until recently, I have hurried past to my office most weekdays without a glance—a little like how after a while you might barely notice the carefully hung family photos on a wall at home.

What does any of this have to do with *From the Vault: A Photo-History of London to 1950*?

About the same time the final touches were being put on this collection, it was announced that 369 York Street had been sold and *Free Press* staff were moving for the fifth or sixth time in the history of the newspaper.

So although the timing is happenstance, we've lately been opening the 'vaults' literally and figuratively around the office, too—and not just to help gather the extraordinary images collected here, the largest part of which were captured by *Free Press* photographers and are held now in the *London Free Press* Collection of Photographic Negatives at Western University's Archives.

Studying that wall of photos again for the first time in a while, it's hard not to be a little in awe of the many kinds of craftsmanship it took to produce quality photographs available day after day to thousands of newspaper readers. One thing is for sure: this is not posting a selfie on Instagram.

First, of course, consider the dexterity, physical and mental—and the bulky manual equipment—needed for a photographer to be in the right place and time for just the right image.

Then, the red glow of the darkroom to develop the film—or, perhaps, glass-plate negative.

But also the noise and ink stains of the press room.

The drawer after long, thin drawer of letters in the typesetting or composing room.

And the heat and grime of the stereotype room. (Thirty years in journalism and I had to look it up: it's the metal platemaking room and, not incidentally, the origin of the meaning of the word as you know it now.)

Like the rooms themselves, many of the skills that the rooms were built to house are obsolete in a digital world.

But ask yourself: would many of the images in this book sourced from *Free Press* archives be with us today if not for the many craftspeople gathering in those rooms day in and day out—and not for any idea so grand as capturing history, but for the more prosaic business of printing a daily newspaper?

That old saying about journalism being a first rough draft of history? Maybe.

But, though our work stations and tools are different today—certainly cleaner—it seems just as unlikely that the faces bending to their work in the photos on the wall then were thinking any more than *Free Press* staff are now of accomplishing anything more than helping Londoners to understand yesterday. Or, in today's newsrooms, when photos and videos and stories are posted all day long over several digital platforms, to understand an hour ago.

We are taking the photos hanging in that corridor with us to our new office. They are a treasure.

As is this collection. Maybe you'll take it with you to your next home, too.

*October 2017*

# FOREWORD

## by Western University Archivist Robin Keirstead

While one might argue whether a picture is indeed "worth a thousand words," for many the sentiment certainly rings true—especially when looking at the range of images presented in such a volume as *From the Vault: A Photo-History of London to 1950*. Photographs can be among the most compelling and evocative of archival documents, especially when presented as a collective visual history. They allow readers to "see" a story, a place, or an event in its original context or at least in the context provided the photographer. At the same time, they also invite readers to "tell their own story," imagining what was happening and why.

The City of London has a rich and storied history and many of the important people, places, and events that have shaped this history have been captured on film. The images selected by the editors of *From the Vault* (primarily—but not exclusively—from the collections of Western Archives) include a mixture of those that are well-known and those that have likely never appeared in print before. They document not only the public face of the City, but also aspects of life behind the scenes, the everyday experiences of ordinary Londoners. They show the evolution of London from its earliest days through to the end of the 1940s, depicting its vibrant downtown and distinct neighbourhoods, its evolving businesses and industries, its celebrations and special events, and the challenges and tragedies that have influenced the city's development.

Given the early technology with which many photographers were equipped, the quality of the images is striking. Whether a professional photographer "on assignment" or a family member simply trying to record a special event, we can marvel at the care with which they composed some of the images, while for others we can be thankful that they were able to capture moments in literally the blink of an eye.

To create such a visual history, one needs access to a wide selection of historic images and it is fortunate for the editors that they could choose from a vast assortment of photographic collections. Indeed, the richness of the collections made their selection no easy task.

The largest single source of images presented in *From the Vault* is the *London Free Press* Collection of Photographic Negatives. Donated to Western University over a period of several years, beginning in 1984, it is one of only a few large photographic collections from major Canadian newspapers available in publicly accessible archives. Currently preserved in Western's Archives and Research Collections Centre, it is one of Western Archives' signature collections. It comprises approximately 1.6 million negatives, covering the period from 1936 to 1992, that include not only those that actually appeared in the paper, but also all others taken by *Free Press* photographers during the period.

Not surprisingly, the *London Free Press* Collection is arguably Western Archives' most popular collection, attracting interest from all manner of patrons, ranging from academic researchers and students, local historians and documentary filmmakers, to members of the public. It is also among the most challenging for Western Archives' staff in terms of preservation and access. Beyond the sheer size of the collection, the physical nature and condition of the negatives require cold storage and special handling procedures. As well, as the original organization of most of the negatives is chronologically by the date of the photo assignment, rather than the date an image appeared in the paper (if it appeared at all) or by subject, successful retrieval often depends on the skill and perseverance of Archives' staff.

While the *London Free Press* Collection is the centrepiece of both the photographic holdings of Western Archives and the photographic history you hold in your hands, it was not the only source of images for *From the Vault*. Other notable photograph collections represented include the Hines Studio Collection, the Leonard Family Fonds, the Ronald Harris and O'Connor and Lancaster albums, the Kingsmill Family Fonds, and the Labatt Brewing Company Collection, as well Western's own regional photograph collection. In addition, the editors were able to round out the selection with images of the City from London Life, London Public Library, The Royal Canadian Regiment Museum, Museum London, and Library and Archives Canada.

Together, the images selected by the editors of this impressive volume provide an extensive—although by no means exhaustive—visual representation of London's history from its beginnings to 1950. The images are a tangible reminder of the immensely valuable collections of photographs and other archival records that are preserved and made available in archives—and libraries and museums—throughout London and its surrounding communities. Without the hard work and dedication of generations of local historians, archivists, librarians, and museum curators, a publication such as *From the Vault* would not be possible. Indeed, without them the contents of the 'vault' would be sparse indeed!

My colleagues and I in Western Archives are pleased to have been able to assist the editors to prepare this impressive volume. We hope you enjoy your trip back in time.

*October 2017*

# INTRODUCTION

Canada's London, on the banks of a river called the Thames, the unofficial capital of Southwestern Ontario—this is the city that over 380,000 people call home. It wasn't always the bustling mini-metropolis that it is today, however. For over 30 years after Lt.-Gov. John Graves Simcoe named it New London, it was a true Forest City, covered thick with trees and only a few scattered European settlers. From these humble beginnings, it has grown into the largest city between Detroit and Toronto, sitting roughly equidistant from each, and boasting its own variety of industries, services, cultural activities—and a proud history to boot.

The North and South branches of the Thames meet at the centre of the city at a location called "the Forks." It was here, where the river unites, that London was born—a spot chosen for its geographic advantage and economic potential. When Lt.-Gov. Simcoe and his party first set eyes on the Forks in March 1793, he envisioned this site as the future capital of Upper Canada. While his plans never quite came to fruition—due to differing ideas from political giant Guy Carleton, First Baron Dorchester—and York (Toronto) became the provincial capital, the future of London was still in motion. Settlers were slowly attracted to the area, sharing the vision that Simcoe saw. For this frontier settlement, the Thames River was essential to everyday life. It provided a means of subsistence and was the primary mode of transportation, connecting the settlers with the rest of the province. With time, as the settlement matured and roads and railways were built, the Thames became London's playground—a spot for fishing, boating, swimming, and the like, especially in the park called Springbank. Of course, devastating floods, such as those of 1883 and 1937, or the Victoria Steamboat Disaster, reminded that life besides the Thames could be precarious. However, even from the days of first settlement, the Thames River was central to London's development—and perhaps even more so, to its identity as a place.

Even though London never became the capital of Upper Canada, the settlement would still find significant standing in the early province. At first, Vittoria in Norfolk County became the capital of the London District, being the site of the district jail and courthouse. After the Vittoria courthouse was destroyed in a fire in November 1825, however, the colonial government decided to move the district capital to the more centrally located Forks of the Thames, to the place named "London" over 30 years earlier. On January 1, 1826, London became the new administrative and legal centre of the London District, with Col. Thomas Talbot overseeing the erection of a new jail and courthouse and Surveyor-General Thomas Ridout instructing Mahlon Burwell to survey a village plot for a village called London. Not surprisingly, some of London's earliest downtown streets are named Talbot, Ridout, and Burwell.

The tiny frontier hamlet in the woods at first attracted men in the building trade, then attracted men who catered to the builders themselves by starting up businesses and hostelries. By 1827, a considerable amount of land had been cleared, streets laid out, and 20 to 30 buildings erected, including a temporary jail and courthouse, tavern, blacksmith shop, one or two shops, and some houses.

Ten years later, when the population of the village was just over 1,000, political events intervened to further spur the development of the London in the bush. The Rebellion of 1837 led in Upper Canada by William Lyon Mackenzie largely missed London, but as a result of the conflict a heightened British military presence was thought necessary in Upper Canada. In 1838, six companies of the 24th Regiment of Foot arrived in London. This was the beginning of the British garrison that would remain in London until after Confederation, departing in 1869. The garrison had a profound effect on the fledgling community as Londoners reaped the benefits of military spending at pioneer businesses. Baker Leonard Perrin received contracts to supply bread and other food to the garrison while Ellis Hyman's tannery received the army leather contract for boots and saddles. The soldiers also had a social impact on the community, organizing dances, sports, and sleighing parties. The officers opened a garrison theatre to perform London's earliest dramatic performances in December 1839. Military men brought news from Britain and other parts of the world in which they had been stationed, making London more connected with the world. The garrison developed London commercially and culturally, so that the community could call itself a town in 1840 when its population reached 1,716.

The town's boundaries expanded to keep pace with its population, laying more streets and carving out new lots in the 1830s. By 1840, the boundaries were extended all the way to Adelaide Street in the east and Huron Street in the north. Suburbs such as London East, London West, and London South developed during this period.

The burgeoning community was on track to cityhood, but needed a catalyst to spur it to the next benchmark of growth. The Great Western Railway

Scene at the fork of the Thames River, circa 1880s.

Company, incorporated in 1845, chose London, as the largest community in the district, to run their railroad through. The first official train arrived from Hamilton on December 15, 1853, and on January 17, 1854, the first train to travel the entire length of the GWR from Niagara to Windsor passed through London—to much fanfare. Once London was on the railway, merchants and industrialists were attracted to the community for its customer base as well as the capacity to transport raw materials and finished products. Not long afterwards, in October 1856, the London & Port Stanley Railway opened, connecting London to the Lake Erie port and further cementing London's role as the region's dominant trade hub. All roads—and railways—led to London. The population rose from 7,157 in 1852 to about 10,000 in 1853. City status was achieved on January 1, 1855 and the population jumped to 15,276 in 1856.

From there, London's industrial might only grew. After oil was discovered in Lambton County in 1857, it was soon being shipped by rail to London for refining and shipped out again after the processing was finished. Oil refining became one of nineteenth-century London's most important industries, spawning secondary industries such as the Canada Chemical Company, which made the sulphuric acid needed for the refining process. Sixteen London oil refiners united to form Imperial Oil in London in September 1880 to better compete with American giant Standard Oil.

Another important London industry was cigar manufacturing. By 1914, over 20 cigar factories in London produced 50,000,000 cigars a year, making London the second-largest cigar-manufacturing city in Canada after Montreal. Rail connections allowed London to import raw leaf tobacco and ship out the finished products. Industry also included several tanneries, foundries, flour mills, and the Labatt and Carling breweries. While industry began in the city's core, it wasn't long before many manufacturers required more space. London's suburb, London East, became the new manufacturing district, as downtown became a home for department stores, grand hotels, and bankers.

Unlike other Ontario towns that developed a strong "Rust-Belt" industrial identity, London attracted white-collar business as well as manufacturing. It developed a reputation as a banking city, a financial and legal centre. Savings, loan, and building societies provided money for mortgages at low interest rates. Canada Trust had its beginnings on Richmond Street as Huron & Erie Savings & Loan in 1864. Ontario Loan & Debenture was founded in 1870 on Dundas Street and was important for over a century until being taken over by Royal Trust.

London was especially known for insurance companies. One of the first was the Middlesex Mutual Insurance Society, organized in October 1858. Many more insurance offices followed, in the early days emphasizing fire insurance, as in the Ontario Mutual Fire Insurance Company or the Huron and Middlesex Mutual Fire Insurance Company. Life insurance also became more popular, the best-known institution being the iconic London Life. When London Life was founded in 1874, there were over 20 insurance companies in London. By 1922, a city directory listed over 160 Canadian, British, and American insurance providers at various London locations.

With its large skilled workforce, it makes sense that London also became a centre for education, training the next generation of lawyers, doctors, and bankers to feed its economy. Numerous schools opened to provide various levels of instruction to Londoners and young persons from the surrounding counties and beyond. Hellmuth Boys' and Ladies' Colleges and Sacred Heart Academy for girls were early schools for those who could afford them. London Collegiate Institute opened in 1878. Huron College opened in 1864, laying the foundation for Western University that officially opened in 1881. The London Normal School, later renamed London Teachers' College, opened its doors to the first student teachers in South London in 1900. Forest City Business College, later known as Westervelt College, opened in 1885 to teach business and office skills.

London was also the go-to place for medical treatment. The London Insane Asylum was known for its innovative treatment programs under its forward-thinking chief, Dr. Richard Maurice Bucke from 1877 to 1902. Victoria Hospital, founded as London General Hospital on South Street in 1875, was renamed in 1897 in honour of Her Majesty's Diamond Jubilee. St. Joseph's Hospital, founded by the Sisters of St. Joseph, originally opened in 1888 in the former home of lawyer, later judge, W.P.R. Street, but built themselves a large addition in 1892. Westminster Veterans' Hospital opened just south of the city in Westminster Township in 1920 to provide treatment for disabled veterans of the First World War. However, the city became known as leader in medical research as well as health care. It was in a house at Adelaide and Queens, in 1920, that Dr. Frederick Banting conceived the idea that led to the discovery of insulin.

The Shute Institute was opened by Drs. Evan and Wilfrid Shute in the former Waverley Estate at Grand Avenue and Ridout Street in 1948 to research the prevention of cardiovascular disease.

After the turn of the century, the city's population continued to grow, both through immigration and the annexation of suburb communities. In 1900, the population was 39,059, and in 1950, it had expanded to 94,027. While most Londoners were of British descent in those days, the city's reputation as a wealthy, white-collar, Protestant city was not entirely deserved. London's prosperous Catholic community had built the magnificent St. Peter's Cathedral as well as a host of smaller churches and separate schools. Moreover, numerous immigrants found their way to the Forks, laying the foundation for the multicultural community of later times. Fugitive slaves from the southern United States sought freedom in British territory before the Civil War and may have chosen London as their home to avoid bounty hunters patrolling towns closer to the border. Casimir Gzowski, an early Polish immigrant, was the engineer responsible for the construction of the early Blackfriars Bridge in about 1842. The first child born to Italian immigrants in London was Joseph Famularo in 1875. The first Jewish wedding in London was celebrated in 1881. Pantelis Karkampasis was the first Greek to settle in town in 1900, the first Ukrainian arrived in London in 1907, and Lem Wong's family became the first Chinese family in London in 1911. These were only the first of the large waves of immigrants who chose to make the Forest City home.

In London, the years leading up to 1950 were ones of great growth, political drama, economic highs and lows, and cultural achievement. Today, the city is fortunate to have a carefully preserved record of its buildings, its events, and its people in Western University's archives. The collections provide a window from which we can view London's vanished past and witness everything we missed—tragic river floods, demolished architecture, horse-drawn delivery wagons, electric streetcars, stores in which we can never shop, streets lined with Ford Model Ts, the day the King and Queen visited town, a massive street party at the end of World War II. Most valuable is the giant *London Free Press* Collection of Photographic Negatives—a veritable dream come true for historians and researchers of London and Southwestern Ontario's history. The *Free Press* was everywhere—documenting fall fairs, school openings, new businesses, devastating fires, bank robberies, sporting events, plowing matches, and 100th birthday celebrations on film—creating (whether they realized it or not) a record of this community, one that lives far beyond that day's paper. Thanks to the work of those eager journalists and roving news photographers—preserved by today's archivists—we can discover a London of a bygone era, our past through photographs in *From the Vault*.

Composing room at the London Free Press, 1936.

# ARCHITECTURE

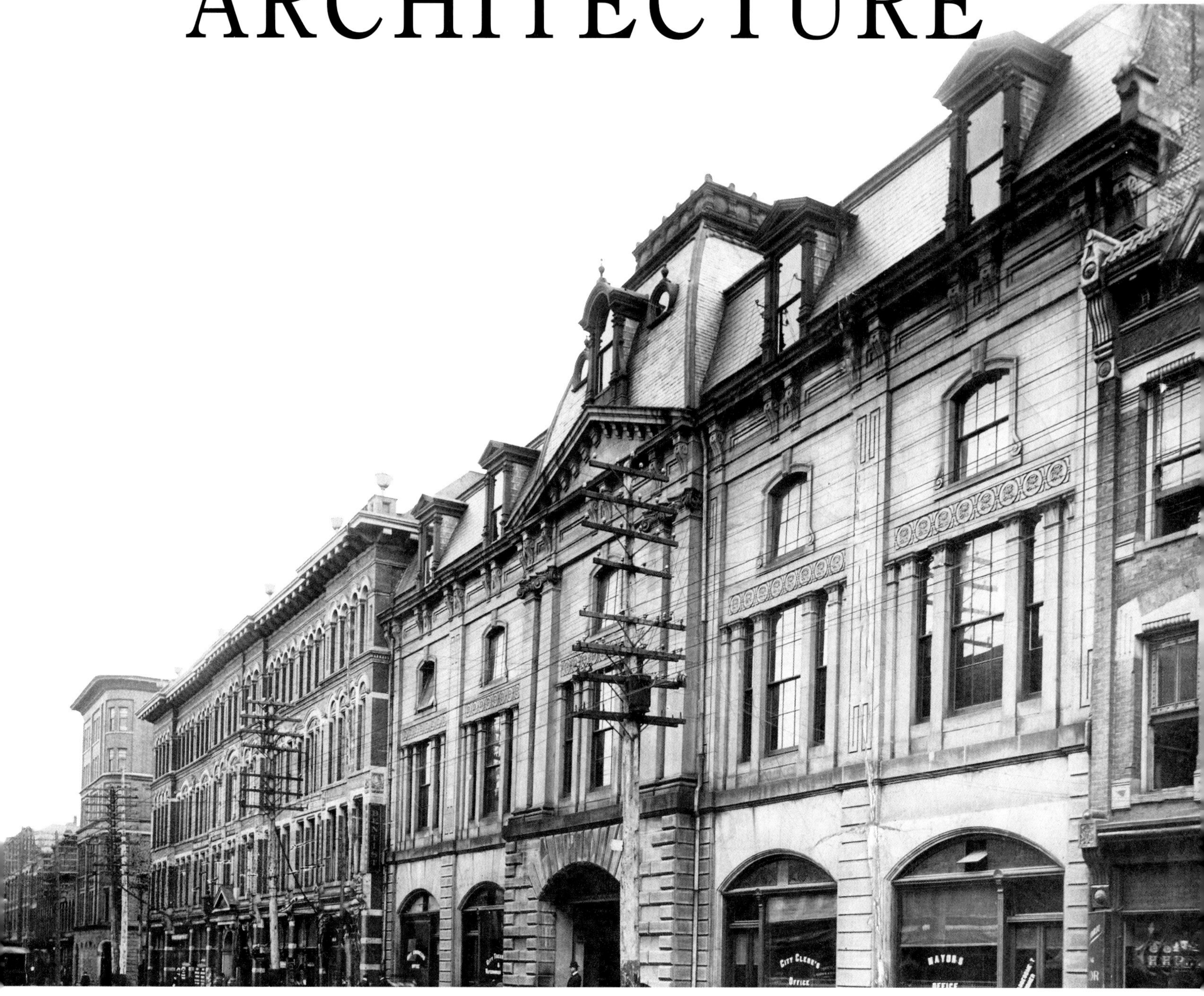

London's earliest buildings have, for the most part, not survived. Many burned down, but most were replaced when their pioneer owners had the means and opportunity to build better, more permanent structures. Our early settlers were no more fond of living in drafty, primitive log cabins than we would be. They replaced them with buildings of frame or brick as soon as possible. Brick, in fact, became the building material of choice for many homes as well as businesses. Not only was it solid and sturdy, it could withstand fire.

Our surviving buildings from earliest times are usually the ones best built—ones not intended to be temporary. The oldest building in London today is the Gothic-style Old Courthouse on Ridout Street next to the Thames, completed in about 1829, but acquiring several additions since. The city's oldest church is St. Paul's Cathedral, itself a replacement for an earlier St. Paul's that burned down in 1844. London's oldest home is Eldon House, built by the Harris family in 1834 and now a museum. The oldest surviving office buildings in the city are those in the Ridout Street Restoration, north of the Old Courthouse and south of Eldon House.

Frequently, our buildings have survived because they were adaptively reused. The Old Courthouse has become the Middlesex County Building; the mansion called Waverley has been repurposed as a retirement home; London East Town Hall is now the Aeolian Hall; many old houses in the core have become offices or have been subdivided into apartments.

London's great architecture, like monumental buildings elsewhere, was meant to awe its viewers. The Old Courthouse and jail were intended to intimidate the citizenry into keeping the peace and obeying the law. The churches, ostensibly built to provide spiritual comfort, might also be said to "remind" Christians into good behaviour. A millionaire's mansion was a physical display of his wealth—and a way to show off to peers. And London's banks and financial buildings were built to reflect the solidity and security of the services they provided. For example, the grandiose head office built by London Life in 1927 was intended to inspire confidence in its policyholders.

Many architectural styles contributed to the buildings of London, Ontario. There's Georgian—sturdy and secure, symmetrical and simple—found in both residential and commercial buildings such as 435 Ridout Street, part of the Ridout Restoration. Gothic Revival, asymmetrical with gingerbread around the eaves, can be found in many of London's older homes, although the most stirring example is the castle-like Old Courthouse. Some builders preferred Greek Revival with columns and elaborate doorways, as seen in the early Mechanics' Institute. There are Second Empire mansions with mansard roofs and dormer windows, as well as irregular-shaped Queen Annes with a variety of decorated surfaces, window shapes, and trim. In the twentieth century, Art Deco came along to strike a modern note in London's core with the Dominion Public Building.

Who were the architects behind these buildings? Many hailed from Toronto. London's first major architectural commission—the old Courthouse—was designed by John Ewart of York (now Toronto). The two cathedrals, St. Paul's and St. Peter's, were built by William Thomas and Joseph Connolly, respectively, both from the provincial capital. But London had many architects of its own, sometimes working individually and often together in partnerships or firms. Samuel Peters Jr. built the first Covent Garden Market building, Grosvenor Lodge, London's first City Hall, the City Hotel (later known as the Belvedere Hotel, still later as the Talbot Inn), and the row housing known as Camden Terrace. The prolific William Robinson designed London's first Crystal Palace, the mansion called Firbrae (later Blackfriars), Christ Church Anglican, the Crystal Block at Dundas and Richmond, St. Andrew's Presbyterian Church and manse, the Bishop's Palace next to St. Peter's Basilica, Reid's Crystal Hall, the 1873 City Hospital, and Springbank Pumphouse. Thomas H. Tracy built the second Mechanics' Institute, First Congregational (later Beecher United) Church, and the Grigg House hotel. George F. Durand was responsible for the second Crystal Palace, Waverley Mansion, the London Club, Talbot Street Baptist, the John Labatt mansion, London East Town Hall, and Colborne Street United Church. Robinson, Tracy, Durand & Co. created London Collegiate Institute. Tracy & Durand built the Masonic Temple and Grand Opera House. John Mackenzie Moore built the Elsie Perrin Williams home known as Windermere as well as London Life. O. Roy Moore built the 1932 Art Deco Kingsmill's department store. Moore, along with Victor J. Blackwell and John MacLeod Watt designed the Dominion Public Building. London was fortunate to have such extraordinary talent in these and other architects.

Most Londoners, of course, didn't live or work in great architecture. They lived in ordinary cottages or above stores and worked in factories or shops. Many of the buildings they called their own could be called eclectic in style, exhibiting characteristics of two or more styles. And many buildings were not defined by any style at all, but simply constructed out of easily available local building materials, such as wood or white brick. But buildings erected by forgotten architects or nameless owner-occupants were often built as sturdily as those built by London's elite architects.

After the Second World War, it was necessary to build many small homes as quickly and efficiently as possible for the large numbers of returning veterans and their families. Practical, unassuming, and built of cheap materials, the houses of the late 1940s were a unique by-product of the war, laying out the foundation for London's suburbs. While lacking the charm of Victorian terraces and office blocks, the small houses of such neighbourhoods as Bellwood Park are also a reflection of London's past.

One of London's oldest and most famous residences, "Thornwood," is pictured here in 1945, when it was 100 years old. On June 26, 1845, Henry C.R. Becher moved his family into the mansion that had its own school rooms, special nursery sections, library, billiards, gun and music rooms, plus 14 bedrooms for staff and servants. By 1945, five generations of the Becher family had lived there.

Looking south at the intersection of Richmond and York streets, 1865. The Holman Opera House is to the right, the Tecumseh House hotel to the left.

Originally military barracks, this imposing structure on the northwest corner of Dundas and Ridout had many uses, eventually being renovated into apartments. This is the current site of the front lawn of Museum London.

Spettigue Hall, 1874–75. Built in 1871 by Joseph Spettigue, this building on the southwest corner of Dundas and Clarence contained a concert hall on the second floor. When James Duffield bought the building in 1891, he closed the theatre and divided the space into a third floor, thus changing the facade.

Amberlay Lodge, 1870s. This attractive clapboard home was built on Wortley Road before South London was annexed by the city, during a time when large park lots such as this were readily available to homebuilders. The home has since been demolished, replaced by a brick structure.

The Custom House, circa 1875. Built on the northeast corner of Richmond Street and North Street (Queens Avenue) between 1870 and 1874, the building was one of the most imposing in nineteenth-century London. The spire in the background is that of North Street (Queens Avenue) Methodist Church. Although the Custom House was demolished in 1971, its ornate iron fence still surrounds the St. Paul's Cathedral grounds.

Dr. Joseph J. Lancaster's octagon house, north side of Dundas Street, east of Waterloo Street, circa 1875. Octagon houses were briefly the rage in the mid-nineteenth century, popularized by the American amateur architect Orson Squire Fowler. Dr. Lancaster stands on the lower steps while Mrs. Lancaster poses at the top and other family members stand on the balcony. The spire in the background is that of St. Andrew's Presbyterian Church.

The Edge Block, southeast corner of Dundas and Richmond, built in 1875 in the High Gothic style by William T. Edge. The building still stands, but now lacks its sign.

North Street (Queens Avenue) looking west from just east of Clarence Street, late 1870s. On the left, or south side, is North Street Methodist Church, while the spire of St. Paul's Cathedral is visible at far right. In the distance are the dark-shuttered windows of the Bank of British North America on the southeast corner of Richmond and North; the Post Office is just to its right; in the middle, far in the distance, the first Mechanics' Institute building on Talbot Street can be seen; and on the north-west corner of Richmond and North stand the Merchant's Bank and Bank of Montreal.

North Street (Queens Avenue) looking east from the roof of the Custom House at Richmond Street, 1873. The first cross street just beyond North Street Methodist Church is Park Avenue (Clarence Street) and the church on the left in the distance is St. Andrew's Presbyterian.

Richmond Street looking south towards Queens Avenue, circa 1875. On the right is the Bank of Montreal and the Merchants' Bank, while on the left is the towered Custom House and the Bank of British North America.

The Odd Fellows' Hall on the northeast corner of Dundas and Clarence Streets, 1880. It was demolished in the 1930s to make way for the Huron & Erie building.

The north side of Dundas Street looking east from Clarence Street, 1880. The Odd Fellows' Hall is on the corner.

Richmond Street looking north from Dundas, circa 1880. The magnificent Federal Bank on the northeast corner was built in 1878.

Col. Hocker's house at the corner of Queens and Wellington looks like a country estate in this undated photograph. The colonel is likely the man standing out front.

The Masonic Temple and Opera House on the northwest corner of King and Richmond was built in 1881 and burned in 1900. Just visible immediately to the north is the first City Hall.

The London Club was built in the Queen Anne style on the south side of Queens Avenue, east of Richmond, in 1881 as a club for London gentlemen.

Norwood House, residence of Bishop Isaac Hellmuth, built in 1871 next to Hellmuth Ladies' College.

A view of London in 1889 with Carling Brewery in the left foreground. Carling Creek runs under Talbot Street to the south of the brewery.

Locust Mount, built in 1853 for Elijah Leonard Jr., who built Western Ontario's first steam engine, on the west side of Talbot Street overlooking the Thames. Once one of London's finest homes, it remained in the Leonard family until 1895. Eventually it landed in the hands of a London developer who demolished the building after it burned in 2007.

Built on the northeast corner of Dundas and Rectory as the East London Town Hall in 1884, this building had many uses over the years. At the time this photo was taken in July 1946, it housed Fire Station No. 2 and Goodwill Industries. It is now the Aeolian Hall.

Waverley, built for Charles Goodhue in 1882, was later the home of the Smallman family. Built in South London on Hamilton Row (Grand Avenue), the driveway extended to Queen Street (Ridout Street). Now the Waverley Retirement Home, the building fronts on to Grand Avenue and the former driveway is the site of an apartment building, Ridout Towers.

Eldon House, July 1892. Built in 1834 by John Harris, it is now the oldest remaining home in London.

Victorian decor in the Eldon House drawing room, 1892.

The imposing London Post Office, circa 1890. Built in 1860 at the southwest corner of Queens and Richmond, it was superseded by the Dominion Public Building on the northwest corner in 1936 and demolished in 1953.

Victoria Hall, on the east side of Clarence Street between Dundas and King, photographed in about 1890. Originally housing a New Connexion Methodist Church, the YMCA purchased the building in 1878, renovated it and renamed it Victoria Hall. They occupied it until 1893 when it was sold to the Salvation Army.

A postcard view of Dundas Street looking east past Richmond Street before 1905. On the left is the Bank of Commerce, built as the Federal Bank by George Durand in 1878.

Canadian Packing Company's cornerstone was laid February 8, 1893, by Sir John Carling in Pottersburg, east of London. The company burned in the early 1900s, but was rebuilt, eventually becoming Coleman Packing.

Hyman Hall, northeast corner of Clarence and Queens, was used as Liberal Party headquarters from about 1905, and is now the London Life parking lot.

Side and front views of the Springbank Pavilion, built in 1898.

Ontario Street looking north from King, 1900s.

York Street looking west from Clarence, 1900s. The house next door and building with the Na-Dru-Co sign have been demolished, but the others stand across from the VIA Rail station in 2017.

St. James Street looking west from Hellmuth Avenue, circa 1910. In the distance is the Church of St. John the Evangelist, built in 1888.

"Buchan House," built in 1872, has had many uses over the years, including the Oakhurst School for Young Ladies and the London Institute of Musical Art. It took on the name Buchan House, after Governor-General John Buchan, Lord Tweedsmuir, after being taken over by the Canadian Legion in 1945. Originally a less pretentious building, the magnificent towers were added by owner Thomas Baker Escott in 1887. It is now My Sister's Place, a women's shelter.

The Thomas H. Carling residence, 677 Talbot Street, circa 1895. Thomas, founder of Carling brewery, was the father of Sir John Carling.

The east side of Wellington Street, across from Victoria Park, in the 1900s. These Victorian houses were torn down to make way for Centennial Hall, Reginald Cooper Square, and City Hall in the 1960s.

Two souvenir postcards show views of the Reid Crystal Hall disaster, July 16, 1907. While the two cards do not agree on the number of people dead, seven is the most likely estimate. Completed in 1873, the building was on the south side of Dundas between Richmond and Clarence. An inquest determined the structure had been damaged by a fire in 1882, weakening its brick walls. As a result of this disaster, building inspection began in London in 1908.

The east side of Richmond Street, looking south past Dundas. The Bank of Commerce, built in 1905, and the Edge Block are shown.

The YMCA building on the west side of Wellington Street between Dundas and Queens, 1914. Designed by the architectural partnership of Moore and Henry, it opened on January 1, 1897. The building was destroyed by arson on January 4, 1981, forcing the ruins to be demolished and the "Y" to rebuild at King and Waterloo. Next door is longtime mayor George Wenige's shop, Bicycle and Motor Sales Co.

The R.A. Brown residence, on the site of what is now Beal Secondary School, circa 1910.

Working-class homes on the south side of Sycamore Street, 1918. The houses could be purchased for $1,200 with payments from $10 to $12 a month.

The north side of Central Avenue looking east from Wellington, 1913.

Looking east along Dufferin Avenue towards Colborne Street, September 1915. The young people strolling along the sidewalk may be students returning home from school at nearby London Collegiate Institute.

Houses at Victoria and Waterloo, circa 1923. This neighbourhood between downtown and the soon-to-be-built University of Western Ontario would become known as Old North.

The Masonic Hall on the north side of Queens Avenue between Clarence and Wellington, 1920s. This is now the site of London Life.

London and Western Trusts was founded by George Gibbons and others in 1896. The company moved into this Neo-Classical building at 353 Richmond in 1921. Eventually the company merged with Huron & Erie, but their name remains on this stately structure to this day.

The Post Office on Richmond Street, July 1927. The date suggests the decorations are for the Diamond Jubilee of Confederation.

The brand new City Hall, northeast corner of Dundas and Wellington, in a 1930 postcard. Built in 1928, incorporating an earlier PUC building, the juncture between the two buildings was disguised with the monumental frontispiece with the city's crest at top. While some called the design "lacklustre," it reflected the values of stability and responsibility the city wished to convey.

Dundas Street looking west in 1934. On the left is the Armouries, Huron & Erie building, and Hotel London.

The Bank of Montreal, CFPL Broadcasting, and the *London Free Press*, southwest corner of Richmond and Queens sometime after 1933.

These four pictures show the construction of the Dominion Public Building on the west side of Richmond Street between Queens and Fullerton, which began in April 30, 1935, and was completed in 1936.

High winds collapsed a partially constructed house on Delaware (Devonshire) Avenue, just south of the city limits, in November 1938. Eight workers were injured by falling timbers. The house was being built by London contractor Harry L. Sifton.

The castellated towers of the Courthouse were badly in need of repair in October 1938—so much so that the *Free Press* reported if they were not repaired shortly they would have to be demolished. The photo shows plaster fallen away and bricks crumbling. The cost of repairs was set at $600, of which the city had to pay 60 percent. Presumably the repairs were made, since the towers are there today.

Kerwood United Church in western Middlesex County was hit by a cyclone the night of July 13, 1939. Wind toppled the large church chimney, causing bricks to fall through the roof into the pulpit. Here, Kerwood resident Harry Easterbrook examines the debris.

246 Richmond Street was built by Dr. O'Flaherty, medical officer of the 83rd regiment at about the time of the Rebellion of 1837. It was lived in by Sir James Alexander, assistant to Col. Wetherall, Commander of the first Royal Regiment. For 73 years it was lived in by the O'Hearn family. Pictured here in May 1939, it was "deserted and alone," condemned by the Board of Health.

A view looking west along Queens Avenue, taken March 26, 1941. On the cross street, Richmond, are from left to right, the HMCS Prevost, the post office, and, on the other side of Queens Avenue, the Dominion Public Building, built 1936. Note that at this time Queens was not a one-way street; it became one-way heading west in 1950.

Kingsmill Terrace or Butler Terrace, on the southwest corner of Queens Avenue and Clarence Street, circa 1940. Owned by Sidney Kingsmill of Boston, "Ma" Butler operated a rooming house in the building. It was demolished in 1957.

The Edge Block, southeast corner of Dundas and Richmond, May 1941. The building was sold in 1929 to the United Cigar Company who still occupied the building in 1941. Note the streetcar tracks in this photo; although the last trolley had been retired in the fall of 1940, the tracks had yet to be removed.

The remains of a building at Thames and King streets, after it collapsed on February 11, 1945. Jacob Miller, salvage dealer, was working in the section seconds before it collapsed due to the weight of too much snow.

Dundas Street, looking east past Clarence Street, in 1941. The Art Deco Huron & Erie Building on the northeast corner of Dundas and Clarence towers above the other buildings. At nine storeys, it was the tallest building in the city when completed in 1931.

Mrs. V.L. Smith and sons Dick and Donald pose in front of their new home at Trafalgar and St. Julien streets. Their house was the first to be completed for veterans under the agreement between the city and local contractors in 1946. The scheme saw the city sell lots to contractors for $1 each—on the condition that they erect a house immediately and sell it to ex-service personnel. Houses were $4,500 and $5,000, depending on the number of bedrooms. Mr. Smith had been a sergeant in the Royal Canadian Army Medical Corps.

In February 1945, 16 wartime houses in Ealing were completed out of a planned 50. The homes, being constructed by Crown Corporation Wartime Housing Ltd., were either 24' x 24' or 28' x 24' and rented at $22 or $25 a month.

In late January, 1945, the veranda on this apartment house on Talbot Street just north of Horton collapsed from the weight of snow from several winter storms. The veranda gave way in two sections one hour apart, startling the 16 families living within.

In late January, 1948, this 80-year-old frame house was moved from the corner of King and Waterloo to a new location on Rectory Street between Little Grey and Little Hill streets. According to City Assessment Commissioner Harry Bennett, part of the house had been built more than 100 years earlier. The home was moved to make way for a new service station.

Richardson's Real Estate was selling this Westmount area home near London for $17,500 in November, 1948.

95 Ridout Street South shown in November, 1948. The *Free Press* reported that U.S. presidential candidate Thomas E. Dewey spent many vacations in this house owned by a cousin, Eleanor Emery, who died that year.

Bell Telephone added two additional storeys on its headquarters on the southwest corner of Clarence and Dufferin in 1949. The extra floors were necessary to house the dial equipment as Bell prepared homes for dial phones.

A view of St. Paul's Cathedral and grounds taken from the roof of the Dominion Public Building on Richmond, May 30, 1949. The Bell Telephone building is being renovated in the background.

A second view from the roof of the Dominion Public Building looking north towards St. Peter's Cathedral. The building at the bottom foreground has had many uses over the years, including London Mutual Fire Insurance and London Conservatory of Music. It is now the Church Key Bistro.

Daring construction workers show off for the camera, perched high up on girders as London Life was being expanded, July 7, 1949.

The former National Grocers Building at 95-97 Dundas was for sale in September 1949. In a prime downtown location next to the Belvedere Hotel (later the Talbot Inn), the building featured four floors with a full basement, 55 ft. frontage, depth of 185 ft., and a freight elevator. Asking price was $60,000 or half the building for $35,000. The site is now the location of Budweiser Gardens.

The Bank of Toronto building on the southeast corner of Talbot and Dundas, September 3, 1949, before its demolition for a modern bank.

A scene on Langmuir Street on October 19, 1949. Attempting to keep up with the post-war demand, fast-working contractors rushed houses to completion before water and sewers were available or roads, curbs, and sidewalks were completed—in hopes that vital services would catch up quickly.

Only one family lived on Easy Street on October 4, 1949. Here Louise Osborne with daughters Gwen, 8, and Carolyn, 6, landscape their yard in the veterans' subdivision on Wellington Road, south of London. Mrs. Osborne named the street herself. When the streets in the subdivision were first named, government officials named them after Churchill, Normandy, and Roosevelt. Veterans, however, had had enough of war and renamed the streets to their liking, choosing names like Winblest Avenue, Greenfield Drive, Eden Avenue, and Willow Drive.

On October 13, 1949, one of the oldest buildings in the city, 229-231 Queens Avenue, was about to be demolished. At the time, it was home to ABC Menders.

An unpublished *Free Press* photograph shows a child playing in an open sewer near a home on Watling Road, Bellwood Park, on August 30, 1948.

# BUSINESS

Within a year after the first log cabin was built at the forks of the Thames, London boasted twenty to thirty buildings. While many of them were homes, London was also developing its first business community. John Balkwill was building a brewery, Peter McGregor operated a tavern in his cabin, a few merchants' shops were operating, and a blacksmith hammered at his forge. The commercial hub of this pioneer London was Ridout Street, a track running north-south next to the river.

London's earliest financial institutions sprang to life on the west side of Ridout Street to the north of Middlesex County Courthouse. As London had been declared the new administrative and legal centre of the London District, banks with head offices in Toronto and Hamilton recognized a need for financial services in the new frontier community. The Bank of Upper Canada was housed at 435 Ridout Street from 1838 onwards while 441-447 Ridout, built by Dr. Alexander Anderson in 1842, was home to both the Gore Bank and the Commercial Bank of Canada by the mid-1840s. Not surprisingly, the buildings became known as "Banker's Row." Today, the Labatt Restoration project preserves this section of London's earliest business district.

The new community's most important early shopping spot was Covent Garden. The market opened November 1, 1845, within the block bounded by King, Talbot, Dundas, and Richmond streets. It was natural to name the spot after the famous market in London, England—after all, every London needs a Covent Garden! Local farmers from across Middlesex County would bring their produce here to supply Londoners' daily needs.

In 1854, the first market building was completed, designed by London architect Samuel Peters, Jr. Inside the building, fruits, vegetables, and meats were sold. Fish were sold in a separate building, where the strong odour would be less bothersome in the summer heat. Covent Garden became the economic heart of the new city and remains one of London's longest-lasting traditions.

The building of Covent Garden also meant that London's business community shifted away from Ridout Street towards the east. Shop owners and artisans collected around the market for the convenience of visiting farmers who often bought provisions while in town. The building of the Great Western Railway station at York and Richmond streets meant visitors to London coming by train usually approached downtown via Richmond. In time, London's main intersection shifted to Dundas and Richmond. When a city hall was built on Richmond in 1855, the street's importance became fixed. Even the financial district shifted to Richmond north of Dundas. The Huron & Erie Savings and Loan Society, a forerunner of Canada Trust, opened an imposing office on the east side of Richmond just south of North Street (Queens Avenue) in 1871.

London became even more of a financial and insurance centre as the nineteenth century progressed. The aforementioned Huron & Erie was organized by 25 local businessmen in 1864. Ontario Loan & Debenture Company, founded in 1870, remained a major firm in London for a century before being taken over by Royal Trust. London Life Insurance, incorporated in 1874, soon became a major force in its field. All these companies constructed offices that inspired confidence in their solidness and stability, but none as monumental as the magnificent beaux-arts style head office built by London Life in 1927. The presence of these institutions gave London a reputation for being a conservative, rock-solid, white-collar city.

London's first stores were small businesses, generally run by the owner with a few assistants. Over time, as the railways, and eventually the airport, allowed businesses to import product in bulk, shops became larger and sold a wider variety of goods. Department stores such as Smallman and Ingram and Kingsmills started out as dry goods firms, but eventually provided a wealth of goods in one convenient location. The store founded by John Bamlet Smallman and Lemuel H. Ingram first opened for business on the south side of Dundas between Richmond and Market Lane in 1877. Their five-storey, L-shaped department store, the largest in southwestern Ontario, was built in 1908, extending from Richmond to Covent Garden. When the store was bought by Simpson's in 1945, many Londoners made their way downtown just to see the magnificent window displays.

Thomas Frazer Kingsmill's store opened on the north side of Dundas Street between Richmond and Talbot in March 1865. Kingsmill brought Londoners a fine selection of overseas goods, making an average of two ocean crossings a year on buying trips for his store. The business was destroyed by fire twice: first, on November 3, 1911, and second, on January 7, 1932. A new Kingsmill's store opened in September 1932, designed by the London architectural firm of O. Roy Moore. The store's Art Deco limestone facade was an iconic part of downtown London for nearly 150 years until its closing in 2014.

By 1950, the dry goods stores had given way to modern department stores and the general stores to supermarkets. Responding to the new post-war culture of consumerism, London's business district was modernizing and expanding. Yet, even from its earliest days, London was a key commercial centre for Western Ontario, ideally situated halfway between the metropolises of Detroit and Toronto.

Covent Garden Market circa 1865, looking south towards King Street. The market building. at right, was completed in 1854. The fish market with its arched doorway can be seen in this photo along with poultry stands, J. Connor's shoemaking shop, and the Market Saloon. Faintly shown at centre background is the Tecumseh House hotel.

Looking east across Covent Garden Market on a Saturday morning, circa 1880s. McCann's Hotel and City Hall with its passageway to Richmond Street are visible in the background.

The Bank of British North America, circa 1875. It was built on the southeast corner of Richmond and North Street (Queens Avenue) in 1856–57. Later it became a branch of the Bank of Montreal. To the right is a glimpse of the Huron & Erie Savings and Loan Society building, later occupied by the *London Free Press*.

The Merchant's Bank, built about 1864 on the northwest corner of Richmond and North Street (Queen's Avenue), is pictured here circa 1870s.

The Bank of Montreal circa 1875, built on the southwest corner of Richmond and Fullerton streets, just to the north of the Merchant's Bank, circa 1865–68. These banks are now the site of the Dominion Public Building.

Bowman & Co. Coal and Wood Yard, established 1876, and located at 246 Bathurst Street is pictured here circa 1890. The carts with "Bowman" painted on the side advertised the business throughout the city.

Wallace Halle & Co.'s Piano Warehouse, circa 1890. The company, which also sold organs, was located in the Masonic Temple building.

William L. Graham's Bon Ton Furnishing Emporium, located at 159 Dundas Street near Richmond, circa 1890. The store sold hats, caps and shirts, as well as other gentlemen's "furnishings." Note the neckties hanging on racks at left.

Burns & Bapty, photographed circa 1890, was a men's clothier at 154 Dundas. Operated by George F. Burns and Harry Bapty, the store's advertising in 1888 announced "First Class Merchant Tailoring. Clothing and Men's Furnishings. Three A1 cutters always employed. The Finest Premises and most complete stock of High Class Goods in Western Ontario."

Lashbrook & Simmons operated a boot and shoe store at 157 ½ Dundas Street, south side, near Richmond Street circa 1887–89. Their shelves were well-stocked, with shoes and boots stacked right up to the ceiling. Upholstered benches in the aisle allowed customers to sit comfortably while trying on footwear.

The London Club, circa 1890. Incorporated in 1880, the club's building was erected on the south side of Queen's Avenue where it still stands. The gentlemen's club membership was a "who's who" of London businessmen who used it to establish business contacts as well as for recreation.

Hats galore at the shop of Henry Beaton, hatter and furrier, in business at 421 Richmond Street, Palmer's Block, in the 1870s and 80s.

Looking east from 184 Dundas Street, circa 1880. Visible on the left or north side is Edy Bros. Photographers, partially obscured. On the right, or south side, is A.E. Pavey & Co. Woolens, and on the far side of Clarence Street, R.S. Williams Music Warehouse next to the Mechanics' Hall.

Looking east from 157 Dundas Street, circa 1880. Alexander Gauld's tailor shop, Manchester House Hotel, and Laing & McPherson Dry Goods are visible. East of Richmond in the Edge Block is Andrew Morphy jeweller.

Gillian McLean's London Hardware Company at 121 Dundas Street, circa 1897. Note the magnificent stained glass transom.

A horse-drawn streetcar passes George G. Wood's grocery store at Dundas and Lyle, circa 1886.

The Carling Brewery was one of Canada's largest brewers when this photo was taken circa 1875–1880. Located close to the Thames River, the building faced Ann Street. Originally located near today's Yale and Harvard streets, the brewery was founded by Thomas Carling in 1843.

A group of businesses at 208-212 ½ Dundas Street, just west of Clarence, circa 1895. From left to right are Edward French's London Fruit Store; William G. Young, jeweller; Frederick W. Goodwin's bicycle shop; and Frank J. Miller's Hair Store that sold wigs and toiletries.

Interior of Morrison Dry Goods, 1903. James M. Morrison operated his business at 636 Dundas.

North Branch Mills, operated by William M. Hilliard and Joseph D. Saunby, circa 1870. Originally built by Joseph Anderson in 1854 on the west side of the north branch of the Thames, it changed hands several times until it was bought by Hilliard and Saunby in 1862. It was later occupied by the Quigley-Welting leather works and burned down in the 1980s.

Dundas Street looking west of Talbot circa 1875 shows the typical three-storey white brick commercial blocks that defined downtown London. The view includes the *Advertiser* Printing Office as well as the millinery shop of Mrs. Forde and Miss Irvine. By the late 1870s, the *Advertiser* had moved to Richmond Street.

Dundas Street looking east from Talbot, circa 1878. About 1885, John A. Rose, bookkeeper at W.T. Rutherford & Co. Cigar Manufacturers, bought the factory and renamed it John A. Rose & Co. The eye-catching overhead banners were a good way for retailers to advertise in late nineteenth century.

The *London Advertiser* building on Richmond Street circa 1879, located just south of the *Free Press* building. Founded in 1863 by John Cameron, it was the *Free Press*'s main competitor until it closed in 1936.

W.M. Allaster's News Depot, then 38 Dundas Street, in the McCormick Block on the north side of Dundas between Adelaide and Elizabeth, circa 1883. After the amalgamation of London East, the McCormick Block became 644-660 Dundas.

Talbot Street looking north from King Street, 1900s. Covent Garden is across the street to the right. Note Wegner Clothing Company's heart-shaped sign, "The Heart of London."

George W. Harkness & Co., chemists, conducted business at 268 Dundas from the 1870s until Harkness' death about 1890. They were the source for Harkness' Bronchial Syrup.

Nicholas Wilson & Company, merchant tailors, conducted business at various locations on the north side of Dundas Street between Talbot and Richmond streets throughout the 1880s and early 1890s.

Interior of George Rowntree's Grocery Store, 340 Richmond Street near York, circa 1900. The store provided seats for customers to better study the well-stocked shelves. An aproned clerk at right appears to be using a meat slicer. The gentleman with the bowtie on the left may be George Rowntree himself.

Cairncross & Lawrence Drug Store, circa 1899, 216 Dundas Street. Opened by James Arthur Cairncross and Lindsay Tyler Lawrence at 256 Dundas in 1886, the store was moved in 1889 to the northwest corner of Dundas and Park (Clarence) when successful enough to require more space. After Lawrence died in 1901, Cairncross continued the business until his own death in 1924, after which his son Roy took over. The store remained in the family for generations, expanding to six locations.

Interior of Cairncross & Lawrence Drug Store.

Dundas Street looking east past Richmond in a 1908 postcard. The Edge Block is visible at the right. The Canadian Bank of Commerce was built on the northeast corner in 1905.

The south side of Dundas Street between Clarence and Richmond in the late 1920s. Businesses include Rowland Hill Shoes, J. Gammage & Sons Florists, National Billiards, Regent Tailors, and Tip Top Tailors.

Dundas Street looking west from Wellington Street, circa 1923. On the north or right side are Anderson & Nelles Drugs, Benson-Wilcox Electric Co., Lascelles Café, R.M. Brisco's sporting goods, George Parkinson's tailor shop, Standard Drug, and Mason & Risch Pianos. On the south or left side is Starr Company phonographs and pianos, the Canadian Café, and Jackson the Cleaner.

Covent Garden Market, 1908. Note the sign for Westman's Hardware, which burned down August 18 of that year.

Covent Garden Market in the 1920s, featuring both cars and horse-pulled sleighs.

North side of Dundas Street between Wellington and Waterloo, early 1920s. Note Arthur G. Westlake's photography studio located at 330 Dundas; his studio was responsible for many of the early photographs featured in this book.

Mason & Risch music store at 248 Dundas Street, circa 1925. The piano department carried many designs of upright, grand, and player pianos while its phonograph department sold Victor victrolas, M&R phonographs, and Victor records. The dog mascot "Nipper" is also present in this display window.

Robert Read and Charles Logan sold coal and wood from their business at 1462 Dundas from 1922 to 1927. Both the trucks and horses and wagons shown here were used to make deliveries.

The Hydro shop on the northeast corner of Dundas and Wellington, 1926. Located in the PUC building, the shop was opened to encourage the use of electrical appliances in the home. The building was incorporated into the new City Hall built 1926–28 after the adjacent Spencer Block was torn down.

Interior of the Hydro shop, circa 1926.

Dundas Street east of Adelaide in the 1920s. This photograph was taken by Henry Hines, whose photo studio appears in this photo. Buildings east of Adelaide were a little less ostentatious than those downtown.

Johnston Bros. bakery wagon delivering bread during World War I. Note the Victory flags.

The interior of Bell Telephone, 479 Clarence Street, in an undated photograph.

The southeast corner of Dundas and Clarence in the 1920s, with Orth Tailoring and Wilmot's Diamonds. South on Clarence is the Savoy Hotel. To the east of Wilmot's is George Boyd's shoes and Archer Electric.

Dundas Street in the 1920s, looking east from the corner of Richmond Street, likely taken from Smallman and Ingram's department store. Visible on the north side are jeweller W.G. Young, Home Dairy Company, London Café, Dowler's, De Luxe Café, and, in the distance, Loew's Theatre. An overhead banner advertises Springbank Amusement Park, which Londoners could reach from downtown by streetcar.

McMahen, Granger & Co., Wholesale Dry Goods, in a 1911 postcard. Built in 1908 by James Granger and A.T. McMahen as their warehouse, the building had an unusual terra cotta facade. It was later used by Gardner Galleries.

Huron & Erie Mortgage Corporation, northeast corner of Dundas and Clarence, circa 1931, soon after the building was constructed. Later the Canada Trust building, it is now TD Canada Trust. Note the revolving spotlight, which once lit the skies of downtown London.

Dundas Street, looking west past the intersection with Richmond, August 1931. Note Smallman and Ingram on the left. In the foreground on the same side is J.P. Cook Shoes and Peters Canadian Restaurant. On the north side, signs can be seen for Metropolitan Store, Graftons, Artistic Ladies Wear, and The Dominion Bank. At right foreground is the Canadian Bank of Commerce.

The second annual banquet of the London District Cooperative Milk Producers was held at Hotel London January 18, 1939. The more than 400 members and guests drank milk as an appetizer. Here Dr. G.I. Christie, President of the Ontario Agricultural College (right), helps F.H. Clarke, provincial secretary of the association, to a glass.

A row of buildings along the 300 block of Clarence Street, known to London as Chinatown, were once home to a Chinese laundry, tailor shop, and Chinese trading company. By the time they were demolished in 1944 to make way for a warehouse, the buildings were among the oldest in downtown London.

Farmer's Advocate building, 122 Carling Street, circa 1935. Originally the site of the *London Free Press* before it relocated to Richmond Street, this building was home to William Weld's monthly agricultural journal from 1920 until the journal folded in 1965. The building is the Marienbad Restaurant in 2017.

Dundas Street looking east from Richmond, 1945. London native Walter P. Zeller, formerly manager of Metropolitan Stores, opened his head office and store on the north side of Dundas east of Richmond in 1928.

In 1877, the dry goods firm of Smallman and Ingram first appeared on the south side of Dundas Street. In time, it grew to be "Western Ontario's largest and most popular department store." This 1941 photo also shows United Cigar Store, Laura Secord, Liggett's Drugs, and Wells Academy ("Register Any Time"). Farther to the west of Smallman and Ingram is Woolworth's, Ontario Loan & Debenture, and, in the distance, London Wines, and Siegel's.

Employees of Smallman and Ingram, just bought by Robert Simpson Co. Ltd. of Toronto, attend a staff meeting on Thursday, December 7, 1944, at which company officials explain future operations at the store. C.L. Burton, president of Robert Simpson Co., speaks to the employees.

On June 3, 1945, the Smallman and Ingram name was taken down, replaced by that of Simpson's.

An example of the artistic display windows for which Simpson's became famous.

Anderson's, "The Home of Red Ribbon Home-killed Meats" and "The Beef with the Flavour," at Covent Garden Market, January 1946.

The Bond Clothes Shop at 189 Dundas Street, between Richmond and Clarence, March 1946. Founded by Sydney H. Vaisler starting in 1938, joined by Harold Vaisler in 1941, the shop sold ready-to-wear clothing for both men and women. The shop closed in 1993 when the brothers retired.

Young Canada clothing store, on Richmond Street just south of King, opened a shoe department called "Shoeland" in their basement in August 1946, just in time for back-to-school shopping. The "shoe boat" featured here created a platform for shoe fittings.

Mara's, next to Kingsmill's on Dundas Street, was the first retail store in Canada to have an interchangeable letter marquee, pictured here on June 17, 1947.

Rowland Hill shoe store opened at 203 Dundas Street, in the spring of 1948. "Canada's Finest Family Shoe Store" started in 1900 in a little corner shop on Wellington Street. At the new location there were 29 employees in four departments: hosiery, men's, women's, and juniors'.

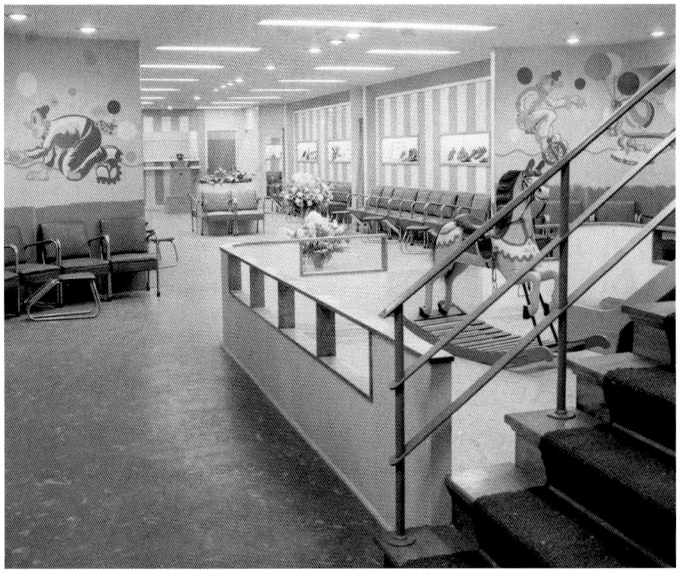

The interior of the juniors' department, at Rowland Hill, with a playroom for children.

The Charles Chapman Company, 88-90 York Street, in October 1948. Chapman, a young artist from Norwich, England, opened an art supply business on Dundas Street between Richmond and Talbot, in November 1855.

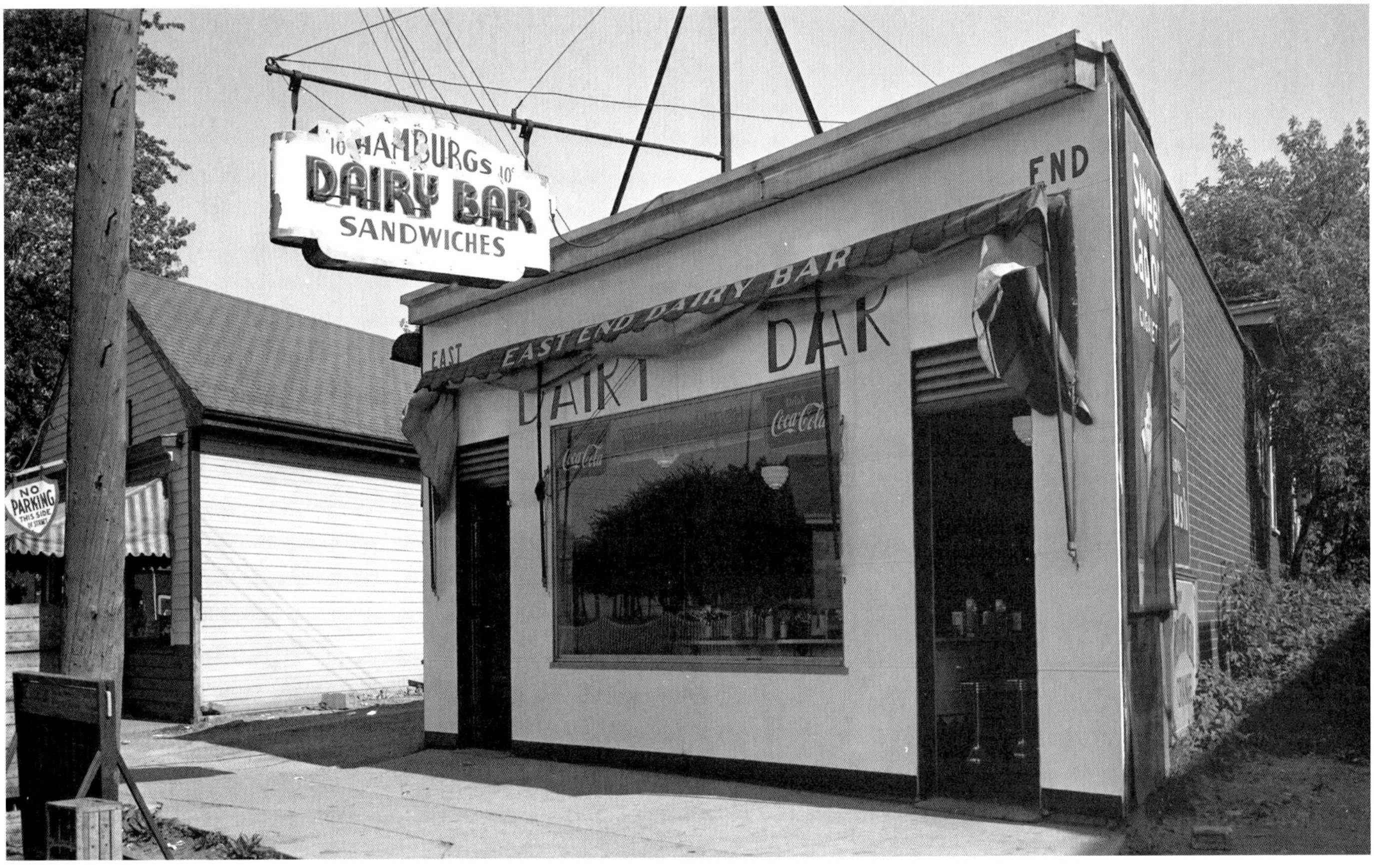


Exterior of the East End Dairy Bar, 772 Hamilton Road.

Staff inside the new East End Dairy Bar on Hamilton Road, June 2, 1948. Proprietor I.J. Hillinger is shown with Mrs. Hillinger, Ruth Phillips, and Eileen Louckes. The Dairy Bar served hot meals, sandwiches, French fries, sodas, and ice cream.

Stuart's Men's Store, 248 Dundas Street, advertises in the *Free Press* in September 1948, featuring their Photo Fit! Made to Measure chart for measuring men for suits.

Stuart's, in January 1949, wants "YOU!" to buy their English woollens, in this *Free Press* promo shot.

A postcard shows the interior of Stuart's.

Liberty Ladies' Wear at 389 Richmond Street went out of business in October 1948. The line in the final days stretched all the way down the west side of Richmond.

When Kresge's opened at 150 Dundas Street, November 4, 1948, hundreds of Londoners lined up for the opening. This photo was taken on Dundas after 9:00 a.m., as large groups milled about near the door.

Supertest Gasoline, March 22, 1949. This location on the northeast corner of Richmond and Pall Mall streets, is now the site of Jack Astor's.

Doug Day, delivery man, hands a loaf of bread from Wonder Bakeries to Mrs. B. Tangredi, November 1948.

Doug's delivery horse, Goldie, pulls a Wonder Bread wagon in November 1948. Goldie "The Wonder Horse," age 18, knew all the stops on all 20 city Wonder Bakeries routes. Wonder Bakeries, with a plant on Carlton Avenue, had over 35 routes in London and district.

Standard Drug at Richmond and Piccadilly, next to Quong Lee Laundry, February 1949. The first Standard Drug store opened on the north side of Dundas between Clarence and Wellington on November 1913 with William Zoellner as president and Percy J. Dunnigan as vice-president. This was one of six London locations in 1949.

Allen Ladies' Wear, 168 Dundas Street, photographed March 20, 1949. The store was on the north side of Dundas Street, just east of Richmond.

Roberts store, 374 Richmond Street, April 21, 1949.

An employee shows off the merchandise in this promotional shot inside Norfolk Lingerie Store, 738 Richmond Street, March 22, 1949.

Crowds crossing at the intersection of Dundas and Richmond, April 2, 1949. The photo looks towards the southeast corner of the intersection where United Cigar Stores, Ainsley, Cook's Shoes, Hunt's Confectioners, and Birks Jeweller can be seen.

Dominion Store under construction, May 13, 1949, on the north side of Dundas Street just east of Maitland Street. The building is still there, now the Marvel Esthetics building.

Staff photo at Johnson-Turner Electrical Repair and Engineering, located at 1184 Frances Street, May 27, 1949.

The second annual Y-Mac Radio Auction was held at CFPL Studio A on May 16, 1949. The runners in front of the tables waited to take the bid slips from the phone operators. The Y-Mac, or International Y's Men's Club, offered nearly $4,000 worth of merchandise for sale, from a $15 wallpaper job to a $1,500 car, all advertised in the *Free Press* in advance.

Club Shangri-La opened at 1905 Dundas Street the evening of June 17, 1949. Operated by proprietor Aston McEachron, a vocalist from the Bahamas, the club offered dining and dancing to Lloyd Kelly and his Club Shangri-La Quartet.

The Market Square, August 27, 1949. The old market building stood until 1956.

The corner of Stanley and Wharncliffe, August 3, 1949. The old building is occupied by Standard Drugs and White's Food Market.

Kingsmill's store founder Thomas Frazer Kingsmill (1840–1915). opened the business as a dry goods store on Dundas Street in 1865. Kingsmill's operated from that spot for 148 years.

His wife, Anne Ardagh (Burns) Kingsmill (1828–1910).

Bellevue Farm, home of Thomas Frazer and Anne Ardagh Kingsmill, June 1890. It is now the site of Middlesex College, Western University. The man in the doorway is identified as Burris Gahan.

Kingsmill's during an expansion sale, circa 1876. The signs read: "Attend the Great Reduction Sale; Summer Dry Goods."

Kingsmill's, circa 1900—before a fire in 1911.

The company delivery wagon on Albert Street, circa 1915.

The fire department attempts to control the destructive fire of January 1932 on the Carling Street side of the store.

An insurance company photograph shows damage to the building after the 1932 fire.

The new Kingsmill's store, rebuilt after the 1932 fire. It was demolished in 2016.

A view of the ladies' fashions department on the second floor in 1932.

Most merchandise was behind a counter, only accessible by sales staff.

A view of the children's department.

Staff at work on the main floor in London Life's 424 Wellington Street head office (later Wright Lithographing), circa 1913. Policyholders could enter the building and pay their premiums at the tellers' wickets in the background.

Men and horses laying the foundation for London Life's new head office, June 16, 1926.

The official ceremony for the laying of the cornerstone for London Life's new head office on the southwest corner of Wellington and Dufferin, August 5, 1926. Standing at left is Edward E. Reid, then General Manager of London Life.

Construction of London Life, January 11, 1927, showing the Wellington Street section of the building.

On September 3, 1927, London Life staff moved their offices and furnishings from 424 Wellington Street, to their new 255 Dufferin location.

London Life mailroom, circa 1935. From left to right are Marjorie James, unknown, Russ Thatcher, Frank Sumner, and Dick Hamill.

London Life Mortgage Department, circa 1937.

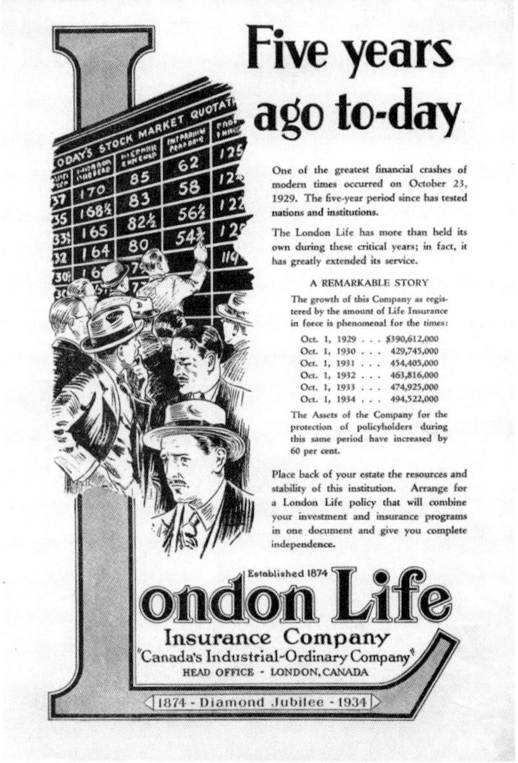


London Life invested wisely in the 1920s and weathered the Great Depression relatively well. This 1934 *Free Press* advertisement extols the progress of the company since the stock market crash.

Stanley Lovell, Corporate Secretary of London Life, demonstrates dictating a letter using an Edison wax cylinder Dictaphone, circa 1928. His desk is so highly polished both he and his Dictaphone are reflected in it.

# CHURCHES & FAITH

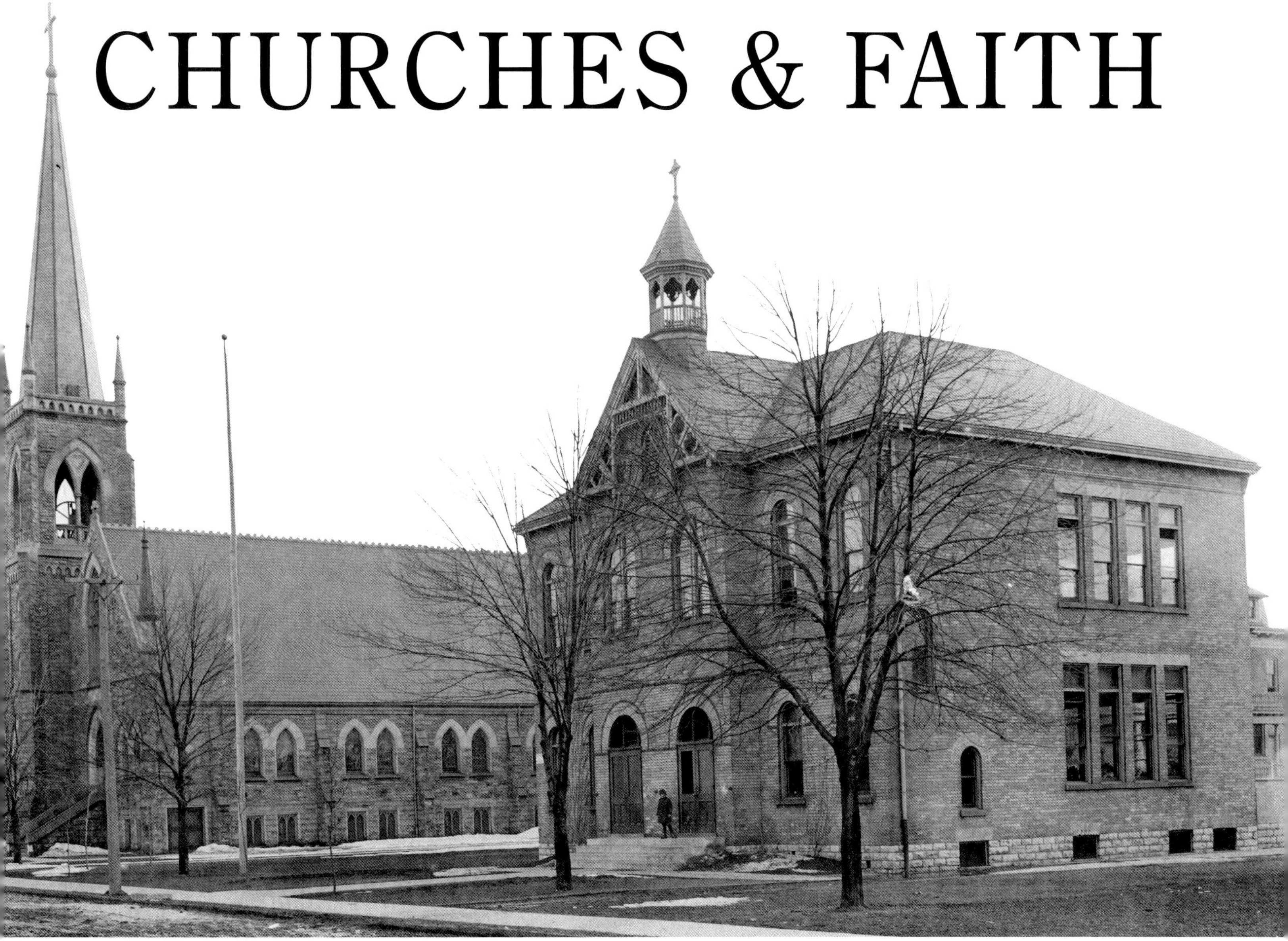

London was founded in an age of faith, making religious congregations among the first organized groups in the new community. Services were at first held in people's homes or in any building suitable for small groups. Within the first ten years of the village's founding, however, there were enough people—over a thousand—to justify the organization of formal congregations.

The Church of England was the official state religion of the mother country and naturally assumed an important position in the growing settlement. This was especially true after the arrival of Rev. Benjamin Cronyn, first bishop of the Diocese of Huron, in 1832. One of Cronyn's first concerns was to construct a proper Anglican meeting place, leading to the construction of St. Paul's Church on the northwest corner of North Street (Queens Avenue) and Clarence Street in 1834. Even the original church, with its seating capacity of 400, must have seemed ambitious for a pioneer outpost. But when it burned down on Ash Wednesday, 1844, Cronyn became determined to build even bigger. The new St. Paul's, dedicated on February 25, 1846, was the foundation for St. Paul's Cathedral, now London's oldest place of worship. Enlarged in the early 1890s from its original proportions, with the addition of transepts and an extended chancel, the 1,000-seat building eventually had chimes, gas lights, an organ, and hot air heating—a far cry from the primitive structure of 1834.

The leading Catholic figure in pioneer days was local resident Dennis O'Brien, whose home held many early services conducted by travelling missionaries. London's first resident Catholic priest was Rev. Laurence Dempsey who arrived in 1833, and opened St. Lawrence's Church about where the Grand Theatre is on Richmond. The growing number of Irish immigrants gave the church reason to grow. A larger, more permanent building called St. Lawrence the Martyr opened in 1852, on the northeast corner of Mark Lane (Richmond) and Duke Street (Dufferin Avenue). The church was renamed St. Peter's Cathedral in 1856, after London became the seat of the Diocese of London, stretching over most of southwestern Ontario. The original building was demolished and a new cathedral dedicated in 1885, a magnificent edifice still standing at Richmond and Dufferin.

The Kirk of Scotland's first representative was Rev. William Proudfoot, who arrived in 1832, and remained a dominant figure in the growing town until his death in 1851. His congregation, organized in 1833, evolved into First Presbyterian Church, the forerunner of First St. Andrew's United.

Methodists also had a tiny church in 1833, but no permanent minister. As their numbers grew and the people became more prosperous, they too built substantial churches such as North Street Methodist Church. When that church burned in 1895, the congregation built what is now called Metropolitan United. The Congregational church was also established at an early date, in 1837, by Rev. William Clarke. The unification of many Presbyterian, Methodist, and Congregational churches in 1925 created Canada's largest Protestant denomination, the United Church of Canada, and many local buildings became United churches.

Houses of worship provided more than religious instruction and spiritual comfort. They were also social havens where groups of like-minded individuals—often from the same homeland or ethnicity—could meet for social support. The African Methodist Episcopal Church, better known as the Fugitive Slave Chapel, opened in about 1849 on the west side of Thames Street south of Bathurst. In 1856, the congregation moved to the north side of Grey Street between Colborne and Maitland. In 1869, it became the British Methodist Episcopalian Church, later known as Beth Emanuel. Long after slavery was formally abolished in the neighbouring United States, this church was a community centre for London's black population. The original Thames Street structure has been moved next to the site of Beth Emanuel and is undergoing restoration.

Church life also provided a source of leisure activities for those who joined the choir, youth groups, and women's organizations. Societies meeting at churches were not always of a religious nature, however, as indicated by the existence of a First Congregational Church bicycle club in the 1890s.

Of course, Christianity was not the only religion practised in London, though it was certainly the most prominent. The first Jewish settlers arrived in the area as early as the 1850s, bringing their faith traditions with them. London's first synagogue was built on the northeast corner of Richmond and Simcoe in 1899, in time for a period of increased immigration, which lasted until the 1920s. As a result of this growth, other synagogues were established, including B'Nai Israel and B'Nai Moses Ben Judah. As with many churches, these congregations began in modest frame buildings and grew into impressive brick synagogues, reflecting the growing affluence of the community.

However, despite the early growth of these religious communities, church closure and demolition is not an entirely recent phenomenon. First Presbyterian Church opened on the southeast corner of Park (Clarence) and Duke Street (Dufferin Avenue) in January 1862. A substantial building, it was remodelled and enlarged over the years, being the first church in the city to have electric lighting. Its site is now the London Life parking lot, the church being demolished in 1938 after the merger with St. Andrews to become First St. Andrews United.

First Congregational Church, on the south side of Dundas between Waterloo and Colborne, was another attractive edifice, designed by London architect Thomas Tracy and opening in August, 1875. Becoming Beecher United after church union, it unfortunately closed in 1947. The building was reused, becoming the first Aeolian Hall concert venue, until it burned down in 1968. Today, only its tower remains as a monument.

Despite these closures, the years up to mid-twentieth century were still an age of expansion for most churches, and many smaller churches were built in the expanding suburbs in the prosperous post-war era. Congregations were able to mark anniversaries of congregations or church buildings—an opportunity to celebrate their history. Many structures, however, have been abandoned in the twenty-first century, leading to discussion as to how to adaptively reuse our ecclesiastical architecture in a secular age.

Bishop Isaac Hellmuth (1819–1901), second Bishop of the Anglican Diocese of Huron. A major proponent of education, Hellmuth founded ladies' and boys' colleges, Huron College, and finally, Western University.

The original frame of St. Andrew's Presbyterian Church opened September 3, 1843, on the northeast corner of North Street (Queens Avenue) and Waterloo. It was replaced by the current building in 1869.

St. John's Chapel was consecrated in 1864 on the Huron College grounds. The architect was W. Kaufman of Toronto, but the building was constructed by London City Engineer William Robinson for about $3,000. The building was demolished, but became the foundation for another church: St. John the Evangelist.

An 1868 sketch of St. Andrew's Church by prolific local architect, William Robinson.

Looking east on Fullarton Street towards St. Paul's Cathedral in the 1800s.

St. Paul's Rectory, northwest corner of Clarence and Queens, circa 1867, with the cathedral in the background. The rectory survived until 1956, but an office building stands on the site today.

Interior of St. Paul's Cathedral.

Old St. Peter's Cathedral, circa 1875. Originally called St. Lawrence Church, the name changed to St. Peter's in 1856. The Bishop's Palace can be seen just to the right.

The Bishop's Palace, later St. Peter's Rectory, built in 1871, was demolished in 2005.

The new St. Peter's Cathedral, from the rooftop of St. Paul's Cathedral, after 1885.

North Street Methodist Church, circa 1873, taken from the roof of the Custom House. The church was on the southwest corner of North Street (Queens Avenue) and Park Avenue (Clarence Street). The building under construction behind the church may be Wesley Hall.

Bishop Cronyn Memorial Anglican Church, 1875. The church, dedicated to the memory of the first bishop of the Diocese of Huron, Benjamin Cronyn, was built in 1873 at the southeast corner of North Street (Queens Avenue) and William Street.

First Church of Christ Scientist, 1900s. This church, located east of Richmond Street on the west side of Victoria Park, was built in the 1880s by a dissident Presbyterian group and nicknamed the "Pepper Box Church" for its shape. It became First Church of Christ Scientist in 1899 and was demolished in 1969. First Baptist Church now occupies the site.

A front view of North Street Methodist Church, circa 1875. Built in 1854, it burned down in 1895. Buildings along the west side of Clarence Street can be seen to the rear of the church.

St. Andrew's Presbyterian Church, now First St. Andrew's United, on the northeast corner of Queens Avenue and Waterloo Street, circa 1878.

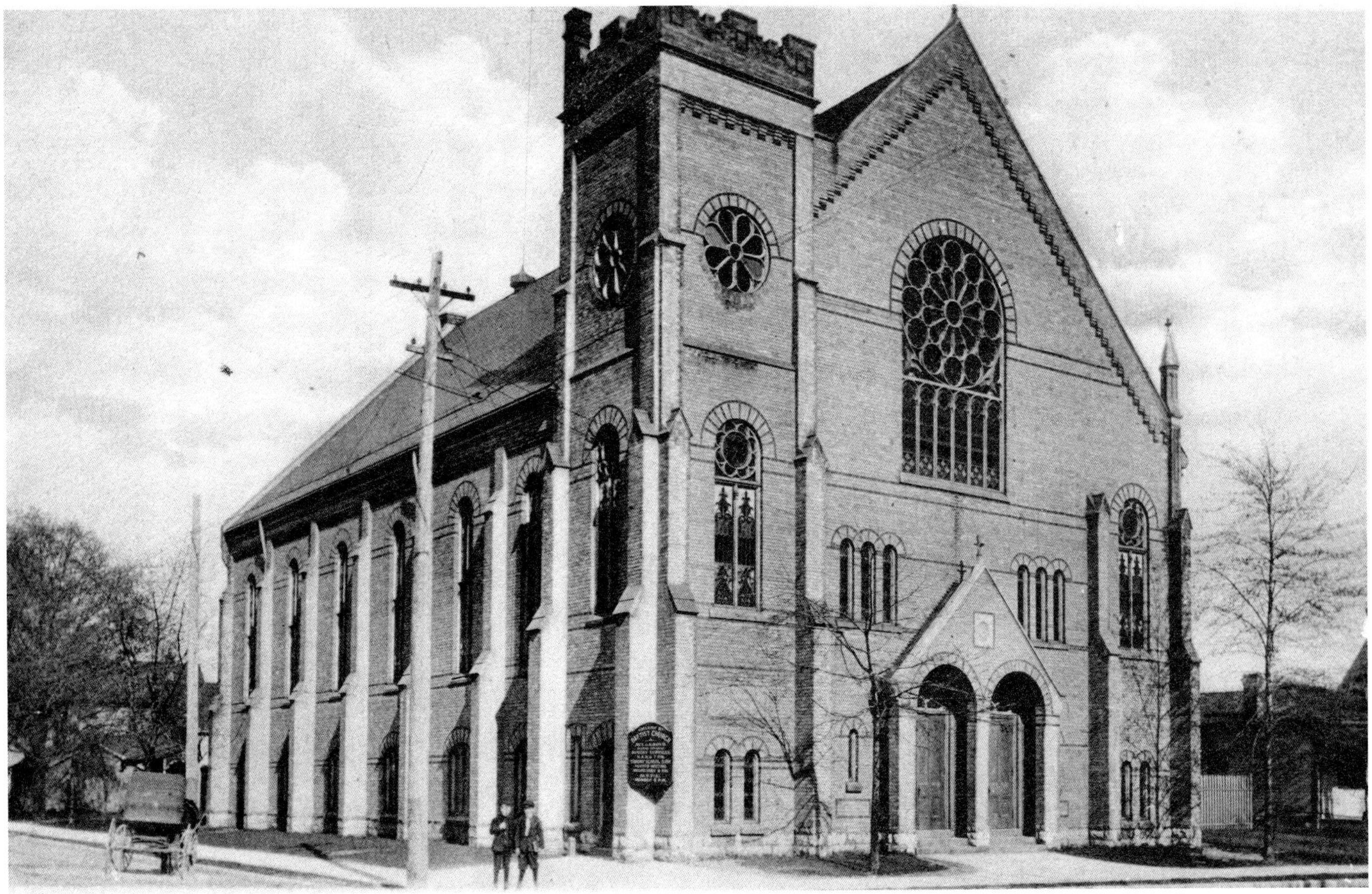

Adelaide Street Baptist Church, 1900s.

Wellington Street Methodist Church, circa 1887. The church was built in 1876 at the time of the amalgamation of New Connexion and Wesleyan Methodists. The church became United in 1925 and in 2017, is The Atonement Fire Baptized Holiness Church of God.

Ridout Street Methodist Church opened its door in 1911. Today it operates as Calvary United Church.

A postcard view of First Presbyterian Church on the southeast corner of Dufferin Avenue and Park Avenue (Clarence Street), 1905. Originally a smaller church, it was remodelled and enlarged in later years, adding its magnificent steeple. The church was demolished in 1938 after the congregation merged with St. Andrew's to become First St. Andrew's United. The site is now the London Life parking lot.

The unadorned interior of First Presbyterian Church.

On October 25, 1938, ministers from 16 Ontario Black churches of various denominations gathered at Beth Emmanuel Church, where plans were made to more fully unite and evangelize the black population in Canada. From left to right are: Rev. R.O. Stewart, North Buxton; Rev. Norval Wilson, Amherstburg; Rev. C.A. Johnson, pastor of Beth Emmanuel; and Rev. C. P. Jones, Oakville.

Dundas Centre Methodist, later United, Church at the corner of Maitland and Dundas streets. The original church on the site burned in 1895 and this new church opened a year later.

The Dundas Centre Choir and Instrumental Ensemble, circa 1909. The Union Jacks suggest a Victoria Day celebration.

Hyatt Avenue United Church in June, 1946. The building, constructed in 1907, stands empty in 2017.

Rev. Lydia E. Gruchy, right, the first ordained woman minister in the United Church of Canada, was guest speaker at a joint meeting of the Women's Association and Women's Missionary Society at Knox United Church in 1938. At left is Mrs. S.R. Byles of Windsor Avenue, with whom Rev. Gruchy stayed during her visit.

The Salvation Army's Horton Street hostel served over 3,000 meals a year in the 1930s. Here Chef William Boyd shows Major F.H. Laing some of the rice pudding he's made for dinner on October 27, 1938.

Ten delegates to the International Youth Conference of the Reorganized Church of Jesus Christ of Latter Day Saints left London by bus on June 9, 1939, for Iowa. The ladies were mainly from the Maitland Street church.

Hope Baptist Church, 1946. Overcrowded and lacking a basement, the church was set to move from this spot on Hamilton Road to a new building down the street, at the corner of Giles.

In June, 1947, Beecher United Church announced it would be closing due to a "lack of congregation." The building, dating back to 1876, was originally First Congregational before church union in 1925. The church became the Aeolian Hall, but burned in 1968. Only its tower remains.

The Family Community Club at Beth Emmanuel Church prepared chicken suppers as a fundraiser to build a Negro Community Centre in February, 1948. From left to right are Christine Jenkins, Jean Anderson, and Mrs. W.L. Berry.

A service at B'Nai Moses Ben Judah Synagogue, in memorial of King George V, in January 1936.

The executive board of the Congregation B'Nai Moses stands in front of their synagogue, located at the corner of Horton and Colbourne Streets, in 1928. B'Nai Moses was London's third Jewish synagogue, and was built in the early 1900s.

Members of Young Judaea perform a hora to celebrate Purim at the Jewish Centre, March 18, 1946. From left to right are Telsa Silverstein, Rifcha Fox, Rita Rosen, Shefra Gangbar, and Sylvia Nelson.

Jewish children celebrate Purim on March 18, 1946, at the Jewish Centre.

Dundas Street Baptist Church, Argyle Park, began as a mission project of Central Baptist Church in March 1948. A year later, the church held two mid-week services in addition to Sunday services, and its Sunday School had nearly 200 children.

These ladies dressed in nineteenth-century costume to celebrate the 100th anniversary of Dundas Street Centre United Church in October 1946. The church is still active in 2017.

The sod-turning ceremony for St. David's Anglican Church on Hamilton Road at Hyla Street was conducted by Bishop F.N. Luxton on May, 1, 1949, while clergy and parishioners look on. An earlier stucco church was demolished to make way for the new building.

Bellwood Park United Church celebrated its first anniversary on April 3, 1949. At the time it was the newest of London's United Churches and was located in a growing neighborhood of wartime homes.

Pictured here in 1926, the African Methodist Episcopal Church, also known as the Fugitive Slave Chapel, was built on Thames Street in 1847. After the historic building was threatened by demolition, community groups rallied to save the church. In 2014 it was moved next to Beth Emmanuel Church on Grey Street and is to be restored.

Members of the children's choirs file up the walk to St. Paul's Cathedral, preceding more than 1,200 London children who attended a May Day service in 1949. The procession, escorted by the Police Boys' Band, marched from Victoria Park to the cathedral.

An ordination service was held at St. Peter's Cathedral on June 11, 1949, in which eleven students of St. Peter's Seminary were ordained to the priesthood by Bishop John T. Kidd of the Diocese of London. Here, the candidates to the priesthood orders are shown prostrate before the altar.

St. Paul's Cathedral, 1949.

# CULTURAL LIFE

In London's early days, residents entertained themselves any way they could: playing their own musical instruments, singing songs, and spending time with friends in homes or taverns—just to escape the hardships of life on the frontier for an hour or two. Over time, however, as London grew into a sizable city, its cultural life flourished, becoming more organized, more frequent, and more professional.

Even in pioneer times, civic and cultural organizations abounded—whether based in politics, religion, ethnic tradition, charity, or the arts—as a space for like-minded individuals to connect. One of the area's first organizations was the London District Agricultural Society, established in 1831—not surprising considering that the village was surrounded by farmland and improving agricultural methods was of major interest. Fraternal organizations were also early developments. The first recorded meeting of a Masonic Lodge was in May 1828. The Independent Order of Odd-Fellows had a branch in London in 1847, and there were five Orange Lodges in London and district by 1848. These early societies encouraged cultural engagement, forming the first foundations of a local arts community.

London's first dramatic performance was staged on December 18, 1839, by officers at a garrison theatre located on the southwest corner of Wellington and North (Queens Avenue). The men performed *Sweethearts and Wives* and *Bombastes Furioso* at what became known as The Theatre Royal. On January 17, 1844, the Gentleman Amateurs—the town's first civilian theatrical troupe—presented George Colman's *The Heir at Law* and James Townley's *High Life Below Stairs* at this theatre. The actors included members of London's elite, such as James Shanly, Jr. and Henry C.R. Becher, men with the means to dedicate time to the theatre.

Eventually, travelling companies found London on their maps, often while making their way between Toronto and Detroit. The first opera in London was performed in 1859 when Cooper's Opera Troupe performed *La sonnambula* at the Covent Garden Theatre, followed the next night by *The Barber of Seville*. One of the leading troupes of their day, the Holman Opera Company, made London their base in 1873, opening the Holman Opera House on the corner of Richmond and York streets. The family of singers and their opera house were overseen by family patriarch George

Holman, who spent part of his childhood in London. In 1881, the Holmans built the Grand Opera House, designed by renowned architect George Durand, on the northwest corner of Richmond and York streets. Seating as many as 1,128 theatre-goers at a time, the Grand provided London with a large enough auditorium to attract world-class entertainers. Stage darling Lily Langtry, known as "The Jersey Lily," appeared in November 1883. Internationally renowned French actress Sarah Bernhardt first appeared in London on April 8, 1896, starring in *La Tosca*—also at the Grand. Profitable for nearly 20 years, the Grand was gutted by fire on February 23, 1900, and rebuilt as an office building. A new Grand Opera House, later the Grand Theatre, opened on September 9, 1901. One of the largest theatres in southwestern Ontario, the Grand confirmed London's role as a leading cultural centre.

Of course, there were other theatres besides the Grand. The Princess Theatre opened on the north side of Dundas, west of Richmond, in September, 1911, featuring both motion pictures and vaudeville performances. Loew's Theatre, also on the north side of Dundas between Richmond and Clarence, opened to a crowd of 2,000 in February 1920. However, perhaps the most significant development for London's local theatre scene was the formation of the London Little Theatre, out of several smaller troupes, in late 1934. The LLT, led by the indomitable Catharine McCormick Brickenden, began to rent the Grand Theatre, where they would stage productions for the next 35 years—including finding national acclaim for their performance of *25 Cents* at the Dominion Festival in 1936.

While the theatre had a large and dedicated following, musical performances were often the most accessible cultural form for the public to enjoy. One of London's first large musical events was a promenade concert for about 800 people held December 14, 1865, in the drill shed on the barracks grounds, later Victoria Park, in aid of London's poor. The highlight was the 60th Rifles 64-piece band, possibly one of the largest and finest on the continent at the time. Over the years, it was discovered that nearly any large building could be used as a concert hall. The London Arena, built in 1923 on the southeast corner of Ridout and Bathurst streets, hosted the orchestras of Guy Lombardo (one of London's own), Woody Herman, Glenn Miller, and Benny Goodman.

London produced numerous visual artists who held exhibitions and provided art education. London artist Paul Peel was one of the first Canadian artists to receive international attention in his lifetime. His father, John Robert Peel, along with Charles Chapman and brothers James and John Griffiths, organized the first art exhibition in London in February 1878, establishing the Western School of Art and Design at about the same time. This school operated out of London's Mechanics' Institute—which had been established in 1835 as the first significant cultural institution in what was then a growing village; in fact, it was the third Mechanics' Institute in Upper Canada. A proto-library and centre of education, its first Greek Revival building opened on Court House Square in 1843. It was a place for local clubs and organizations to meet, and here, London's first Board of Trade was organized in 1857. Later, the Institute was on the south side of Dundas between Clarence and Wellington, built in a grand Second Empire style by local architect Thomas H. Tracy in 1877. It was there the Western School of Art and Design had its offices and held art lessons on weekday evenings in the 1880s and 1890s.

In May 1895, the Mechanics' Institute merged with the Free Library Board to form London Public Library. The Mechanics' Institute became the Music Hall, and a new public library opened on November 26, 1895, on the southwest corner of Wellington and Queens to provide culture and learning to the next generation of Londoners. This building was in turn replaced by the Elsie Perrin Williams Memorial Library and Art Museum in 1940. The library, in its various forms, has probably done more to provide Londoners with amusement and instruction than any other institution. It even had a "bookmobile" delivering reading materials to parts of the city not served by a library branch.

A unique feature of London's central library was its marriage with a permanent art gallery. Indeed, before there were formal galleries, many buildings and businesses held art shows. Paul Peel famously exhibited his painting at the Tecumseh Hotel in 1890. Smallman and Ingram's department store exhibited nearly 50 paintings of local artist Clare Bice in April 1936. While the Western Fair opened the city's first exhibition space in 1913, London art finally received a proper home at the Elsie Perrin Williams Memorial Library in 1940—joined two years later by the McIntosh Memorial Art Gallery at Western University, featuring a selection of World War I paintings from the National Gallery of Canada.

One thing is certain: early Londoners were not starved for culture. Despite its proximity to the glamour and glitz of Toronto, London's arts scene flourished in the first half of the twentieth century, solidifying its place on the nation's cultural map for generations to come.

In November, 1938, members of the Canadian Order of Foresters paraded from Adelaide Street and Hamilton Road to Egerton Street Baptist Church where Rev. P. D. Cameron addressed the gathering on "Religion, Relation, and Reality."

This Christmas card from the Fotoforum Photographic and Stereoscopic Society of London wishes friends a Merry Christmas and a Happy New Year, 1941.

Chinese Freemasons Banquet held at Wong's Café on Richmond Street, 1944.

Stratford Orangemen led a London church parade east along Dundas Street on July 4, 1948. Fifes played "Finnegan's Wake" and "Rise Sons of William" as nearly 400 men and women, representing Orange Lodges from London and district, marched to Maitland Street Baptist Church in the London Orange Lodge annual church parade.

Men shovel snow in front of the Moose Temple on March 25, 1947. The fraternal organization, founded in 1888, had branches across North America and is still active in London today.

Shriners from all over Western Ontario met in London for a "spring ceremonial" on May 21, 1948. A parade, headed by the Mocha Mosque brass band under the direction of Fred J. Weekes, started at the Masonic Temple and made its way to the London Arena.

The British Companions Club meets at the YMCA on July 21, 1949. Seated from left to right are Violet Nelson, Marjre Kilroy (secretary), Connie Waddell, and Mrs. Rand Ford (president). The group of 60 British war brides assisted newcomers from England settle in Canada. Here, they sort a donation of 300 comic books to be sent to the United Kingdom.

London's Mechanics' Institute and Museum, on Talbot Street, circa 1860s. A precursor to the London Public Library, it was meant to be a self-improvement centre for "the working classes," offering lectures, concerts, exhibitions, and a lending library.

London's first public library building opened November 26, 1895, on the southwest corner of Wellington Street and Queens Avenue. It closed its doors on September 20, 1940, replaced by the Elsie Perrin Williams Memorial Library and Art Museum.

The children's section of the new public library pictured in November, 1940. With its wood panelling and fireplace, the *Free Press* called it "one of the most impressive in all of Canada."

Elsie Perrin Williams, circa 1910. Daughter of London manufacturer Daniel S. Perrin, Elsie left her estate, "Windermere," to the City of London when she died in 1934. The city, however, broke her will in order to use her money for other projects, including the building of the Elsie Perrin Williams Memorial Library and Art Museum on Queens Avenue.

The new $285,000 Elsie Perrin Williams Memorial Library and Art Museum opened the afternoon of Friday, October 4, 1940. The new library could hold 48,000 volumes and also featured an auditorium and children's library. Here visitors view the art gallery on the second floor, containing a loan exhibition of Canadian art.

Londoners read books and magazines at London Public Library in March, 1945.

A Citizen's Forum, titled "Canada in the Postwar World," chaired by R.T. Bell in an office at the London Public Library, 1945.

Listening to gramophone records in the LPL listening room, March 1945. Two of the patrons are in uniform. The London Public Library was the first in Canada to offer music recordings.

Staff member Barbara Morphy reaches for a film in the motion picture film section of the library, March 1945. Patrons could borrow 16mm films, beginning in 1942.

The brand new cabin trailer, the first of its kind in Ontario, was used to distribute books throughout the Middlesex County library circuit in October, 1940. The trailer held more than 1,000 books and had electric lights and a stove.

Mrs. Mary Barber, county librarian, seated behind the folding desk inside the trailer.

Mountsfield School pupils line up to return books to the County of Middlesex bookmobile in December, 1948. Besides Mountsfield, the green truck went to three other suburban schools: Argyle, Manor Park, and Broughdale.

Rental statues available from June Sadler, London Public Library, December 4, 1948. In 1942, head librarian Richard Crouch and curator Clare Bice started the lending Library of Canadian Art, where patrons could borrow artwork to display in their homes.

Guy Lombardo and his London Winter Gardens Orchestra, circa 1923, taken on stage at Loew's Theatre. The group was not renamed the Royal Canadians until after they left for the United States in 1924 to pursue a recording career. Guy is at far right while Carmen Lombardo is third from left and Liebert Lombardo is fourth from left.

Frank Crowley and his orchestra in the 1930s. Crowley was a London native, having graduated from De La Salle High School. He and his band played throughout the Great Depression at such venues as the Masonic Temple and Springbank Pavilion. He died age 34, December 12, 1943, in Windsor.

The Johnny Downs Orchestra, 1946. A talented teenager, Johnny Downs organized his first band in 1939 when he was only 17. This local band played at dance halls throughout London and Western Ontario, including Port Stanley's famous Stork Club.

A large student choir performs at the Grand Theatre in 1920. The choir director was Edgar William Goethe Quantz, director of music in London schools. He also held positions as organist and choirmaster at various churches.

The jitterbug was all the rage in London dance halls in July 1940. Thelma Bartlett of Byron and Ray Millson of London show off their "jitterbug costumes"—loose clothes, flat-heeled shoes, and bare arms. The other essential for the new dance was "hot music" supplied by an orchestra.

London Chamber Orchestra performs at the Aeolian Hall, the former Beecher United Church, in December 1948. Gordon Jeffery is at the organ. London's newest concert venue could seat 550 persons.

London Promenade Orchestra, in one of its first concerts, October 1946, with conductor Raymond Neal. The orchestra took its name from the "promenade" concerts popular in England during the war years. Still active today, it is the oldest orchestra in London.

The "famous Lucan Male Choir" performed under their director, Mrs. Harold Sturgis, at the Middlesex Seed Fair and Export Show, March 1948.

Also performing at the 1948 Middlesex Seed Fair and Export Show, the Lucan dancing girls were members of the Anglican Young People's Association (AYPA) from Holy Trinity Church, Lucan. They appeared with the Lucan Male Choir "in a full scale Minstrel Show."

Arguably London's most famous artist, Paul Peel is pictured here sketching at Pont-Aven, France, circa 1885. To the right of the tree is his fiancée, Isaure Verdier, while to the left of the tree is his sister Mildred Peel. Paul is at far left, kneeling.

While the Western Fair was in progress on September 10, 1912, Ontario Agriculture Minister James S. Duff opened this Art Gallery at Queen's Park. It was designed by the firm of Watt & Blackwell who also built the McCormick Biscuit factory on Dundas Street East. This building was London's first permanent art gallery.

Boris Volkoff, founder of ballet in Canada, paid a short visit to the London School of Ballet on March 24, 1949. Here he examines the pose of Colleen Kenney and Patsy Steel, Grade 8 ballet students.

London Ladies' Choir reorganized in January 1949 after an inactive period during and after the war. Their weekly rehearsal with Earle Terry, superintendent of music for London schools, was held at the CNR office.

Crowds attend the cornerstone-laying ceremony for the new McIntosh Memorial Art Gallery at the University of Western Ontario on June 30, 1941. The money for the new gallery was provided by the late Wilhelmina Morris McIntosh. Arthur R. Ford, chairman of the building committee, stressed the value of the gallery to the university and to London: "This afternoon marks another step forward in the progress of the university of which we are so proud."

London artist Clare Bice, curator of the Elsie Perrin Williams Memorial Art Museum at the library, is seen putting the finishing touches on a painting in his studio, March 22, 1947. When not painting, Bice illustrated children's books.

Artist Kathleen Hart in her Byron studio March 30, 1948. The *Free Press* photo was taken at a time when Warner Brothers was featuring the artist in a newsreel. Born without hands and feet, Kay held her brush between her elbow-length arms as she stood on two artificial limbs.

London artist Paul Peel was born in 1859 at 238 Richmond Street, shown in this 1948 photo when it was about 100 years old. The house has since been demolished.

A performance at the London Asylum concert hall in 1903. Whether the performance is for or by patients is not known.

The Masonic Temple opened September, 1881, on the north-west corner of Richmond and King. A multipurpose building, designed by George Durand, it contained a 1,128-seat concert hall called the Grand Opera House in its upper storeys.

Holman Opera House, northwest corner of York and Richmond streets, October 1874. Built by Ellis Hyman in 1866, it seated about 580 people, but was torn down in 1881 when it was replaced by the Grand Opera House.

Over time, a canvas mural covering the proscenium ceiling in the Grand Theatre loosened due to dampness. The painting, showing Grecian ladies, was probably by the Detroit artist Henry Droishagen and added when the theatre was built as the Grand Opera House in 1901. Here, William Griffin, Grand Theatre maintenance man, is shown re-pasting the mural in February 1949.

The London Little Theatre's production of Canadian play, *Twenty-Five Cents*, garnered them first prize at the Dominion Festival in 1936. Directed by Catharine McCormick Brickenden, the actors pictured here, mid-scene, are: Marvyn Kenyon, Kitty Bletz Walker, Jack Glennie, and Margaret Glass, from left to right.

On June 10, 1948, Patricia Theatre manager Tom McKnight used a "gorilla" to advertise one of his features, the film *Congorilla*. McKnight, in straw hat with cigarette, looks perturbed as the police officer on duty at Dundas and Richmond makes out a jaywalking ticket for the "star" of the movie.

Mayor George Wenige (left) and Chief of Police Earl Knight pause before one of the posters advertising Naked City, as they enter Loew's Theatre. The semi-documentary film starring Barry Fitzgerald opened April 15, 1948, giving an "accurate and thrilling" account of the work of the New York homicide squad.

Hundreds of Londoners lined up on November 17, 1948, hoping to get tickets for Purple Patches, UWO's Annual Revue, held at the Grand Theatre on November 22–27.

Three postcards show the 1908 Old Boys' Reunion Mardi Gras, a carnival held August 3–8 that year. The last reunion, the city's seventh, had been held in 1905. Buildings such as the Edge Block, pictured here, were decorated for the occasion.

In March, 1939, St. Joseph's Day celebrations were held by the Polish Nationalist Association at the Polish Community Hall on Hill Street. Dancing girls performed traditional dance under the direction of Mrs. Antonette Bladek. Back row from left to right: Janina Lupa, Stella Wielgosz, Jozefa Bogal, Jozefa Wielgosz, Bronice Stanczak. Front row from left to right: Helen Szymla, Sofi Adamski, Celia Wielgosz, Janina Kula, Janina Baron, Caroline Kula, Wanda Ciamaga, Elizabeth Adamski.

Cutting the haggis to bagpipe music on Robbie Burns Day, January 25, 1939. The event occurred at Hamilton Road Presbyterian Church where the ladies prepared a haggis dinner for the congregation. Here Annie Henderson, President of the Ladies' Aid, cuts the haggis after it was piped in by Pipe Major Peter Russell (right). Church elder William Sibbald (left) carried in the haggis.

The Canada First Conservative Club held their annual "hard times" masquerade party at Highland Golf Club on the evening of October 28, 1938.

On Sunday, September 9, 1945, a Chinese play was performed free of charge at Loew's Theatre. The occasion marked the Chinese victory celebration at the end of World War II.

Springbank's miniature Railway closed temporarily on July 24, 1949, after the operator, James Kennedy, was warned by the OPP that he would be liable to prosecution under the Lord's Day Act for running the ride on a Sunday. The warning was part of a province-wide "purge" against miniature railways, miniature golf courses, archery courses, and other grounds open on Sunday.

Ethel Benstead was crowned Queen of St. Matthew's Church Summer Festival by Mayor Allan Johnston on July 5, 1939. From left to right: Pat Watt, trainbearer; Mayor Johnston; "Queen" Ethel; Rev. A.A. Trumper, rector; Evelyn Morley and June Broadley, attendants; and five-year-old Bobby Moody, who as "Prince Charming" carried the crown.

# FIREMEN

Destructive fires were one of the greatest threats to pioneer London. The earliest known fire was in November 1832, when the Dickinson blacksmith shop burned down along with most of its equipment. Seven years later, London faced its first major blaze, when in February, several buildings on the south side of Dundas between Ridout and Talbot were destroyed. The Great Dundas Street Fire broke out in October 1844, this time on the north side of the street between Ridout and Talbot—but it managed to spread and destroy buildings on the south side as well. On April 13, 1845, the Great Fire of London destroyed nearly 30 acres of property, perhaps one fifth of the town. More than 100 homes and businesses were engulfed by the flames that started rising in the Robinson Hall Hotel stables. The fact that the Great Fire did not reach the west side of Ridout Street is indicated by surviving pre-1845 structures, such as the Old Courthouse, the Ridout Street Restoration, and Eldon House.

Needless to say, early town officials did their best to prevent such conflagrations. In June, 1850, the town passed a bylaw forbidding the use of frame buildings downtown, encouraging builders to use the local white brick. Another early bylaw prohibited cigars and pipes in stables and outhouses and ordered that candles in such places be enclosed by a lantern. No able-bodied passerby was allowed to stand and gawk at a fire, council insisting that those who refused to fight fires be penalized with a jail sentence. In 1838, each ratepayer was required to keep a leather bucket for bucket brigade purposes. By 1842, water tanks were situated at street corners, householders forbidden to remove water for personal use. Yet, the reality was that these measures were of little use in a major fire.

One particularly desperate measure was carried out on February 7, 1851, when a fire started in a building owned by Maurice Baker on Talbot Street. The idea was to control the outbreak by tearing the structure down before the fire inside could spread to a neighbouring building. While it seems impossible that a building could be torn down faster than it could burn, this tactic was apparently effective.

Devastating fires continued to be a problem for Londoners throughout the nineteenth century and into the twentieth. Fires were easily caused by overheated stoves, faulty furnaces, lightning strikes, and substances like turpentine, when left uncovered. The oil refineries of London East were especially vulnerable to fires. On January 23, 1867, Thompson & Hendershott's oil refinery lost 30 barrels of oil when a workman entered with a lamp in his hand, resulting in instant ignition. Perhaps ironically, the Ontario Mutual Fire Insurance Company opened on Richmond Street that same year.

Fire often spelled the end for businesses. The partnership of George Jackson and John Elliott, formed in 1850, ended when their foundry burned down only one year later. Prominent industries and stores were not immune; even Labatt's burned on March 5, 1874, with a loss of $50,000, only $20,000 of which was covered by insurance. Kingsmill's was entirely destroyed on January 7, 1932, and had to be completely rebuilt that year.

Beyond the destruction of property and assets, fire often had deadly consequences. The first recorded death of a London fireman was in 1855, when 22-year-old John Eskdale of the Hook and Ladder Company was trapped inside a blazing home on Talbot Street and burned to death. The Westman Hardware Store fire on August 18, 1908, took three lives, including that of Fire Chief Lawrence Clark. On March 3, 1934, a fire at the Hunt Milling Company on Nightingale Avenue cost the lives of District Chief Stanley T. Scruby and Lt. Arthur R. Hartop when powerful water jets kicked up flour dust inside the mill, causing a huge blast.

Unfortunately, another cause of fires was arson. Crosby & Dart's fanning mill shop near the southwest corner of Richmond and Hitchcock (Dufferin) burned down, along with all tools and materials for 300 fanning mills, August 7, 1874. The partners rebuilt on the same site, offering a £50 reward for the arrest of the arsonist. The outcome is unknown. In 1849, the store Laurason & Chisholm on the northwest corner of Dundas was burned by an arsonist. Town Council itself offered a reward of £350, a sizable sum in the mid-nineteenth century. The reward was never claimed. Some speculate that the string of arson could be traced to the early fire companies, the members being paid cash for each fire they attended; however, with no evidence, the fires could just as likely be the work of pyromaniacs.

The earliest record of a volunteer fire company is in November, 1841, when men were called to a chimney blaze in Dennis O'Brien's block. The city's first permanent, paid fire brigade—the Forest City Fire Company—began service in 1873 with its own team of horses. London's first hand pump fire engine was purchased in 1844, donated to the town by affluent merchant George J. Goodhue. Described as a "garden sprinkler," it was destroyed in the Great Fire "when after a minute's work, it was abandoned and disappeared in a general ruin." The town persisted in purchasing firefighting equipment, however, hoping for better results. In 1867, a four-wheeled hose cart and 600 ft. of rubber hose were purchased from the New York Fire Department. By 1879, there were nine fire hydrants in the city, scattered at various downtown intersections. Fire alarm boxes were installed in the 1880s at locations such as Dundas and Adelaide, Richmond and Fullerton, and Queens and Waterloo.

Previously, hand pumpers were drawn by firemen on tow ropes, or a team of horses could be commandeered from a passing farmer to pull the equipment. The first ladder was purchased in 1895, mounted on a horse-drawn truck and raised by cranks operated by six men.

In 1911 tests were conducted by the fire department to learn if there were advantages to using the newfangled motorized fire trucks then replacing horse-drawn apparatus. On three separate runs, the horses arrived first. This was likely because early motorized trucks had to be cranked to start while horses were "raring to go." Despite these results, the first motorized fire truck was purchased by the city in 1912 and christened "Kaiser Bill" in an unusual moment of pre-war tolerance. But there was great resistance to replacing the department horses, the animals seemingly being regarded by Londoners as heroic as the firemen themselves. The department's last horse, Doc, did not retire until about 1928.

London's first proto-fire hall—little more than a storage space for the fire engine—was located on the north side of North Street (Carling) between Richmond and Talbot in 1847. The Central Fire Hall was built on the north side of King between Richmond and Clarence in 1853. As London's suburbs were annexed, it was necessary to provide firefighting outlets in each area. The city's next fire station opened in the former London East Town Hall at Dundas and Rectory. The third was built on the north side of Bruce Street, just east of Wortley, about 1890, after the annexation of London South. Fire Halls 4 and 5 were built in 1908 on the southwest corner of Colborne and St. James and on the east side of Adelaide between Grey and Hill. All four later buildings may be seen to this day, although none are now fire halls.

While firefighting is certainly an essential service to this day, for early Londoners, fires were a constant menace to the growing town—threatening livelihoods, infrastructure, and even personal safety.

London's Central Fire Hall, in the foreground, was located on the north side of King Street between Richmond and Clarence, pictured here in the 1850s.

London Fire Brigade, 1870s, lined up along Queens Avenue just east of Richmond Street. The building on the left is the Custom House.

A fire broke out at the Labatt Brewery in March, 1874, starting in the engine room. It rapidly spread throughout the brewery, reducing it to rubble. Despite the devastating loss, John Labatt rebuilt it by December of that year.

London Central Fire Station, circa 1873. The equipment includes two steamers, two hose reels, and a ladder wagon.

Firemen pose outside the Central Fire Station in this early photograph. Note the hats with section numbers.

Carling Brewery after a fire on February 13, 1879. The brewery reopened for business on May 29 of that year.

Department staff before the Central Fire Hall on King Street, circa 1889.

A scene from the Westman Hardware fire of 1908, preserved on a souvenir postcard. The devastating fire took place in the Cronyn Block on the south side of Dundas Street. The view shows firemen battling the blaze from the rear on Market Square. The fire took the lives of Fire Chief Lawrence Clark, Fireman Henry M. Wein, and Sgt. John "Jock" Cockburn of the 7th Regiment.

The funeral procession for Fire Chief Lawrence Clark reaches the corner of Dundas and Richmond, August 21, 1908.

Firemen battle a blaze at the Masonic Temple, in February, 1900, seen here looking south on Richmond.

The postmortem of the Masonic Temple fire, 1900. Despite firefighters' best efforts, the building—home to the Grand Opera House and offices—was gutted. One of the tenants, Dominion Savings, purchased the building after the fire to rebuild.

London Fire Department trucks on King Street, circa 1915.

The Fire Insurance Underwriters organization conducts water pressure and flow tests on Fire Department apparatus in front of the J. Darch & Sons building on Talbot Street.

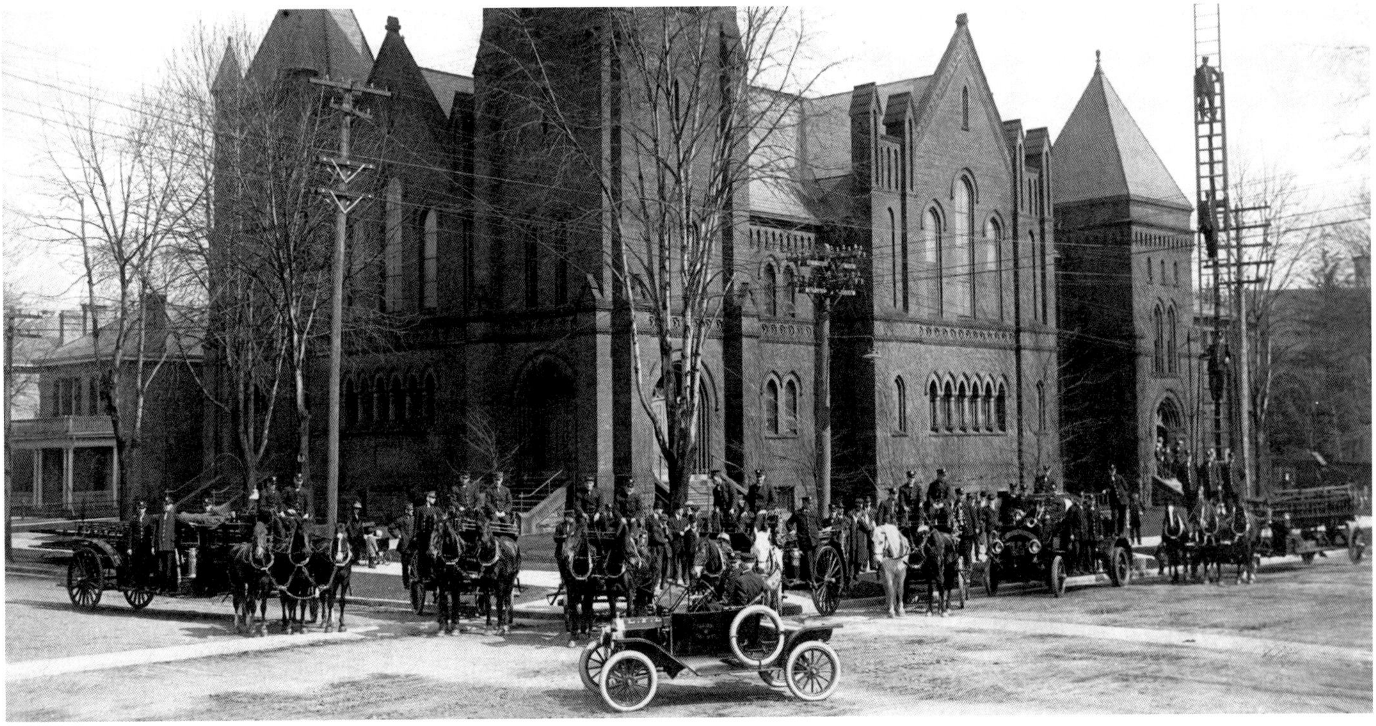

London Fire Department poses in front of First Methodist Church (now Metropolitan United) at the corner of Wellington Street and Dufferin Avenue in 1913. At centre, Fire Chief John Aitken sits in the first Fire Chief Car, a 1913 Ford Model-T Runabout. Aitken's face is turned away from the camera. Also present in the picture is the department's first motorized truck, a 1912 Seagrave Chemical Combination that carried hose and 40 gallons of water.

Fire Hall No. 5 on the west side of Adelaide Street between Grey and Hill streets. The tower, located at rear, was for the "look-out-man" to spot fires. By the 1950s, this system was replaced by a telephone and mechanical alarms.

A postcard of the 1911 Dundas Street fire that destroyed seven of London's finest businesses. The fire started in Chapman's dry goods store.

Blacksmiths hired by members of the London Fire Department, 1914. They were hired to make shoes for the department horses or to make tools.

Ruins of the Grand Trunk freight sheds after the fire of March 6, 1920. Of undetermined origin, the blaze destroyed all but the bonded warehouse. All stored freight was destroyed by either fire or water.

"Doc," last horse of the London Fire Department, retired at the age of 32 in about 1928. He had served with the department since 1903.

Now Aeolian Hall, the main floor of this building in East London served as Fire Station No. 2 from 1885 to 1946.

A fire at Yocum Faust chemical plant at the corner of Piccadilly and St. George destroyed $25,000 worth of fish and castor oils and industrial chemicals. In this photo, firemen on the lower roof are trying to pour water on the top of the building.

Representatives of London district fire brigades attended a two-day Firemen's Training School at UWO in May, 1941. Training included lectures on arson and sabotage, information about incendiary bombs and warfare, and various practical demonstrations such as those seen here.

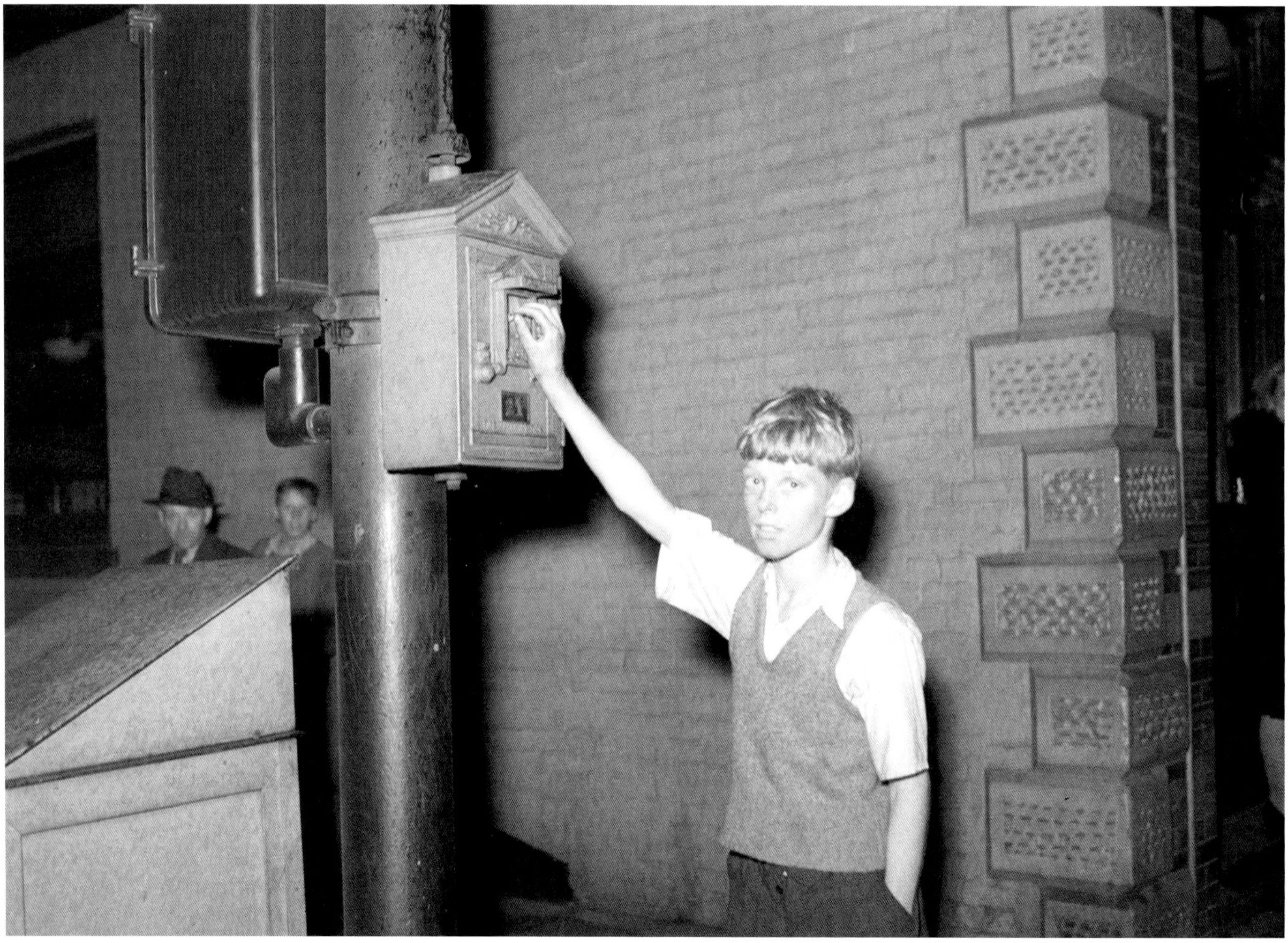

On October 15, 1942, the London Fire Department fought a blaze at Charles Chapman Bookbinding on Dundas Street, west of Talbot. Twelve-year-old Edward Ede was the hero who raised the alarm from a call box.

Firemen at No. 4 Fire Hall salute as the hearse carrying Firefighter James Moir passes by in 1949. Moir, who worked at No. 4 Fire Hall, had passed away from natural causes.

Flames raced through a General Steel Wares building on the south side of York Street in February, 1948, causing $50,000 worth of damage.

The prompt response of city firemen prevented a more serious fire on July 11, 1948, at Wong's Restaurant next to the *Free Press* building. Reportedly, customers in the billiard room in the basement were told the building was on fire, but continued playing.

Firemen pose at the East End Fire Hall on Florence Street, September 26, 1949. Pictured from left to right are, Captain Norm Gillathy, Harry Cudmore, Keith Newman, and Jack Johnson.

On January 22, 1949, at about 8:00 a.m., a loaded ten-ton semi-trailer careened off Highway 2 and crashed into the Rendezvous roadhouse, setting fire to the building and trapping the driver in his cab. Driver Ralph Bailey, 23, was dead before firemen could reach him. The restaurant owner and his family escaped the wreckage of their Crumlin business. Coils of fence wire the truck was carrying are shown strewn about in this picture.

# HOSPITALS & HEALTH CARE

In the nineteenth century, most Londoners who were ill received treatment—if any—in their own homes, called upon by local doctors. Hospitals were left as refuges for the very poor and for the quarantined sick during epidemics. Medical treatment was fairly primitive and life expectancies by the turn of the century were grim at 50 years of age. Indeed, one record from 1832 details a Dr. Patrick Donnelly, who died during a cholera epidemic when, attempting to treat his patients, he himself became a victim of the disease. In the generations that followed London's founding, healthcare infrastructure grew rapidly in the town as the age of modern medicine began—with the Forest City often pioneering the way.

One of the earliest medical centres in London was a cholera hospital, built along Hamilton Road in 1854, possessing four wards with accommodation for ten patients each. Although this building burned down in 1857, other primitive hospital buildings existed in London over the next decades until more permanent institutions were established.

London General Hospital was built in 1875, and renamed Victoria Hospital at the time of Queen Victoria's diamond jubilee in 1897. Built on South Street west of Colborne, the hospital expanded its services and departments until, by the early 1900s, it had special wards for children, consumptives, and contagious diseases, as well as quarters for surgeons and staff. Nursing training for women was provided by the hospital from 1883. When an expansive new wing opened May 26, 1941, the opening ceremony featured Dr. Leonard G. Rowntree, a London native who that same year was appointed head of the medical division in the U.S. Selective Service board by President Truman.

With the burgeoning of humanitarian initiatives in late Victorian times, it was not long before other hospitals were established to serve London's growing population. In 1888, St. Joseph's Hospital opened, operated by the Sisters of St. Joseph on the north side of Grosvenor between Richmond and Wellington. It had humble beginnings, with only four doctors and room for 24 patients, but "St. Joe's" also expanded as needs arose and funds became available.

Other medical institutions included the Home for the Incurables, founded in 1894 by the Women's Christian

Association. It later evolved into Parkwood Hospital on the south side of Grand Avenue. The Queen Alexandra Sanatorium opened in Byron in 1910 to treat tuberculosis, eventually being renamed Beck Memorial Sanatorium in 1949. An Institute of Public Health opened next to Victoria Hospital in 1912. On May 1, 1920, Westminster Hospital opened in a new building at the southeast corner of Commissioners and Wellington. Westminster was a Department of Veterans' Affairs hospital that provided rehabilitation and treatment for those injured overseas. Here, London artist Selwyn Dewdney and his wife Irene pioneered the use of art therapy for psychiatric patients in Canada. The War Memorial Children's Hospital opened on the northwest corner of Colborne and South streets in 1923. The rise of these institutions made London the centre for medical care in Western Ontario.

One hospital of particular importance was the Lunatic Asylum, which received its first patients in November, 1870. The building's name became more euphemistic over the years, changing into the London Asylum for the Insane, before finally being renamed the Ontario Hospital in 1932. Its most famous superintendent was Dr. Richard Maurice Bucke who served as its head for decades, almost until his death in 1902. A reformer who believed treating mental illness meant treating the entire person, Bucke encouraged his patients to take part in organized sports and receive what would now be called occupational therapy.

Women played a greater role in health care after nursing became viewed as a respectable female career in the nineteenth century. Most nurses received their training in hospitals to begin with, living in special residences built on site. In 1906, the London branch of the Victorian Order of Nurses was founded, with the redoubtable women's activist Harriet Boomer as president of its board of directors.

London also became known for medical research and discoveries. Dr. Frederick G. Banting, while living in a house on the southeast corner of Adelaide Street and Queens Avenue on October 31, 1920, conceived the idea that led to the discovery of insulin. Doctors Evan V. and Wilfrid E. Shute, along with Arthur Vogelsang, claimed in May 1946, that high doses of vitamin E could relieve heart disease. In 1948, they opened the Shute Institute for Clinical and Laboratory Medicine at Waverley, the former Goodhue mansion on the northeast corner of Grand Avenue and Ridout Street. There, they undertook further research into preventing heart disease.

Of course, the story of medicine in London was not without its setbacks. A branch of the Anti-Vaccination League opened in November 1909. The patent medicines sold by druggists were largely useless. Moreover, many Londoners would have nothing to do with the hospitals, regarding them as places to get sick, not cured.

Nevertheless, the story of medicine in London is generally one of progress, as Londoners followed the general path of Canadians elsewhere, learning research methods, finding and using cures and controllers, providing physiotherapy, vaccinations, and x-rays. Gradually, as well, came the idea that everyone should be treated, not just those who could afford the best care. Children were vaccinated in the schools as were members of the armed forces. Medical care became preventive care, as the public were educated about best health practices through classes and hospital tours. By 1950, a well-informed London was an increasingly healthy London.

Main building at the London Lunatic Asylum, circa 1875. The asylum admitted its first patients on November 18, 1870, under Superintendent Dr. Henry Landor.

Dr. Richard Maurice Bucke, at centre, Superintendent of the London Asylum from 1877–1902, sits with members of his family on the steps of the medical superintendent's house, 1899. Bucke was a health care reformer who encouraged asylum patients to take part in organized sports and experience occupational therapy. Bucke is also famous for his friendship with American poet, Walt Whitman.

The main building, with its signature bell tower, of Victoria Hospital on postcard, circa 1907.

London's General Hospital opened November 3, 1875, on South Street. Renamed Victoria Hospital in honour of Queen Victoria's Diamond Jubilee in 1897, the hospital was vastly expanded, nearly filling a city block, when it was rededicated on November 16, 1899.

Pictured here in the 1870s, this building was constructed as a home by William Barker in 1854, and became Mount Hope Orphanage in 1869. Once situated on the west side of Richmond Street between College and Grosvenor streets, it was demolished in 1963.

Children and staff gather on the lawn of Mount Hope Orphanage, circa 1870. The Sisters of St. Joseph operated the home, which also became a refuge for the sick, destitute, and elderly.

St. Joseph's Hospital, circa 1892, on the north side of Grosvenor east of Richmond. The hospital opened in 1888 in the former home of lawyer (later Judge) W.P.R. Street, visible at far right. The hospital was founded by the Sisters of St. Joseph who came to London in 1868 and were encouraged to open a larger medical facility following the success of Mount Hope Orphanage. Today, St. Joseph's is one of London's major hospitals.

The old west wing of Victoria Hospital, with the nurses' residence at right, circa 1917.

A scarlet fever quarantine sign such as this would be fixed to any home where the dangerous communicable disease had struck.

The Victoria Home for Incurables is pictured here in its second home at 703 Dundas Street, which opened in 1903. The Women's Christian Association founded the home on Hamilton Road in 1894. In 1921, it would move to "Parkwood," the former residence of John R. Minhinnick on Grand Avenue, which would grow into Parkwood Hospital.

The Queen Alexandra Sanatorium for the treatment of tuberculosis opened in 1910, overlooking the Thames near the village of Byron. In 1949, it was renamed the Beck Memorial Sanatorium, and remained open until 1972.

After the First World War, many soldiers returning to Canada were stricken with tuberculosis. Here, recuperating veterans lounge outside a pavilion at Queen Alexandra Sanatorium—a photo included in a 1917 fundraising campaign for the sanatorium called "How Big Is Your Heart?"

The Cliff Infirmary at the Sanatorium. The man standing in the bowler hat may be Dr. Delmar Alan Craig, Medical Superintendent from 1913 to 1917.

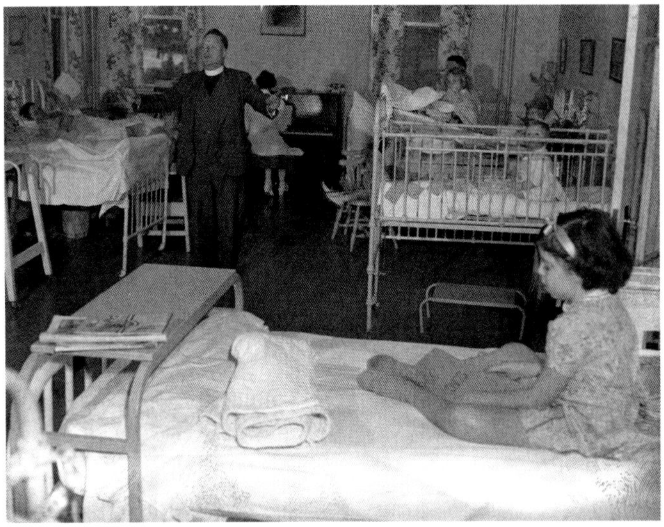

Canon Alford Abraham of St. Andrew Memorial Anglican Church conducted "Sunday School" on Tuesday afternoons at War Memorial Children's Hospital in 1949.

War Memorial Children's Hospital opened on South Street in 1922, located across from Victoria Hospital. Today, while the Children's Hospital continues at a new location, this building sits empty.

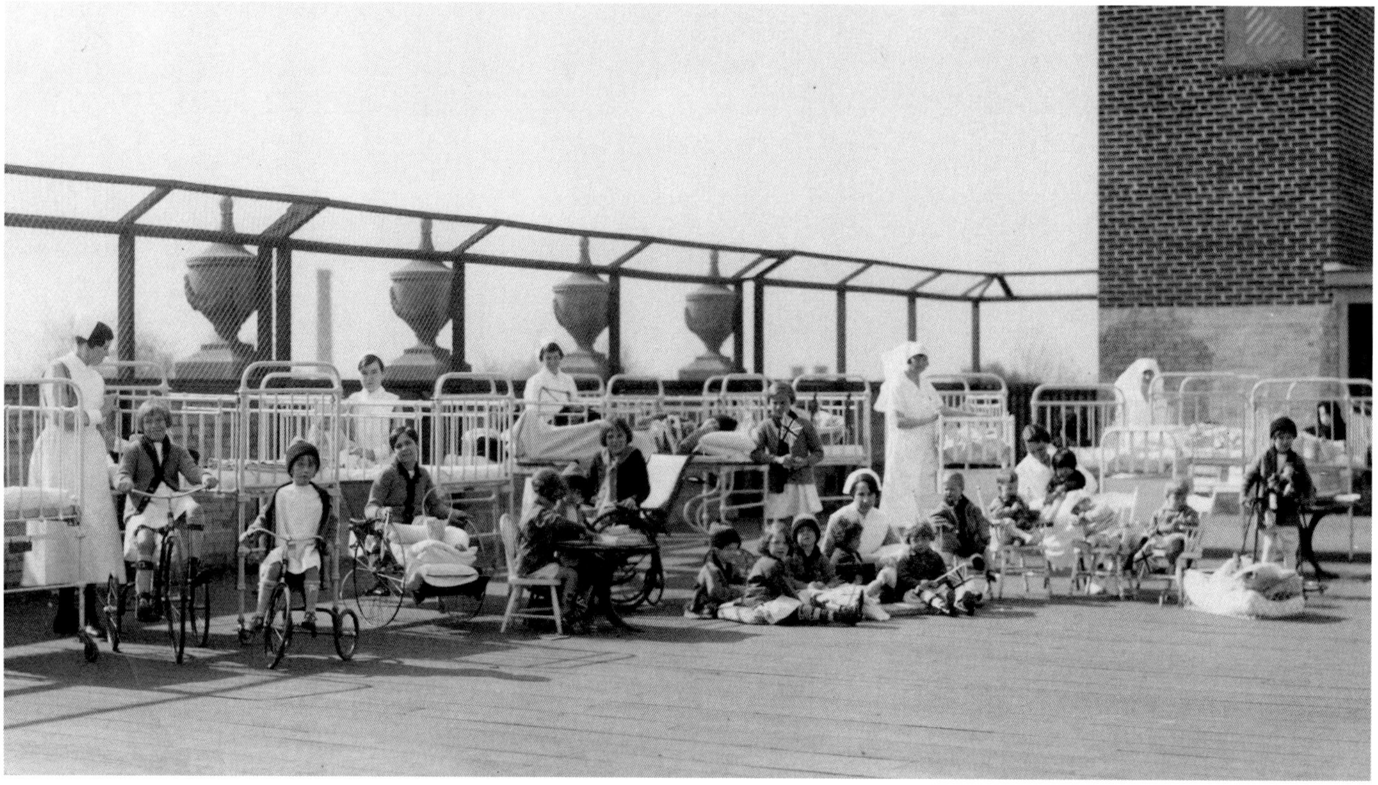

Nurses and young patients at War Memorial Children's Hospital in the late 1920s. Built with funds raised by the Imperial Order Daughters of the Empire, the facility opened with a 60-bed capacity.

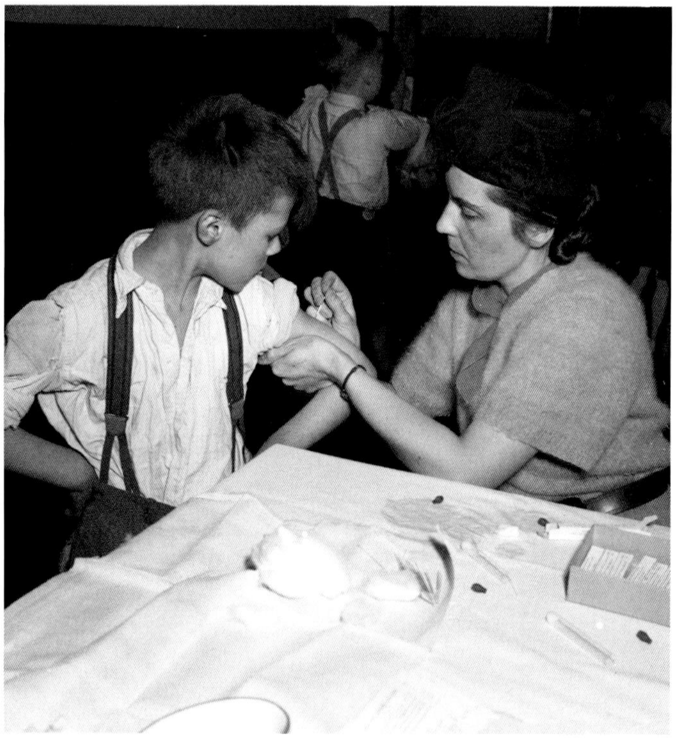

On January 4, 1939, 65 doctors injected smallpox vaccine into thousands of babies and young children. The program was extended to secondary schools the next day. Altogether, about 90% of London's children were immunized. By the mid-1940s, smallpox was eradicated in Canada.

180 Western undergraduates heard Nobel Prize Winner Sir Frederick Banting (centre) lecture in the Medical School auditorium on November 21, 1938. At right is Dr. C.B. Stewart, of the National Research Council and at left is Dr. F.J.H. Campbell, dean of the Faculty of Medicine. In his speech, Banting said devoting one's life to medical research was the greatest possible contribution towards the welfare of mankind. Banting co-discovered insulin and how to isolate it from the pancreas in 1921.

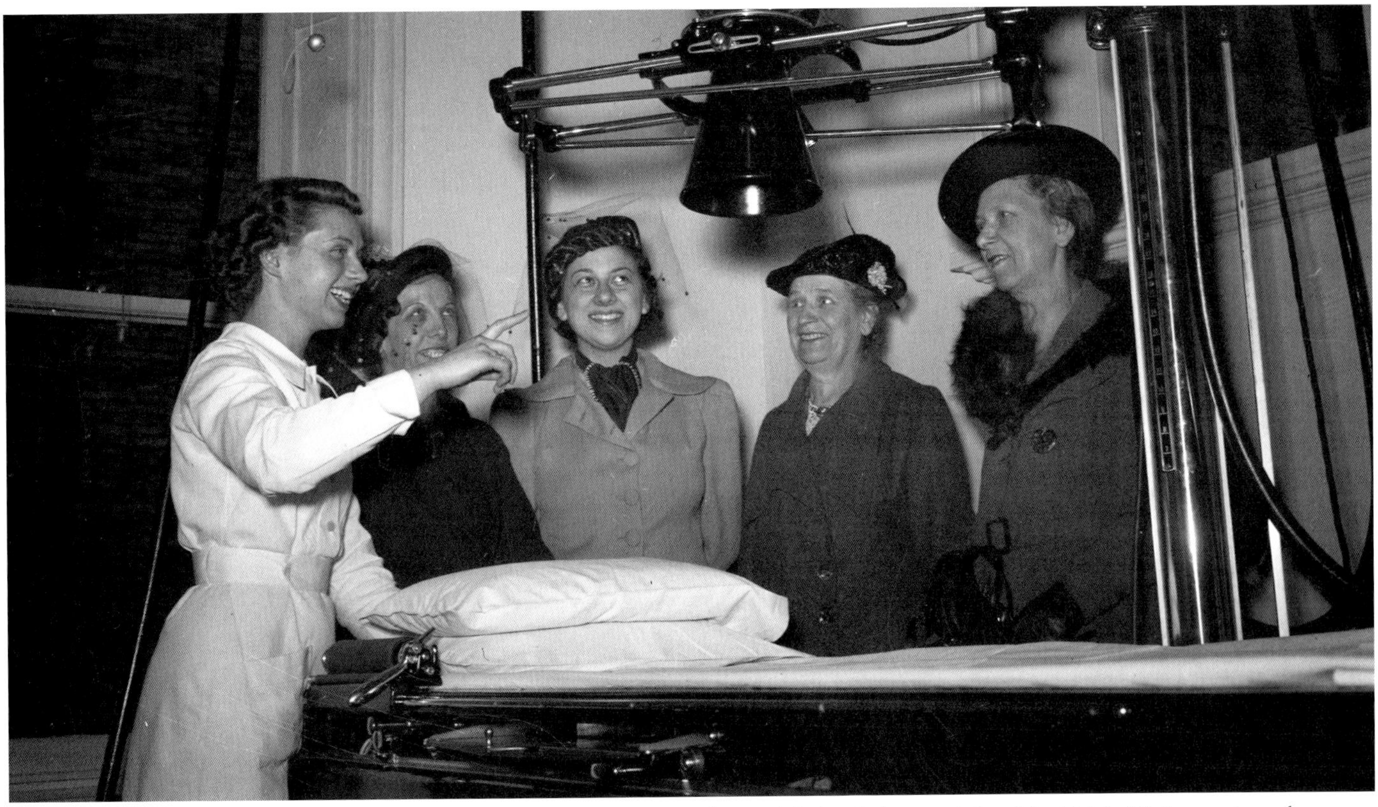

Hospitals opened for citizens' inspection to mark Florence Nightingale's birthday on May 12, 1939. Visitors view the x-ray apparatus in the radiology department at St. Joseph's Hospital. Staff member Netta Semchism explains the equipment to, from left to right, Elizabeth Toohey, Muriel Codling, Emma Moule, and Annie Moule.

On April 4, 1939, the *Free Press* covered the funeral of Mrs. Domenic Pallaria—likely Ontario's largest woman at 500 lbs. Pallaria, wife of a jeweller who lived at 345 Clarence Street, was only 27 when she died. Here pallbearers pull her casket into St. Peter's Cathedral for a requiem mass before interment in St. Peter's Cemetery.

St. John Ambulance nurses and cadets from Sarnia, Ingersoll, St. Thomas, and London marched to First St. Andrew's United Church on June 25, 1939. Pictured here is a section of the ambulance brigade.

London nurses of the St. John Ambulance nursing division also paraded through London's streets on June 25, 1939.

Therapeutic swim classes were held for local children who were physically incapacitated by infantile paralysis during a polio epidemic two years earlier. Here, a group takes to the water at the heated YMCA pool on January 7, 1940.

Gene Autry's wife Ina holds a picture of the famous singing cowboy for him to autograph for the little patients at Children's War Memorial Hospital, during a visit to the city in 1940. Autry wrote "Keep Your Chin Up" on the photo of himself riding his horse Champion. The signing took place at a City Hall reception that included Premier Mitch Hepburn among the crowd of 5,000.

Westminster Veterans' Hospital, April 1941. Building began in 1918 on the southeast corner of what are now Wellington and Commissioners roads, allowing the hospital to admit its first patients on May 1, 1920. The hospital expanded during World War II to treat the sick and injured from nearby training camps. After the war, the focus returned to long-term and acute care for veterans with disabilities.

Construction was underway on a new north wing at Victoria Hospital in November, 1939. In the 1930s, overcrowding at Victoria peaked at 35 percent above capacity, necessitating an expansion.

Victoria Hospital opened its new addition on May 26, 1941. The new wing could accommodate 400 patients.

A civic dinner was held in Hotel London at noon on May 26, 1941, to celebrate the opening of Victoria Hospital's new wing. Here, Major W.J. Heaman speaks, while Dr. Leonard Rowntree is the guest of honour.

The new $80,000 six-storey wing at Victoria Hospital, shortly after opening in 1941. This and other buildings on the site were demolished in 2014.

In October, 1942, Dr. W.J. Weekes, age 86, claimed to be the oldest practising doctor in Ontario. The doctor is shown here in his office at 436 Waterloo Street with his black bag, in which he carried the ingredients for making his own prescriptions. Weekes graduated in 1886 from Western's medical school, part of the first class of students to take their complete medical training at UWO. After a brief stint in Thorndale, he practised in London for 48 years.

Children battling the "T.B. Scourge" were often treated at home by the 1940s, but children treated at the Queen Alexandra Sanatorium were those who required surgery, braces, and bedrest. Some of the children pictured in the *Free Press* feature were First Nations children from northern Ontario, a long way from their families and friends.

Dr. Wildred Shute (left), Dr. Evan Chute (seated), and Dr. Arthur Vogelsang made headlines in the *Free Press* in May, 1945, after they announced that concentrated doses of vitamin E provided relief from heart disease. Evan and Wilfred established the Shute Institute in London in 1948.

Westminster Hospital patients attend exercise class, April 1948. Many of the hospital's patients were veterans of the Second World War.

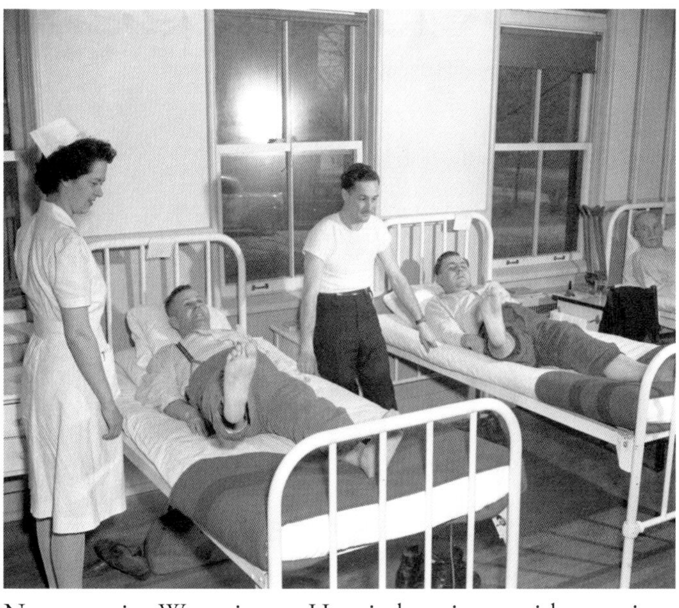

Nurses assist Westminster Hospital patients with exercises, April 1948.

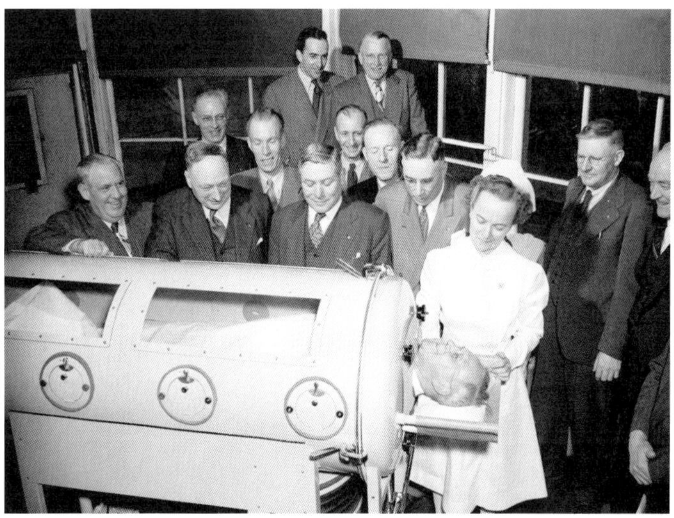

In March, 1949, Mayor Ray A. Dennis took a "trial spin" in an iron lung used for fighting polio donated to Victoria Hospital by the London Lions Club. Nurse H. Bell attends to the mayor while various Lions club members and officials look on.

The McCormick Home for the Aged, pictured here in 1949, was located at 1050 Richmond Street. This care centre dated back to the Home for Incurables in 1894.

On June 1, 1949, Governor-General Viscount Alexander of Tunis laid the cornerstone for the new Crombie Pavilion under construction at Beck Sanatorium, formerly Queen Alexandra.

# HOTELS & TAVERNS

Not surprisingly for a frontier town, some of London's earliest businesses were hotels and taverns. Indeed, the very first building at the Forks of the Thames was Peter McGregor's tavern—a shanty built on the southwest corner of King and Ridout streets in 1826. As the story goes, McGregor placed a tree stump by the front door and sold whisky to travellers from a jug he kept on it. He soon faced competition after Abraham Carroll built his ostentatiously named "Mansion House" on the north side of Dundas, between Ridout and Talbot, by November 1827. Perhaps in response, McGregor expanded, leasing a large frame building on the southeast corner of Ridout and Dundas, which housed workers building the Courthouse and jail. He converted it into an inn called the King's Arms, and later, Robinson Hall.

Like many early settlements, taverns and hotels were natural centres of community life. The first ball held in London was at the King's Arms on March 13, 1833, the business by that time being owned by William J. Hawley and his brothers. Two years later, a formal St. Patrick's Day dinner was held at the Mansion House Hotel. London's high society was born. Beyond grand balls and social gatherings, bars and hotels were often where early political dealings took place, as an informal gathering place for the city's movers and shakers. During the Upper Canada Rebellion, Reformers held a clandestine meeting on December 8, 1837, in Joseph Flanagan's tavern on the southwest corner of Dundas and Talbot streets. Apparently, they were planning a common defence in case they were attacked by the Tory forces in the area.

Many of these early hotels survived well into the modern age, some even into the new millennium. In October 1853, Peter McCann opened McCann's Hotel, later known as the Western Hotel, on the northwest corner of Richmond and Fullerton streets. It was not demolished for a new development until 1989. In 1855, Richard Carruthers opened Brock's Hotel on the northwest corner of Talbot and York streets. This establishment was expanded over the years and underwent several name changes until it became the Brunswick Hotel about 1912. That building burned in 2008 while awaiting demolition. A remarkable survivor from early days is the Hotel Richmond, which dates back to the Revere House in 1860, and is still open for business at the northeast corner of Richmond and King today.

Over time, London's guest houses and drinking holes became larger and grander, as befitted a growing city in need of accommodation for new arrivals. Since most visitors arrived by train after 1855, it made sense to have a large hotel conveniently near the station. In 1858, the Tecumseh House, the largest hotel in British North America, opened on the southwest corner of York and Richmond streets. Over the years, its guests included various dignitaries and luminaries like Cornelius Vanderbilt, Emperor Dom Pedro II of Brazil, Sir John A. Macdonald, Walt Whitman, Louis Riel, and the Prince of Wales (later King Edward VII). It closed its doors in 1929, outdated and unable to compete with London's luxurious new hotel, Hotel London. A wrecking crew finished dismantling the old, iconic hotel in September, 1930.

Perhaps one of the most famous London institutions, Hotel London opened its doors on July 25, 1927 on the southeast corner of Dundas and Wellington. Boasting 350 rooms, it also provided modern conveniences like bars, lounges, a barber shop, flower and gift shop, and ladies' hat shop. It immediately became *the* place for banquets, luncheons, dances, and conventions, truly a gathering place for both Londoners and visitors for decades to come. Indeed, long after the city boasted more sophisticated infrastructure, from a grand City Hall to beautiful opera houses, hotels and taverns remained important social and political spaces—arguably to this day.

A 1948 photo of the Swartz Tavern, built circa 1822 as a stage coach stop. The tavern, by this date a privately occupied home, was on the south side of Brick Street (Commissioners Road) east of Westminster Hospital and west of the L&PS tracks. Built by Bartholomew Swartz, a veteran of the Napoleonic Wars who came to Canada in 1813, it was burned by the London Fire Department in 1975.

Ward's Hotel, Springbank, circa 1880. Mike Ward built this hotel in 1880 on the north bank of the Thames a little east of the Springbank pumphouse. The resort was a centre of summer sports and a destination for steamboats operating on the river. Bought by the city in 1896, it was demolished in 1923.

The Tecumseh House, circa 1890. Built on the southwest corner of Richmond and York streets in 1856, it was for decades London's largest and most luxurious hotel, boasting 160 rooms.

The Tecumseh House, circa 1920. The hotel closed in September 1929, having served 2,555,000 guests, according to the *Free Press*. It was demolished within a year.

Looking north on Richmond Street from the corner of King Street, circa 1860s. The Revere House (Richmond Hotel) is on the right. John Ferguson, furniture maker and undertaker, was located across the street on the northwest corner until 1870. The west side of the road was later the site of the Masonic Temple.

Western Hotel on Richmond Street just north of Fullerton, circa 1875. The building also served as Westervelt College for many decades, but was demolished in 1989 for a retail complex.

Hotel White, northwest corner of Dundas and Wellington, circa 1880s. John A. White opened the hotel in 1881. Later names for this building were the Horsman Hotel and Metropolitan Hotel. Most of the building was demolished in 1957 for a Bank of Montreal building, but the west or left section was preserved, housing The Scots Corner and Fine Art Custom Framing in 2017.

Dundas Street looking east past Talbot showing the City Hotel (a.k.a. Belvedere Hotel or Talbot Inn) on the southwest corner, 1900s. Across the street on the northwest corner is another hotel, the London House.

Evans House, London Junction (Pottersburg). The hotel burned in February 1913.

The Victoria Hotel stood at the corner of Dufferin and Wellington before First Methodist Church (now Metropolitan United Church) was built on the site in 1895. It was operated by Edward Morkin who went on to open another tavern on King Street between Ridout and Talbot. The sign near the front door says Boarding. Note the nearby advertisement for Oak Hall Clothing.

The Duke of York Hotel on the south side of Dundas just east of Adelaide, circa 1912. The building is still standing as the St. Regis Tavern.

The Richmond Hotel on a rainy day, January 21, 1942. Built in 1860, with the name the Revere House, the hotel enjoyed a prime location in the business district, close to the railway station and Covent Garden. The Richmond is still open for business.

Former White Ox Inn, 495 Hamilton Road, June 1950. The inn was built on land owned by Tilley Hubbard who settled there 1819. Used as a cholera hospital during the epidemic of 1832, the building was a hotel for over 50 years and a stop to change horses on the Hamilton-London stage coach line. A private home after 1896, it was demolished in 1982, at which time it may have been the oldest building in the city.

The Grigg House hotel, northeast corner of Richmond and York streets, in the 1890s. First called the "America House," it was designed by Thomas H. Tracy, and built for John McKinnon in 1879. Later, it was known as the Grigg house after proprietor Samuel Grigg. It was the first hotel in the city with running water.

The Grant House hotel on the north side Dundas just east of Wellington, circa 1890. It was founded by J. C. Grant, circa 1886.

The Cobble Stone Inn, Byron, Westminster Township, circa 1940. At one time the Bungalow Tea House, it later became the Hermitage Club, which is still open for business on Springbank Drive.

Opened in 1890 as the Grand Pacific, the CPR Hotel on Richmond Street is pictured here upon its February 1948 sale to James Melnick Ltd. of Toronto. To avoid legal trouble with the nearby railway, the proprietors declared that CPR stood for "Comfort, Peace, and Rest." The hotel eventually became the Ceeps, an iconic London bar and haunt for Western students to this day.

The Riverside Hotel, seen here mid-demolition in March 1947, was "one of the city's prominent gathering places in bygone days" according to the *Free Press*. Located in Petersville, later London West, the hotel flourished in the days when it was outside the city limits. The famous London Tecumsehs baseball team could be seen playing from its windows.

Hotel London on April 1, 1949, southeast corner of Dundas and Wellington. London's grandest hotel, built in the Renaissance Revival style by London Realty Co., opened on July 25, 1927. A true downtown landmark, it provided London with space for banquets, meetings, parties, and entertainment until it was demolished in 1972.

# INDUSTRY

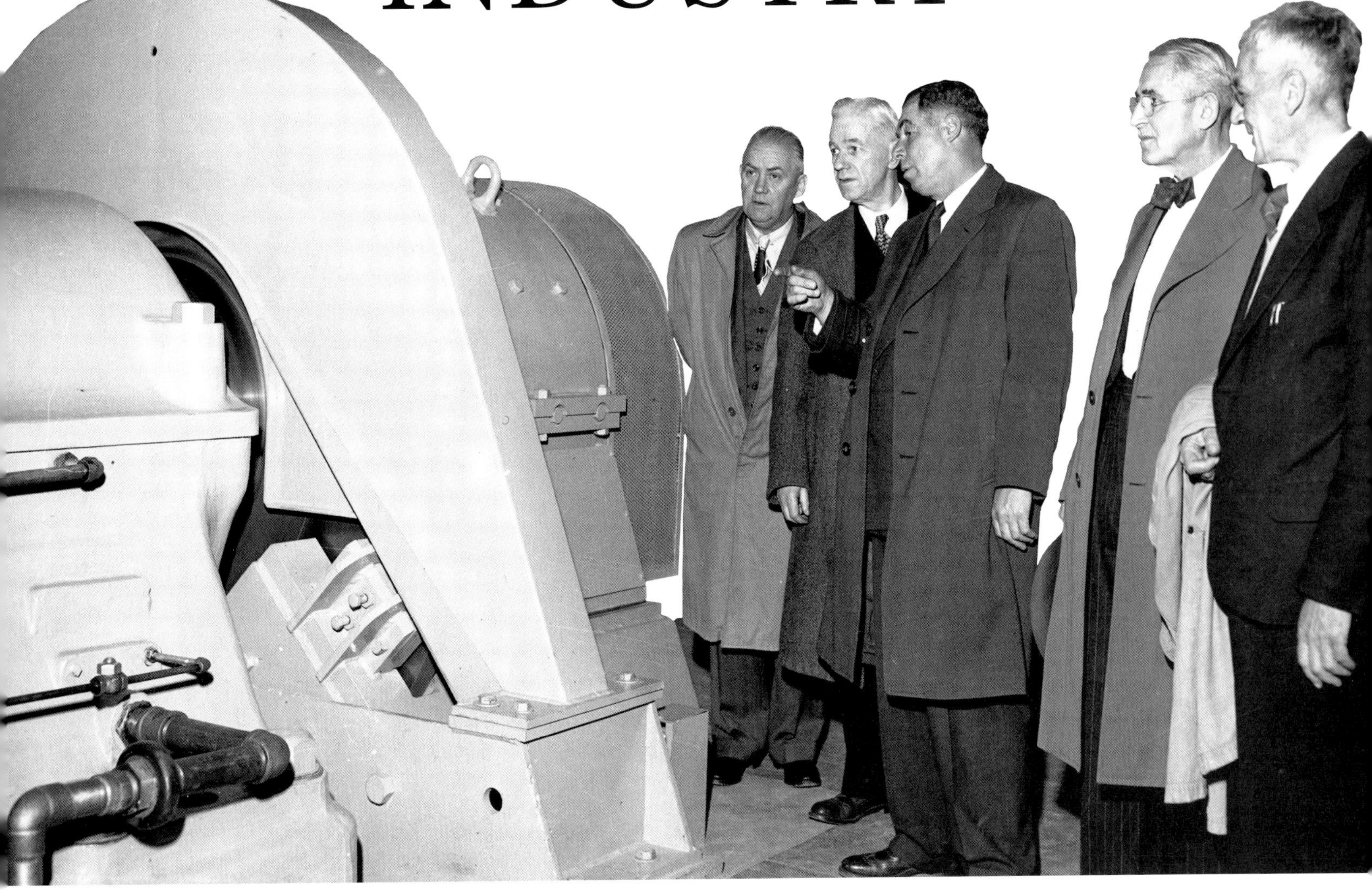

London's early manufacturing sprung up right alongside the original town site near the river forks. As the nineteenth century progressed and factories grew larger, noisier, and smellier, most production moved away from downtown to what became known as "the east end." The town's prime location next to the Thames River made it an attractive site for many young industries, turning London into a manufacturing hub for a diverse range of products.

Mills, especially flour mills, were among the earliest pioneer industries. One of the first operations, known as Blackfriars, was owned by Robert and Thomas Parke on what is now Harris Park. Operating from the 1830s, it ceased production in about 1912. Another well-known mill was that of Charles Hunt who founded City Mills at the corner of York and Talbot in 1854, later moving east to Nightingale Avenue.

Oil refineries were among London's most important nineteenth-century industries. Soon after oil was discovered in Lambton County in 1857, it was shipped to London for processing, making London the original "Oil Capital of Canada." In its 1860s heyday, the oil industry had about 50 refineries in London. Eventual competition from American refineries forced about 16 businessmen in London and Petrolia to amalgamate as Imperial Oil in 1880. In 1884, the City of London denied Imperial's request for a grant to build a pipeline into the city, responding to Londoners' complaints about the explosions, fires, and stench that arose from the refineries. Imperial chose to move its offices and refineries closer to the oil fields, first to Petrolia and later to Sarnia.

Cigar factories were prevalent in Victorian and Edwardian London. In 1914, over 20 cigar manufacturers operated in the city, producing 50,000,000 cigars that year and making London second only to Montreal in Canadian cigar production. London's extensive rail connections allowed the city to import raw leaf tobacco and ship out the finished products. While some tobacco was grown locally, most was imported from the United States and Cuba.

One of London's biggest employers, McClary Manufacturing Company was founded in 1847 by Oliver McClary, soon joined by his brother John. McClary produced stoves, furnaces, and enamelled and galvanized tinware, exporting the products as far as Britain, the West Indies, and Australia. Purchased by General Steel Wares in 1927, the factory on the southwest corner of Wellington and King streets was torn down in 1955 to make way for Wellington Square Mall.

Empire Brass Manufacturing Company (EMCO) started out as a small plumbing business on the west side of Talbot Street north of Carling in 1903. Moving to Dundas Street east in 1908, it was typical of industries that started downtown but were encouraged by City Council to move from the core to the east end.

London also became known for textile mills such as Holeproof Hosiery, Penmans, London Hosiery Mills, and Middlesex Mills. Other industries revolved around the railway. The CNR car shops built and repaired passenger and freight cars. General Motors built their diesel locomotives in London as well, with their factory opening in 1950.

But perhaps the most all-encompassing manufacturing theme in London was food—foodstuffs of all kinds, from bakeries and confectioners to soda beverages and beer. One of the earliest of the big food manufacturers was Daniel Perrin who, in the 1860s, established his own bakery and soda water factory, the Forest City Steam Confectionery and Biscuit Works, on Hamilton Road. By 1881, the firm of D.S. Perrin & Company was located in the heart of downtown, on the north side of Dundas between Ridout and Talbot. It had 500 employees by the time it was bought by its main competitor, Frank A. McCormick, to form the Canada Biscuit Company in 1926.

Rival baker McCormick's dates back to 1858, when Thomas McCormick founded the Dominion Steam Confectionery and Biscuit Works on the north side of Dundas between Clarence and Wellington. They evolved into the McCormick Manufacturing Company in 1879. McCormick's also employed a great many Londoners, between 100 and 150 in 1888. In 1913, the company built the Snow-White Sunshine Biscuit and Candy Factory on the north side of Dundas in the east end. Called the "Sunshine Palace," the eight acres of floor space at the new location were a testament to the popularity of London's very own cookie industry.

Another confectionery was that of John and Duncan McDermid, founded in the Somerville Box Company building in 1911. O-Pee-Chee, as the company came to be called, produced candy and gum as well as sports cards from the 1930s. Many Londoners still fondly remember the taste of "Gypsy Gum" and "Thrills."

In 1907, the Battle Creek Toasted Corn Flake Company established a head office and plant on the northwest corner of Grey and Adelaide streets to manufacture Kellogg's Toasted Corn Flakes. In about 1913, the company moved to a new larger building on Dundas Street at Festubert Avenue (later Kellogg Lane). The new location had over 50,000 square feet of workspace and employed 60 workers. In 1924, the company was renamed Kellogg Company of Canada Limited and remained a major employer in London until 2014.

Gorman, Eckert & Co., founded in 1883, conducted business in several locations downtown before moving to the east side of Rectory Street between Florence and the CNR in 1910. From here, they imported coffee, spices, and mustard, while manufacturing baking powder and extracts. In fact, by this point, they were the largest olive packer in the British Empire. The company remained at this location for more than 80 years, eventually becoming Club House Foods.

No discussion of London industry is complete without mention of the oldest business of all—Labatt Brewery. London had other breweries, of course—most notably Thomas Carling, who set up business on Carling Creek in 1843, making beer using an old family recipe from his native Yorkshire. But none were as long-lasting as the brewery begun by John Balkwill in London's earliest days. After several owners and partnerships, John Kinder Labatt became sole owner of the London Brewery, as it was known, in 1855. Labatt's took many medals for its product, especially its India Pale Ale, which won the gold at the International Centennial Exposition held in Philadelphia in 1876 and at the International Exposition held in Paris in 1878. After achieving international success, the company never looked back. Although now part of a multinational conglomerate, in the twenty-first century, Labatt Breweries is by far the longest continuous industry in London—a famous representative of the many factories and manufacturers that called the Forest City home over the years.

The vast Carling Brewery on Talbot Street, circa 1880. Established in 1843 by Thomas Carling near the present intersection of Harvard and Yale streets, the expanded plant, pictured here, was taken over by sons William and John (later Sir John) Carling.

Atlantic Petroleum Works, Hamilton Road, 1875. The refinery was established in 1866 by Herman and Isaac Waterman when London's oil refining industry was in its heyday. The factory covered four acres.

George Moorhead's Furniture Factory, north side of King Street between Richmond and Clarence, circa 1875. Despite, or perhaps because of, its huge size the company failed in 1878 and was bought by Frederick Ardiel Fitzgerald and Charles P. Smith.

John Campbell's Carriage Shop, 77-85 King Street, circa 1890. This prominent manufacturer and businessman was mayor of London several times.

Hunt's City Mills, 1910. Located on the south branch of the Thames River, west of Labatt Brewery, the City Mills operated at this location (albeit in different structures) from 1854 to 1917, when the company moved to East London to take advantage of cheap hydro. This factory was demolished in 1957.

The interior of Tune's Soda Water Works. The company employed eight men and shipped as far west as Windsor and east to Ingersoll and Woodstock.

Daniel Simmons Perrin, one of London'a most successful early manufacturers, circa 1895. His famous bakery/confectionery, D.S. Perrin Co., started on Horton Street in 1863. Peaking with 500 employees, Perrin merged with his competitor, the McCormick Manufacturing Company, in 1926.

A spill at the GTR coal chutes, Glencoe, in the early 1900s.

Kellogg's, Dundas Street, circa 1920. Dating back to 1913, the plant operated on Dundas Street until 2014.

Interior of Hyman's Tannery, west side of Richmond Street between Mill Street and the CPR tracks, circa 1895.

Line, McDonald & Co. cigars, circa 1900. Harry Line, Robert D. McDonald, and Thomas H. Weldon's cigar factory was on the east side of Clarence Street between King and York—one of many cigar manufacturers in London at the time.

W. Ward Cigar Manufacturers, located at 64 Dundas Street east of Ridout, 1900s. By 1920, the company had moved to King Street. Ward's was the last of London's cigar manufacturers to remain open, closing in 1952.

Holeproof Hosiery, southwest corner of Bathurst and Clarence Streets, circa 1920. Originally established on King Street in 1911, their socks were guaranteed to be worn for six months without developing holes. Later known as Kayser-Roth, the company's building still stands.

Ford Motor Company plant, Waterloo and Pall Mall, 1923. This location, open from 1914 to 1945, was conveniently built beside the CPR line for access to the boxcars that delivered partially assembled cars from plants in Detroit. The cars were assembled and sold here in the showrooms facing Waterloo Street. Henry Ford dropped in twice, in 1920 and 1926. The building is now Siskinds Law Firm.

Workmen near the Ford plant mix concrete and pour it into wooden forms to construct a sewer. The purpose may have been to carry Carling Creek underground on its journey to the Thames.

J.A. Tancock, veterinary surgeon and blacksmith, 96 King Street, north side, just west of Talbot. Tancock may have had competition from the blacksmith next door, William H. Clampitt—not to mention the Clinton Motor Car Co. just down the street. Note that King Street is paved with bricks in this 1910 photograph. This block is now the site of Budweiser Gardens.

The Spramotor Building, 1912, with wagons lined up out front. The company manufactured spraying equipment for painting and agricultural use.

An early photograph of McClary Manufacturing Company. The huge downtown factory was London's largest employer with 1,500 men in 1915. Note the sign in the background, to the right.

Stoves being constructed inside McClary Manufacturing Co., circa 1914.

Established 1902, the London Rolling Mill Co. produced bar iron from molten scrap iron. In 1928, workers began to make steel bars in a new electrical process. The plant closed just before World War II began in 1939.

The Beatty Brothers plant at the corner of William and York streets. The company had made washing machines in the old Wortman & Ward foundry since about 1912.

The Hydro Shop assures its customers that the "Modern Santa Claus" uses electric appliances to make an "Electric Xmas" in December 1915. The shop was established by the Board of Water Commissioners (PUC) to encourage the use of electrical devices in the home and build a customer base for power from Niagara Falls.

"The New Way" to travel versus "The Old Way" according to The Hydro Shop. As the home of hydro pioneer Adam Beck, London was a leader in embracing this new form of electricity.

McCormick's, circa 1923. The new Snow-White Sunshine Biscuit and Candy Factory was built on the north side of Dundas in 1913–14.

Members of McCormick's staff pose at the front entrance to the factory, 1928. Frank A. McCormick is standing in the back row, likely the one at centre.

McCormick's staff making Molley-O chocolate bars, 1948.

McCormick's, seen from the air, September 19, 1947.

R.G. Edgcombe Co. advertises Carriage Hardware and Wholesale Automotive Equipment, 88-90 York Street, 1927. Established by Richard Gerry Edgcome in 1920, the business was comparatively short-lived, closing about 1928.

New coach being made at CNR Carshops, 1948.

Interior of the CNR Carshops, London's largest industrial plant, November 1938. The building extended over a third of a mile from just east of Rectory Street to Egerton Street and was over 900 feet wide. Workers in this plant kept thousands of CNR passenger coaches safe and running in good condition. The payroll was over $60,000 a month.

Hygrade Corrugated Products Limited, seen from above in 1940. The company opened on the block bounded by Adelaide, Pall Mall, and William streets and the CPR tracks in April 1927. The first company in Canada to manufacture corrugated paper boxes, the business employed 30 people.

An aerial view from about 1940 shows Penmans on the right and London Can Company on the left. The factories are on Thames Street where it intersects with King. Penmans opened a branch in London in 1919 to perform finishing on hosiery and underwear.

Empire Brass Manufacturing Co., later known as EMCO, in July 1946. Founded in a small building on Talbot Street, the company expanded to a new location on Dundas Street East in 1908. The expansion can be attributed to the early twentieth century housing boom requiring plumbing supplies for indoor bathrooms.

Horses, wagons, and delivery men in front of Silverwood Dairy headquarters on Bathurst Street, circa 1937. While the company, founded in London in 1903, also used trucks, it maintained this home delivery fleet of wagons until the late 1950s.

An aerial view of the Kellogg's plant, 1941. Train cars can be seen lined up on tracks to the left of the building to ship the company's products.

A display of new London-made products in the Hotel London coffee shop on February 3, 1947. Many of the products in the exhibit were made by returning veterans establishing their own businesses.

Hunt's Flour Mill, photographed from the air, 1947. Originally located on the Thames just west of Labatt's in 1854, the building was moved to the east end in 1917 to take advantage of cheap hydroelectric power.

An aerial view of London's East End manufacturing district September 19, 1947. Kelvinator can be seen at centre with Coca-Cola to its left, McCormicks is at right, and Hunt's Flour Mill is in the top left corner.

Grapes arrive at London Winery, October 1948. The winery was founded in 1925 by Arthur and Joseph Knowles, south of the city on Highway 2.

Dennisteel, 1948. Originally, Dennis Iron & Steel Works, the company was founded on King Street in 1868. Incorporated as Dennisteel in 1936, it was by that time on the north side of Dundas west of Ridout where Museum London is now located. Bankrupt in 1964, Dennisteel was demolished in 1965.

A horse-drawn delivery wagon pulls into the Canada Bread factory, South Street west of Wellington, 1948. Canada Bread operated a London factory until 2003.

A group tours London Hosiery Mills during its "open house," June 1948. Here Victor Tremblay "boards" stockings—the process in which the nylon and silk legwear was shaped.

J.R. Shuttleworth & Sons Hat Manufacturers, 1948. The factory was located next to Beecher United Church, of which only the tower remains today.

Staff at Neals Bakery, later Wonder Bakery, fill cookie boxes, November 1948.

Coleman Packers Plant in East London, photographed from the air on September 19, 1947. The building was located on First Street in East London.

An aerial view of the extensive General Steel Wares downtown plant, December 1949. The plant was bounded by King Street (seen at bottom left), Wellington, York, and Clarence streets. The CNR can be seen at centre.

National Dry Ltd., manufacturers of Wishing Well Soda Pop brand, at 303 Richmond Street near the railway underpass, June 1949.

General Motors' new parts warehouse at 127-133 Queens Avenue, August 31, 1949. Described as a "modern wholesale parts depot," it was founded to distribute factory-approved parts and accessories for Chevrolet, Pontiac, Oldsmobile, Buick, Cadillac, and Vauxhall cars as well as GMC and Chevy trucks to GM dealers across Western Ontario.

Officials turn the sod for the General Motors Diesel plant to be built east of London in London Township on September 21, 1949. From left to right: Homer Hardy, Reeve of London Township; company president and general manager E.V. Rippingille; and Mayor Ray Dennis.

Gorman, Eckert & Co., December 1948. The company was located on the east side of Rectory Street between Florence Street and the CNR tracks after 1910, importing spices, coffee, and mustard, plus manufacturing baking powder and extracts. Today, the company is Club House Foods Ltd.

London's oldest and most well-known industry, Labatt's, is pictured here in 1873, with the surrounding neighbourhood. The Labatt brewery buildings are in the centre and the Labatt home is visible to the right.

John Labatt II at his office desk, circa 1906. Under his leadership, Labatt's grew into the largest brewery in Canada.

A wagonload of Labatt beer out on delivery, circa 1880.

Coopers (barrel-makers) outside Labatt's own cooperage.

A view of Labatt's, circa 1875.

Labatt & Co. Custom House Brokers staff in 1914.

The new 1932 office building. The date 1832, engraved above the door, likely refers to the year when John Balkwill's London Brewery gained partners—years before Labatt joined the company that eventually bore his name.

Company advertising from 1938 that boasts of Labatt's famous India Pale Ale and the "deep-well water of London, Canada so unusually suitable for brewing."

Labatt workmen pose outside the brewery in 1914, surrounded by barrels and kegs.

Aerial view of a greatly expanded Labatt, circa 1940.

A local driver benefits from the Labatt Road Courtesy Program in 1948. The Labatt vehicle says the driver is also trained to deliver first aid if necessary.

Women worked at Labatt during World War II, as they did in many other factories.

# LABOUR

London's reputation as a white-collar city built by banks and insurance companies is not a complete—or accurate—picture. The unskilled and skilled labourers, who put in long hours in often unpleasant conditions, are frequently left out of the narrative. Moreover, they were not always treated fairly by their employers. As the world of work began to change from the turn of the century through the Great Depression and Second World War, labour unions took an increasing hold, as the plight of the ordinary worker became an important social issue.

As early as the mid-nineteenth century, London had a small, but vocal, labour movement—and their share of labour unrest. In December 1845, London's earliest known organization of workers formed when more than 100 master and journeyman carpenters met to oppose the establishment of machinery that would reduce the need for manual labour. On May 3, 1872, workers founded their own political party when the Workingman's Progressive Party was organized. At the time, the culture of work was precarious—owners and managers faced few legal confines for working conditions, pay rates, or firing practices. These labourers were galvanized to action by the imbalance of power, which favoured the demands of business and industry over workers' rights.

One of the earliest recorded strikes in London's history took place on February 11, 1856, when the journeyman printers employed at the *London Free Press* and other city newspapers walked off the job. The *Free Press* refused to recognize or sign an agreement with the newly formed London Typographical Association, which demanded a wage of 28 cents per 1,000 letters or $10 a week. The going rate was 25 cents per 1,000 letters or $9 a week. *Free Press* owner Josiah Blackburn offered a rate of 26 cents per 1,000 letters, but was turned down. The newspaper reacted by advertising for six young women to learn the business of typesetting—a seemingly progressive move, but it was actually a move to undercut wages, as women would only earn $4 to $6 a week. How the situation was resolved is unclear, but by the fall of 1856, the strike was over and the city news printers were back on the job.

The best known labour standoff in early London started on October 27, 1898, when Branch 97 of the Amalgamated Association of Street Railway Employees of America called its first strike against the London Street Railway Company. Not all workers walked off the job—some men were in the barns and repair sheds—but the company was inconvenienced enough to agree to a 1/3 of a cent wage increase to 15 and 1/3 cents per hour.

With that, the strike ended in November and that should have been the end of the matter.

However, on May 22, 1899, the London Street Railway Company workers again chose to strike, after management refused to honour its previous agreement and attempted to break up the union. 79 motormen and conductors walked off the job without notice, beginning the most acrimonious labour dispute in London history. The directors hired "strike-breakers" to replace the workers on the picket line, inciting an angry response. Riots broke out sporadically from June to September, bitter strikers causing damage to streetcar stock. Trams and their strike-breaking crews were guarded by constables carrying loaded revolvers. Many Londoners sided with the strikers, boycotting the street railway and strutting proudly to work wearing signs that read "We Walk." On July 8, a mob of thousands, some merely thrill seekers, took control of downtown London from about 2:30 p.m. until the local militia was called out to restore order at midnight. Mayor Dr. John Wilson read the Riot Act for the first and, so far, only, time in London's history. In May 1900, the directors decided not to rehire the striking workers.

While the strike was a failure for the streetcar operators, it did lead to the development of the London Trades and Labour Council, whose first assembly was held at City Hall on December 7, 1900. Some labour organizers managed to elect members to City Council afterwards as well.

For some years, London had a monthly labour newspaper, the *Industrial Banner*. Founded in 1892 and edited for 28 years by London labour leader Joseph T. Marks, the *Banner* was one of the first newspapers in Canada to champion the rights of the working class. Marks, once a young tinsmith on the Great Western Railway, became a founding member of the London Public Library Board, established to promote literacy among the working classes. Around 1913, the paper moved to Toronto.

On September 3, 1894, Londoners observed the first official Labour Day holiday in Canada. 3,000 workers converged on Market Square that day to hold the first Labour Day parade on the downtown streets. In the years that passed, it became traditional for the parade to march to Queen's Park, now the Western Fairgrounds, where participants would enjoy various sporting activities and contests. As the decades passed and workers gained increased rights (and women worked outside the home in growing numbers), Labour Day remained an opportunity to reinforce solidarity among workers and their families, while celebrating the gains they had achieved that year. For many modern Londoners, Labour Day may just be another holiday—the unofficial end of summer—but in earlier times, it had great social significance.

London electric workmen erecting poles on Ridout Street in 1893.

In 1899, 79 motormen and conductors from the London Street Railway Company went out on strike for improved pay and working conditions. Like many early employers, owner Henry Everett responded by replacing his staff with "strike-breakers." Here, the local militia parade down Dundas Street—called in to (forcibly) restore the peace. Never fully resolved, the labour unrest continued until the employees organized into a new union in 1917.

Union no. 97, the London chapter of the Brotherhood of Painters, Decorators, and Paper Hangers, poses here during the Old Boys Reunion, 1900. Each member is wearing his uniform and membership ribbon.

Apprentices at E. Leonard & Sons Boiler Workers pose during their lunch break, 1907. At the time, provincial legislation mandated that children be in school until age 14, but after that, many boys would enter the workforce.

Women workers at Holeproof Hosiery, 1914. Many of the factory's 200 workers were women, as sewing was considered an "appropriate" job.

Workers at Hourd & Company, 1914. The factory produced folding chairs and tables, crokinole boards, and toilet seats.

Workmen lay sewer pipes in an undated photograph.

Workers in an unidentified late nineteenth-century slaughterhouse.

Paving Talbot Street, circa 1905.

Masons building St. Martin of Tours Roman Catholic Church on the northeast corner of Duchess Avenue and Cathcart Street in 1911. Bricklaying was one of the highest-paid building trades, but required men to work out of doors and men could only work an average of 200 days a year due to weather conditions.

A workman wearing a "sandwich apron" pickets the Superior Restaurant, 670 Dundas Street, in August 1939. He wished to make the restaurant owners sign a contract allowing a 60-hour work week with one day off in seven.

During a heat wave in late July 1940, men had to work in temperatures upwards of 150°F at one of London's foundries. Here, the men are carrying white-hot metal from a blast furnace to moulds, a job which took them about an hour and a half each afternoon.

Roger and Cecile Varmini, married in March 1938, started a cross-country trek (carrying all their worldly possessions in a pack), looking for employment. Hailing from Abitibi, Quebec, the couple were dubbed the "hitch-hiking honeymooners" by the *Free Press* upon arrival in London in January 1939. Until the Second World War brought increased employment, many young workers like the Varminis—Roger was a mechanic—struggled during the Great Depression.

The ACCL (All-Canadian Congress of Labour) takes part in Labour Day festivities on September 1, 1939. Opposed to American interference in the Canadian labour market, the group merged with the Canadian sections of the Congress of Industrial Organizations in 1940 to form the Canadian Congress of Labour.

Carpenters, apprentices, and labourers working at Bellwood Park veterans' housing project went on strike beginning June 17, 1947. They demanded a pay increase of 15 cents an hour from $1.10 an hour for experienced workers. Here, the workmen congregate in front of uncompleted houses while negotiations take place between their union representatives from the International Brotherhood of Carpenters and Joiners and Housing Enterprises Ltd. On June 12, the men returned to work, after Housing Enterprises guaranteed the wage increase.

Labour Day celebrations on September 2, 1940, included a parade, baby show, military drill, competitive sports, motorcycle racing, and musical entertainment. The parade started at Market Square and continued along King Street to Queen's Park, where most of the events took place.

First-prize float in the 1940 parade went to the National Beverage Workers for "There'll Always Be an England"—a timely message in the middle of the Second World War. William Walmsley played John Bull, accompanied by an English bulldog.

An imitation army tank is actually another float produced by the National Beverage Workers in 1940. The poster on the side declares: "You Serve by Serving," advertising War Savings Certificates.

Labatt Clown Band in the Labour Day parade, September 6, 1948. Thousands lined Dundas Street from the Armouries to Queen's Park in London East to watch the annual parade. Later, at the park, people gathered for sports, contests, and entertainment.

The 1949 Labour Day parade marches east on Dundas Street past the English Street intersection. The former London East Town Hall, now the Aeolian Hall, is in the distance.

# LAW & ORDER

In London's earliest days, policing was difficult—the pioneer outpost was a town of saloons and drifters. There was not enough funding in the frontier community for a regular police force. Moreover, there was no job security for policemen, since the force changed after municipal elections took place each year.

Nor were good officers necessarily easy to find. William O'Reilly was London's first chief constable. On July 16, 1855, he was fined 10 shillings and costs in London Police Court after being found guilty on a drunk and disorderly charge. Needless to say, he was dismissed by City Council soon afterwards. It was Police Chief William T.T. Williams, appointed in 1877, who developed an appropriate police force for the growing city during his long career that lasted until 1920. Under his tutelage, officers on night duty were armed and all officers began to wear helmets. The first horse-drawn patrol wagon, dubbed the Black Maria, went into service in February 1889. The police purchased their first motor vehicle, a Cadillac patrol wagon, from London Motor Sales in 1913. The city provided Williams funding for a central police station on Carling Street in 1882, a building used until 1930.

One would think London's imposing Gothic Courthouse and jail would be enough to strike fear into the heart of any would-be wrongdoer. Yet many criminals of all kinds spent time there after its completion in 1829. Many famous trials, including those for murder, took place in the courtroom and many culprits were afterwards hanged—in the early days, publicly. The first execution, in 1830, was that of Cornelius Burley for the shooting death of Constable Timothy Pomeroy in 1829. The last public hanging was that of Thomas Jones in 1868. The only woman hanged was Phoebe Campbell, found guilty of the axe murder of her husband in West Nissouri Township in 1871.

Compared to many larger cities, London was seldom considered a hotbed of criminal activity—at least, not before 1950. However, the Forest City has witnessed its fair share of robbers, smugglers, kidnappers, and murderers—not to mention first-rate mischief.

No one in London history was more famous for breaking and entering than "Slippery Jack," a character who entered the homes of many Londoners at night, rearranging furniture and tickling people's feet in 1867–68. "Jack" was actually two men, Bill Symonds and John Crosbie, who are said to have made a bet that they could enter a London home once a week for a year yet evade capture. Their bet was made with members of the Hellfriar's Club, a similarly roguish group of local young men, all apparently with too much time on their hands. While the crimes of "Slippery Jack" were fairly harmless and easily sensationalized, London would soon become infamous for a much bloodier act.

When the notorious Donnelly Massacre occurred in Biddulph Township near Lucan on February 4, 1880, London and Middlesex suddenly found themselves on the continent's crime map. Five members of the "Black Donnellys"—an Irish Catholic immigrant family notorious for being small-town criminals, accused of countless infractions—were murdered by a vigilante mob of their neighbours. However, Middlesex County's most famous trial resulted in no hangings, not even anyone found guilty. The police arrested James Carroll for the murder of Johanna Donnelly. Carroll's first trial, held in 1880, ended in a hung jury. The second trial, in 1881, ended with his acquittal. Afterwards, indictments against another two men, Thomas Ryder and John Purtell, had to be dropped. No one was ever found guilty of Middlesex County's most famous crime.

Another of London's most dramatic nineteenth-century crimes occurred on April 1, 1898, when James Tuttle, manager of the touring Wesley Stock Company, was shot to death on the stage of the Music Hall by American actor William D. Emerson over $35 in unpaid wages. Most theatre-goers thought they were victims of an April Fools' joke when the curtain was raised and a bleeding corpse lay in centre stage. Emerson was later acquitted, despite having shot Tuttle in the face at point-blank range.

When prohibition began on September 18, 1916, it was not with the approval of most Londoners. After all, a city with two major breweries could not be expected to approve of an alcohol ban. Rum-running was not as popular here as it was in the Border Cities, but incidents between the police and "rummies" did occur. On January 24, 1921, five London officers chasing rum-runners were ambushed on Hamilton Road. The authorities were left behind while the "rummies" escaped.

London's first recorded bank robbery was on December 1, 1920, when the London South branch of the Merchants Bank of Canada was robbed. $700 was taken in the hold-up at the branch on the east side of Wortley between Craig and Bruce. Perhaps London's most dramatic bank heist, however, was that made by the city's (and Canada's) first aerial bandit. A man successfully escaped by airplane after robbing the branch of the Bank of Toronto on the southwest corner of Richmond and John streets in June 1931.

One of London's most notorious crimes was the kidnapping of brewery president John Sackville Labatt, abducted while driving his car from Sarnia to London on August 14, 1934. A ransom note left in his car demanded $150,000 from his brother Hugh. While John was held in a Muskoka cottage for three days, a media frenzy erupted, causing the kidnappers to panic. Released by his abductors, John Labatt walked into the Royal York Hotel in Toronto where his brother was attempting to gather the money. Pandemonium erupted as a crowd of reporters realized who had walked in the door, ending the ordeal on an equally sensational note.

While not all London crime was this dramatic, the city's underworld grew alongside the community—but so did the police force, which, armed with new technologies (radio patrols were introduced in 1941) and an increasing level of professionalism, strove to stay one step ahead.

Originally in City Hall on Richmond Street, police headquarters moved into a former fire station on Carling Street in 1874. This new Central Police Court and Station was built on the site in 1882 and was used until a new building was constructed on King Street West of Ridout in 1930. This building then became London Printing and Lithographing.

The Middlesex Courthouse and Jail with surrounding buildings. This photo was taken before 1878 when the Courthouse was renovated with a new entrance facing Ridout Street. The building at right was built about 1865 for Middlesex County Council.

Dr. Rufus Bratton (1821–1897) was a physician, Confederate army surgeon, and member of the Ku Klux Klan who committed serious crimes against southern blacks after the Civil War. On the U.S. federal government's most wanted list for the lynching of black leader Jim Williams in South Carolina, Bratton fled to London and sought asylum in the Revere House. Arrested by American authorities here in London in 1872, he was returned to the United States. The Canadian government called the arrest a kidnapping and demanded Bratton's return. Looking to avoid an international incident, American authorities allowed Bratton to return to London where he practised medicine for a time.

George Edward Harlton, a chicken thief, shot and killed traffic officer John "Jack" Waddell on Egerton Street on September 12, 1925, while Waddell tried to arrest him. Harlton was arrested in Washington State two years after the murder. Pictured here during his trial in January 1929, he was sentenced to death, but received a reprieve.

County Constable Corsaut escorts a handcuffed Daniel "Gypsy" Reynolds from his cell in the county jail on December 22, 1911. Reynolds was facing his preliminary hearing after being arrested for the murder of Fred Culver at Graham's Hotel on Hamilton Road.

The Home Bank of Canada in the village of Melbourne was robbed by four men on April 11, 1921. The robbers shot local resident Russell Campbell to death while trying to escape.

Here one of the Melbourne bank robbers, Sydney Murrell, is lashed to a post after being caught by a local posse. Sydney and his brother William escaped from London jail and fled to California. Syd was arrested two years later and extradited to London, where he was convicted of murder and hanged on April 10, 1924.

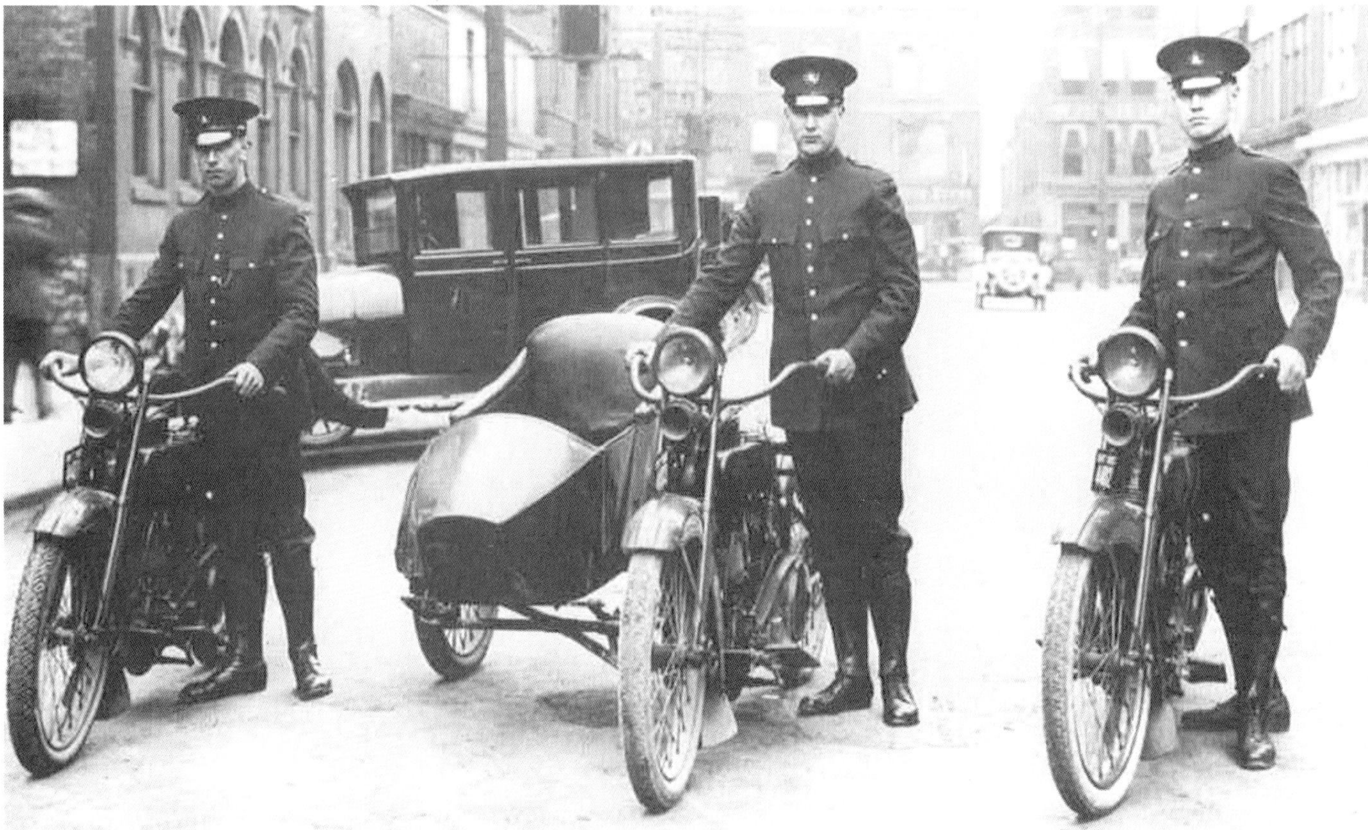

The London Police's motorcycle squad poses on Carling Street, 1932. From left to right are Tomas McMaster, Charles Noltie, and Gawin Monahan.

The London police got their first vehicle in 1913: a Cadillac patrol wagon and ambulance. It is pictured here in 1923 with Constable Walter Harpue, Sgt. John Mackay, Constable Charles Langferd, and Constable Gawin Monahan.

London's police force poses for a group photo in January, 1933. W. Harry Down, likely the man front and centre, was chief of police at the time.

WEATHER
Lower Lakes — Partly cloudy today and Thursday with a few local thundershowers.

The Sarnia Canadian Observer

HOME EDITION

INCORPORATING THE SARNIA DAILY OBSERVER AND THE SARNIA WEEKLY CANADIAN

Vol. XVI—No. 251 | Sarnia, Ontario, Wednesday, August 15, 1934—12 Pages | THREE CENTS

PROVINCEWIDE SEARCH FOR JOHN S. LABATT CONTINUES

London beer tycoon John S. Labatt was kidnapped en route from his summer home in Sarnia to a business meeting in London on August 14, 1934. Held for a $150,000 ransom for three days by "Three-Fingered Abe" and his accomplices, Labatt's snatching inspired a media frenzy until he was released unharmed three days later. Three men were arrested and charged, though one of them, David Meisner, was misidentified by Labatt and wrongfully convicted—only to be exonerated and released 15 months later. As a result of the traumatic incident, Labatt became a recluse until his death in 1952.

*London Free Press* reporter Frank Rowles points at the spot near the corner of Pall Mall and Miles streets where the body of 65-year-old widow Annie Templeton was found on March 28, 1939. At first, police thought she had been the victim of a hit and run, but her clothes were tidy, she wore no coat or hat, her arms were folded across her body, and there was no broken glass. She had been living with friends, George and Jessie Taylor of 502 Pall Mall Street. According to Mrs. Taylor, Templeton's will left the Taylors all her money. After blood was found on the front steps of the Taylor home, 50-year-old Jessie was arrested for murder. With a husband on relief, 11 children to feed, and the promise of inheritance, Jessie fractured her friend's skull with a piece of kindling. However, the deceased had lied and left her money to a local church instead. Although condemned to hang, Taylor's sentence was commuted to life. She served 12 years in Kingston Penitentiary.

On August 12, 1939, a lone bandit held up the Royal Bank at Dundas and Quebec streets. After threatening teller S.G. Finn with a revolver, he escaped with $1600. Taking a taxi to Queens and Clarence, he got out and disappeared. Here Mr. Finn and Miss M.E. Hovey pose with a Reward sign.

Exterior view of Royal Bank of Canada at Dundas and Quebec, after the holdup.

A view of the interior of the robbed bank.

Detectives go over the escape taxi, looking for fingerprints of the Royal Bank Bandit. Note sticker on car for the recent Royal Visit of 1939.

Escaping in a hail of bullets with about $1200, a lone gunman robbed the East London branch of The Dominion Bank at Dundas and Rectory streets on January 29, 1940. Teller A.J. Nash and ledgerkeeper J.S. Carpenter fired a fusillade of shots after the bandit, who escaped by car.

Bullets fired into the bank window were not from the criminal's gun, but from that of two employees hoping to attract attention to the holdup.

A revolver range opened at the police station in April, 1941.

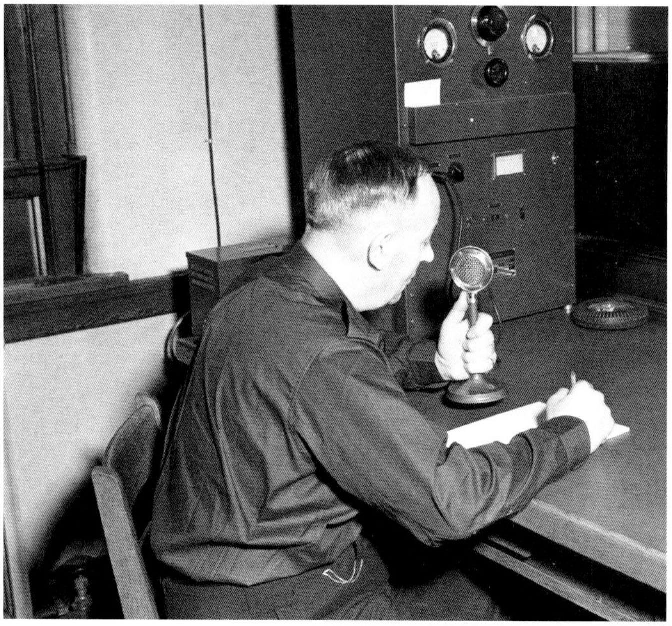

Desk sergeant George F. Tomblin at London Police Department headquarters, detailing a patrol car using the station's brand new radio patrol system, May 1941.

London police acquired a radio patrol system in early May, 1941. Here Inspector Percy Last sits at the wheel of one of the patrol cars, talking to police headquarters using his microphone.

Constable Fred Hart models the new LPD uniform in early May, 1941. His uniform includes a perforated hat, open collar, ID number, blue shirt, and black tie—all of which will keep him "cool and smart" on the beat.

When a prowler tripped over a box of tools in the cellar of the Rae home at 1249 Trafalgar Street in August, 1943, house guest Mrs. Art Pyman grabbed Mr. Rae's shotgun and fired. Here, she proudly brandishes said shotgun for the *Free Press* after successfully scaring the intruder away.

An officer directs traffic at the corner of Richmond and Dundas Streets, 1950. London had its first traffic lights installed in 1925; they were operated by an officer in a tower.

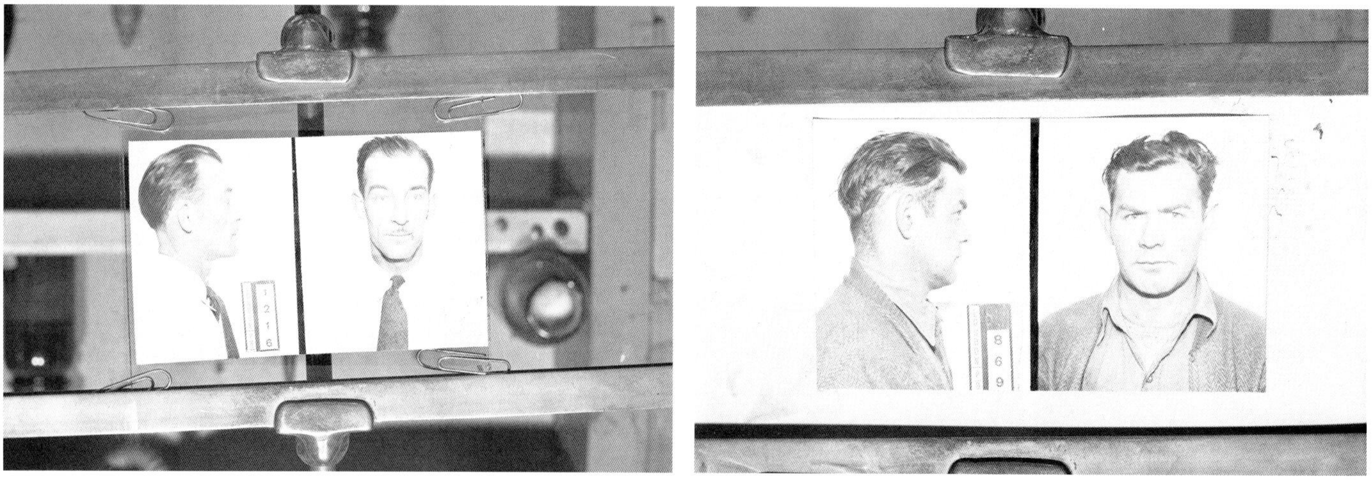


London Police Department mug shots of unidentified perps from December, 1943.

Chief Dispatcher Floyd Haight charts the positions of the 26 provincial police cars patrolling the London division in March, 1948. Map work was part of the new provincial police two-way radio system that officially opened March 25.

An abandoned piece of fishing line caused the drowning of six-year-old Robert (Bobbie) Keith on May 13, 1949. The boy slipped into the Thames from a narrow ledge below Hunt's dam at the Richmond Street bridge. His body was recovered three hours later after the fire department rescue squad dragged the river for two and a half hours, as seen here. Firemen Tom Allison, James Sneddon, and Constable Wallace Blanshard from left to right are in the boat.

Trains out of London bound for the border crossing into the United States at Windsor or Sarnia had Canadian customs officers as of March 1948. Some of the "customs examiners" were women including Olive Pretty, a veteran of the RCAF women's division, pictured here, with Canadian and U.S. customs officers who also worked on border crossing trains.

Bob White inspects the antenna on his police radio car, March 5, 1948.

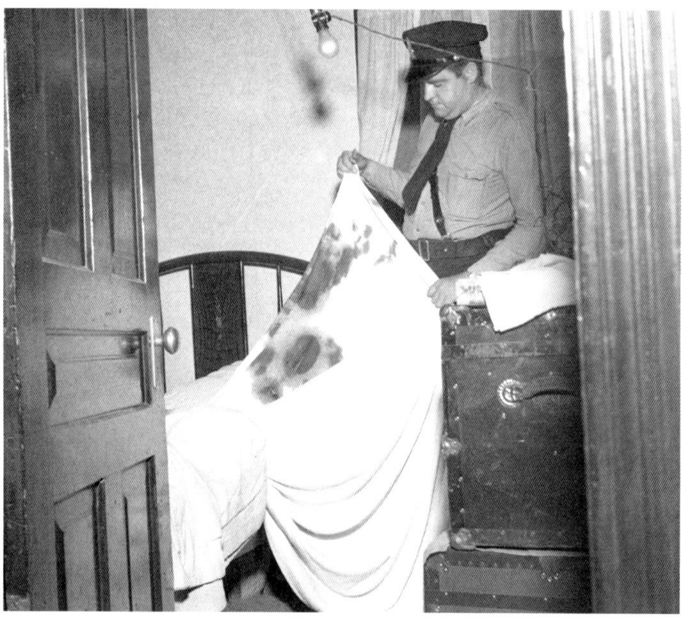

A Japanese-Canadian woman, Mrs. Masa Kato, was stabbed while alone at 114 Inkerman Street in June 1949. The 69 year-old was in bed when a male attacker entered the home shortly before midnight. Escaping along Layard Street, Mrs. Kato collapsed in front of the home of fireman Samuel E. Purcell. She was taken to Victoria Hospital with several gashes to her head.

Mrs. Kato lived with the Yamura family, shown here packing to return to Vancouver, following the violent incident.

# LONDON FREE PRESS

On January 2, 1849, the first issue of a fledgling newspaper called the *Canadian Free Press* appeared in London, Canada West. Published by a 25-year-old Scottish printer-editor named William Sutherland, the four-page paper competed with publications called the *London Times*, *Western Globe*, and the *Evangelical Pioneer* for the attention of the approximately 5,000 citizens of the town.

As early as May 28 of that year, Sutherland faced his first trial in the news business. His office on Dundas near Ridout in the O'Brien Block was set on fire by a mob unhappy with his support for the Reform Party and his advocacy of responsible government. Sutherland, who slept in his building, escaped unharmed. The city's offered reward of 50 pounds for information about the arsonists was never claimed. Undaunted, Sutherland published his next weekly edition on time, moving the paper's office to a building on Ridout north of Dundas.

While surviving that storm, Sutherland failed after an attempt to convert the *Free Press* into a daily paper. Perhaps London was not yet ready for a daily, since the paper lasted only 40 more issues under Sutherland's editorship. A young English journalist named Josiah Blackburn took over the paper in 1853, buying a $500 mortgage on the property. He then renamed it the *London Free Press*—and the rest, as they say, is history.

In 1854, Blackburn moved into a building on Carling Street, a site now occupied by the Marienbad Restaurant. He later moved to Richmond Street into a building across from Carling Street's east end, which is also still standing. In 1931, the *Free Press* expanded by moving farther up Richmond, taking over an old Bank of Montreal building. It was at the Carling Street location, however, that Blackburn succeeded in the experiment at which Sutherland failed. With a staff consisting only of himself and six others, Blackburn began to publish a daily paper on May 5, 1855. The four-page *London Free Press* and *Daily Western Advertiser* usually contained two pages of advertising, but perhaps the commercial content was the key to making the paper successful. It certainly provides a useful record of London's mid-nineteenth-century business community for today's historians.

Over the next century, the Blackburn name became synonymous with that of the *Free Press*, as well as with innovation and progress in London's media. The *Free Press* was undoubtedly London's most important news and communications vehicle. News arrived by telegraph so that readers could read news taking place virtually anywhere in the world; articles could be supplemented with more detailed material arriving in the daily mail. By early twentieth century, the *Free Press* was the information beacon of southwestern Ontario, nothing escaping its notice. Even today, the paper remains an important source of facts about local tragedies such as the Donnelly Massacre, the Victoria Disaster, and the Flood of 1937, as well as a host of lesser-known events. In its time, it was how Londoners accessed the world around them—learning the latest in the war effort, tragedies like the sinking of the *Titanic*, and virtually all other major world happenings. In 1939, 50,000 papers were printed daily and delivered throughout London and southwestern Ontario.

In his youth an ardent liberal, Blackburn later developed a conservative stance, which was reflected in the pages of the *Free Press*, which, for example, adopted the cause of Sir John A. Macdonald's National Policy. However, from 1863 to 1936, there was completion from the *Advertiser*, a daily evening newspaper with a liberal bent. The *Free Press* took over its main competitor on February 15, 1926, when Joseph Atkinson, publisher of the *Toronto Star*, sold the *Advertiser* to the *Free Press* for $112,500. The *Advertiser* operated for another ten years, despite being owned by its former competition. When it closed in 1936, the *Free Press* became London's only daily paper.

Josiah died in 1890, leaving his paper to his two sons, Walter and Arthur. In 1920, Walter died and Arthur became president. Arthur added to the media empire by founding radio station CJGC in the *Free Press* building on Richmond in 1922. The station closed in 1933 as a result of the Depression, but Blackburn re-launched the station later that year with a new label, CFPL. When Arthur died in 1935, his 21-year-old son Walter J. took over as publisher of the paper. A less-famous, but equally talented, member of the family was Victoria Grace—Josiah's daughter and Walter and Arthur's sister—who in 1900 became the paper's literary and drama critic. From 1918 until her death in 1928, she was assistant managing editor of the paper. To the world she was known by her pseudonym, "Fanfan."

Well-known managing editors of the *Free Press* included Malcolm G. Bremner, Alfred E. Miller, and Arthur R. Ford. Bremner, editor-in-chief from 1890 to 1910, started as a *Free Press* reporter in the 1860s. Having being sent to cover the Fenian Raids, he is said to have slept in the field before the Battle of the Ridgeway in 1866 so as not to miss the action—not only making him an early Canadian war correspondent, but one willing to go beyond the call of duty! Miller, who became managing editor in 1910 and remained so until his death in 1920, avoided the city hall disaster of January 3, 1898, by arriving too late to complete his assignment. Ford became editor-in-chief in 1920, but found time to teach journalism at Western, start Western's journalism school, and eventually become chancellor of the university.

Certain dates or editions stand out in the history of the *Free Press*. On May 8, 1875, an evening edition was added to the daily paper. The earliest photograph—that of 19-year-old jockey Otto Wonderly—appeared July 31, 1901. The first action photograph, taken by Arthur Blackburn, was that of the ending of the King's Plate horse race in Toronto in 1906. The first Sunday paper was probably that published on August 2, 1914, to announce that Germany, France and Russia were at war. A popular, long-lived feature called "Looking over Western Ontario" first appeared on October 8, 1921. On Sunday, September 3, 1939, a pale apricot-coloured four-page extra was published announcing "CANADA IS NOW AT WAR" in a one-and-a-half-inch headline. The largest edition of a newspaper printed in Canada appeared on June 11, 1949, when the *Free Press* issued a 232-page edition to celebrate the paper's centennial. It was a far cry from the four-page first issue Sutherland printed in 1849—and a signal that the *London Free Press* would remain the paper of record for Londoners for years to come.

Newly arrived English immigrant, Josiah Blackburn, pictured here circa 1860, purchased the *Canadian Free Press* from William Sutherland in 1853, renaming it the *London Free Press*. The Blackburns, London's first family of media, would own the newspaper for generations, until 1997.

Composers at work, 1909.

Press room, 1910.

Arthur Stephen Blackburn and Walter Josiah Blackburn, who inherited the *Free Press* after their father Josiah's death in 1890, have a meeting in the publishers' office, 1910.

Advertising department, 1911.

Typesetting department, 1911. Here, operators work away on linotypes—an innovation that greatly sped up the process of typesetting from placing each letter manually.

Editorial department, 1915.

Accounting department, 1915. Note the London Life calendar hanging on the wall.

Circulation department, 1915. As early as 1901, the *London Free Press* boasted a circulation of over 10,000, putting it in league with newspapers like the *Globe*, the *Toronto Star*, and the *Evening Citizen*.

*Free Press* building on Richmond Street, 1922. The newspaper operated out of this location from 1868 to 1931. Note the news bulletins posted for the public on the front facade.

An expanded (and tidier) editorial department, 1922.

The offices of the advertising department, pictured here in 1922, was located just east of the main *Free Press* offices on Richmond Street.

The exterior of the *Free Press* printing plant, 1922.

Workers bundle and package copies of the *Free Press* for delivery in the mailroom, 1922.

The *Free Press* delivery fleet lineup, 1922.

Composing room, 1934. Here, printers are arranging type columns, advertising plates, and illustration plates to set up a page of that day's paper.

Stereotype (composed printing plates) casting in progress, circa 1934.

The press room, 1929. This printing press was made by R. Hoe & Co., out of New York City, as indicated by a sign, partially visible in the background, to the left.

The *Free Press* moved into this new building, also on Richmond Street at 442-446, in 1931. The studios of CFPL were housed on the third floor.

These children have a little help with their *Free Press* deliveries on London Street, 1945.

Editor Arthur Ford works in his office, 1941. Beyond his work as editor-in-chief, Ford also founded Western University's School of Journalism and was known to be a confidant to various prime ministers from Robert Borden to Mackenzie King.

The *Free Press* plane, a twin-engine Cessna called the News Hawk, used in part for aerial photography, is seen here in 1946.

Worker in stereo department, circa 1947.

A tour of the press room, 1940s.

Using the microfilm machine, 1947. The newspaper being viewed is from 1945, discussing the surrender of Japan.

The photography department, 1940s.

Typesetters work away at linotype machines in an updated composing room in the 1940s. The linotype was the primary technology used by newspapers across North America until they became obsolete in the 1970s.

Walter J. Blackburn at his desk, 1948. Walter inherited the family business, at age 21, upon his father Arthur's death in 1935, becoming the publisher of the *Free Press* and owner of CFPL radio.

The first "birthday party" of Luke Worm (the little worm mascot featured in each editorial cartoon by *Free Press* artist Merle Tingley) is celebrated at the ten-forty club. From left to right are Arthur Brown and Walter Blackburn, with Tingley at far right. Tingley was the editorial cartoonist at the *Free Press* from 1948 to 1986.

# MIDDLESEX COUNTY

In the early days of Upper Canada, the province was divided into districts and counties. On January 1, 1800, the London District came into existence, formed from parts of earlier districts called Home and Western. Within the new district was the County of Middlesex. While districts existed for administrative purposes, the counties served as electoral ridings for the first provincial parliament as well as for militia organization. When the Forks of the Thames became the administrative and legal centre of the London District on January 1, 1826, it created the basis for the fledgling village of London to become the future administrative centre of the county as well. It would be 1850 before counties took on the local government responsibilities formerly held by the districts.

The County of Middlesex took in what is now Elgin County up until 1850. Middlesex did not, however, include the northern townships of Biddulph and McGillivray until 1865 when they were removed from Huron and added to Middlesex. This latter step was because the county seat, London, was closer to the townships than the Huron County capital of Goderich.

Many histories have covered the story of the settlers in Middlesex and Western Ontario. The trees were cut, pioneer industries and businesses were founded, farms were established, and small schools and churches dotted the countryside. There was much excitement in the 1850s over the newly built railway lines that guaranteed prosperity to the communities through which they passed. Bustling crossroads and hamlets failed when bypassed by the railways, forcing the inhabitants to relocate to localities on the lines. By 1850, Middlesex was very different from when European settlement began. From a small number of scattered individuals, it had transformed into the basic settlement that would still be evident one hundred years later. The landscape changed from a forest criss-crossed by "Indian" trails to being covered by farms and communities connected by an elaborate network of roads and railway tracks. As canoes gave way to stagecoaches, to trains, and finally to automobiles, a cross-country journey that once took days took only a few hours.

Over the decades, London has expanded at the expense of the county. Between 1885 and 1912, there were several annexations as London suburbs like London East, London West, Pottersburg, and Chelsea Green became part of the growing city. Gradually, the farm population of Middlesex declined as the population of city dwellers increased.

The county had a different culture than the city. It was a place where the life ways of earlier times continued, where traditional pastimes such as making maple syrup, conducting log-sawing contests, and attending village fall fairs continued into mid-twentieth century. Londoners, on the other hand, prided themselves on adopting a "big-city" attitude, distancing themselves from their county neighbours.

Despite this, the *London Free Press* attempted to remind Londoners that there was a county—many counties—surrounding the city. The newspaper was an information beacon, shining its light all over Western Ontario. Its readership far exceeded the city limits and it bragged of being "Western Ontario's Foremost Newspaper" on its front page. For Middlesex, it included news and sports in the towns of Strathroy and Parkhill and the villages of Ailsa Craig, Lucan, Newbury, Wardsville, and Glencoe, covering seed fairs, plowing matches, country fairs, and other aspects of farm and village life. From October 8, 1921, the newspaper included a popular historical page, "Looking Over Western Ontario." The section continued until late 1992, tracing pioneer families, buildings, and communities, and becoming a popular resource for future historians.

The Sisson family home factory in Byron, Westminster Township, after the devastating flood of 1883 wrecked the building. A wooden bridge over the Thames stands in ruins at the left and a distillery on the right in the picture is also damaged.

The first residence south of the tracks at Newbury, Mosa Township, in 1852 was still standing in September 1949, featured in the *Free Press* "Looking Over Western Ontario" section.

Sissons Saw Mill, Byron, Westminster Township, circa 1870. The mill was located in what is now Springbank Park.

Byron dam, grist mill, and miller's cottage, circa 1903. The first flour mill and dam at Byron were built in the 1830s.

Meadow Lily Mills, north bank of the Thames east of London, 1886–90. The business was owned by William Plewes as indicated by the "P" for Plewes above the date, 1886, on the front facade. Plewes bought the mill in 1870, rebuilding it after it burned down in 1885. The mill burned twice more, in 1891 and 1901, after which it was not rebuilt.

Station at Hyde Park Junction, London Township, 1900s. This once-busy station on the Grand Trunk closed in 1967.

The flour mill owned in pioneer days by Walter Oliver on Oxbow Creek, near the Kilworth Bridge in Lobo Township. Settlers came as far as 30 miles to grind grain at this mill in the 1830s.

The main street of Mount Brydges in Caradoc Township, seen here, is a typical 1900s village street. The view shows C.J. Farr's General Store and Mitchell's Taylor Shop.

A home (possibly the rectory), Presbyterian Church, and schoolhouse, from left to right, at the hamlet of Hyde Park, 1900s.

The store of Walter C. Reeve, General Grocer, in Hyde Park. General stores carried a bit of everything, including dry goods, as Reeve's sign indicates. Built as the Old Countryman's Inn, circa 1860 on the southeast corner of the Hyde Park intersection, this store was dismantled in 1925.

Crowds gather in the village of Delaware to attend the annual Delaware Fall Fair. Visitors at village fairs would see exhibits of crops and livestock, crafts and baked goods, not to mention meet their neighbours from miles around.

A Calithumpian Parade makes its way north on Main Street in Glencoe on August 11, 1908. The CPR ticket office is visible at right.

Main Street, Glencoe, 1908. The McAlpine House hotel is the first building on the left.

Fairgrounds near Glencoe, September 30, 1908.

Memorial Hall and Public Library, Glencoe, circa 1912.

Town Hall and Opera House, Glencoe, 1900s. Built in 1898, the building was demolished in 1962.

A postcard featuring Dorchester, located southeast of London on the Thames River, 1909.

The village of Dorchester, 1907. J.H. Birch dry goods is visible at right.

The busy main intersection of the village of Melbourne is featured in a 1910 postcard. The crossroads community developed on Longwoods Road at the Ekfrid-Caradoc Townline.

A country road near Melbourne, an idyllic spot for a Sunday drive.

Looking north on the Proof Line Road at Arva's main intersection, 1912.

Middlesex County's 10th Annual Plowing Match near Ilderton in October 1938.

Prize for the best team and equipment at the match went to J.S. Fletcher of Ilderton.

The Caradoc Fruit Growers' Association depot on the railway line in Caradoc Township, October 1938.

The Caradoc apple harvest.

Apple barrels being loaded onto a train.

Miss Dora Smith, Strathroy beauty shop operator, won $75,000 in the Irish sweepstakes in October 1938. Here she answers one of the hundreds of congratulatory phone calls she had after the news arrived by cable.

A jumbo crop of tobacco was raised in the summer of 1939 by Valere Brabant on his farm two miles east of Dorchester on Hamilton Road. His plants were 3½ feet high and he expected to harvest his bumper crop within 10 days.

Mrs. Fred Moore (nearest the camera), Ruth Lyons, Shirley Roulston, and Eleanor Mahler "tie" the tobacco crop grown on the farm of Harvey Wales and Arthur Malott near the village of Delaware in March 1946.

Workers haul bales of tobacco on the Wales & Malott farm in Delaware, 1946.

An aerial view of Lucan, a village of 650 people in March 1946. The main road is the Proof Line or Highway 4, now Richmond Street.

Arnold (left) and Donald Scott make syrup in a kettle over a fire on the Scott farm, March 19, 1947.

By March, 1947, Belton general merchant James Box had operated the hamlet's general store and post office for 42 years. The business had changed little since he opened it in 1905.

The Belton Lumber Yard, 1948. The hamlet of Belton developed around the CNR crossing on Concession 5, West Nissouri Township.

At the Oneida Indian Fall Fair in October 1948, the Oneida Indian Band performed in costume. Here, three younger bandsmen receive a few words of instruction from the band leader, Simon Doxtator. The others are, from left to right, Arnold Antone (13), Frederick Jamieson (19), and George Hill, Jr. (12). George won first prize for his clarinet solo.

Log-sawing contests remained popular in country communities into the twentieth century. No. 9 Mosa Schoolhouse near Glencoe was filled to capacity on April 13, 1948, for an evening of fun and music sponsored by the Women's Institute. The log contest was the highlight of the event. Here two partners in the open "free-for-all" class sweat it out over a 16-inch hardwood log.

Sheila Robinson and her dog Whiskers enjoy the view of the distant London skyline, April 1, 1949.

# MILITARY

Londoners have a proud history of defending their country and empire in times of peril. In the earliest days, the military presence consisted of the local militia. Legislation passed in 1793—before the first log cabin was built at the forks of the Thames—made every able-bodied male between 16 and 60 a militiaman. The men received neither pay nor equipment for their "voluntary" service and had to attend an annual training day for military exercises. They were also expected to supply their own muskets, powder, and shot; those who did not register for service were fined. Nevertheless, most men in the London area seem to have been willing to be called up to defend their homes and families, if the need arose. And it did. Between 1812 and 1866, the Middlesex Militia was mobilized 16 times to deal with crises such as the Rebellion of 1837 and the Fenian Raids from across the American border.

After the Rebellion of 1837, it was considered necessary to have a heightened British military presence throughout Upper Canada. Therefore, although the Rebellion was almost non-existent in the London area, six companies of the 24th Regiment of Foot arrived in 1838. This was the beginning of the British garrison that would remain in London until after Confederation, not departing until 1869. The various British regiments stationed in London were always well received, since they brought spending money, news from the outside world, and some organized social life in the form of theatrical performances, dances, and sports. The barracks were located on the Military Reserve, rechristened Victoria Park by Governor-General the Earl of Dufferin in 1874.

The absence of British troops didn't mean the end of a military presence, however. Rather, London was made the headquarters of Military District No. 1 in 1868, responsible for the militia units across Western Ontario. The last years of the nineteenth century also provided Londoners with the opportunity to defend both the new Dominion and the Empire. When the Northwest Rebellion, led by Louis Riel, broke out in 1885, the 7th Fusiliers were called up as part of the fighting force to put it down. The company of 21 officers and 244 non-commissioned officers and men headed west, but took so long getting to Clark's Crossing on the Saskatchewan River that the rebellion was over by the time they arrived. Despite their lack of fighting experience, they still received a triumphant reception upon returning to the city.

On January 6, 1886, federal cabinet minister John Carling agreed to sell his farm to the city for $40,000 on the understanding that it would be traded to the government for the remaining militia grounds adjoining Victoria Park. Carling's farm was a natural spot for a training ground since it had been used for that purpose before. In 1864, for example, 30,000 people from as far as Windsor, Hamilton, and Goderich enjoyed the spectacle of a review of volunteers and regular troops on Carling's farm.

Also in 1886, the cornerstone was laid for an Infantry Training School, later known as Wolseley Barracks, on Carling Heights (as the farm became known) and the school opened for regular training in 1888. The Infantry Corps School became The Royal Canadian Regiment in 1901, and the first tank school in Canada opened on the site in 1936.

In 1856, the 1st London Volunteer Troop of Cavalry was formed. The unit merged with other cavalry troops in 1872 to form the 1st Regiment of Cavalry and in 1892, took the name First Hussars. "1H," as they were branded, moved into the new London Armouries in 1905, giving London's military a downtown presence. The First Hussars fought in the Boer War, the First World War, and landed on the beaches of Normandy on D-Day in the Second World War.

The Boer, or South African, War provided Londoners with another fighting opportunity. On October 25, 1899, a contingent of volunteers from Military District No. 1 departed from London for South Africa after being addressed at the Grand Trunk station by Prime Minister Sir Wilfrid Laurier. The men were from the First Hussars, The Royal Canadian Regiment, and the Middlesex Regiment. The Boer War was also one of the first wars that provided women with a means to publicly participate. On the home front, Harriet Boomer organized a branch of the Red Cross to assist the soldiers. After the war, ladies of the IODE raised $1,800 to construct the Boer War Memorial in Victoria Park in 1908. The statue was unveiled by none other than Prince Arthur, Duke of Connaught.

HMCS Prevost was founded in 1938 as the London division of the Royal Canadian Naval Volunteer Reserve with quarters on the second floor of the Darch Building on Talbot Street. The location was conveniently next to the Market Square for parade ground activities. But after the outbreak of the Second World War, a move was made to the Carling Block on the northwest corner of Richmond and Carling streets. The building was named after a War of 1812-era ship called HMS *Lady Prevost*. During the Second War World, Prevost enrolled 4,480 officers, men and women into the Royal Canadian Navy.

The military had a very visible presence in London, more than your average Canadian city—leading a patriotic citizenry, which rallied time and again in support of King and country.

Lt.-Col. James Shanly's Volunteer Militia Field Battery, 1866. George B. Harris of Eldon House sits on the white horse.

The officers' quarters at the barracks, 1867. These barracks were located at the south end of the infantry square, now Victoria Park.

Stables at the barracks with men from H. Battery, 4th Brigade, Royal Artillery, circa 1867.

Artillery sleighs on the London Military Reserve with the 4th Brigade of the Royal Artillery, circa 1866. On the left is the frame Infantry Barracks Hospital while the west end of the soldiers barracks is visible to the right.

Regimental games at the Infantry Drill Grounds featured the 63rd Regiment on May 24, 1864. This view looks south from the south end of the military reserve. The churches visible in the background are First Presbyterian (left) and North Street Methodist church.

An artistic depiction of the officers of the 7th Battalion Fusiliers at Clarke's Crossing during the Northwest Rebellion, 1885.

Three local soldiers pose with playing cards, 1895.

Fox Hunt at the Infantry School Corps, circa 1890. In addition to drills and soldiers' training, popular activities such as fox hunting were conducted on the grounds surrounding the Infantry School Corps, known as Carling Heights.

The Infantry School Corps building, circa 1888. The building was renamed Wolseley Barracks in 1894.

Soldiers pose before Wolseley Barracks, circa 1900.

Military parade through downtown, on Dundas between Ridout and Talbot, looking east, circa 1900.

London Garrison church parade passes the McCormick Manufacturing Company on Dundas street, 1909. The Armouries can be seen in the background.

Cavalry drill, Carling Heights, circa 1910.

Postcard view of the south facade of the officer's quarters at Wolseley Barracks, circa 1910.

Through the efforts of Major James Shanly, two Russian guns captured in Crimea at Sebastopol were brought to London in 1860. Years later, they were installed in Victoria Park, as seen in this 1911 photograph.

This postcard gives a view of both exterior and interior at Wolseley Barracks.

Unveiling the soldier's monument at Victoria Park, May 29, 1911. Prince Arthur, Duke of Connaught, was officiating.

Paardeberg Day, February 27, 1913, marked the first decoration of the Soldier's Monument.

Cadet Instructors Corp lines up at Carling Heights in 1913.

The First Hussars train at Port Stanley in these undated early twentieth century photographs.

This military funeral held Sunday, July 26, 1914 was held for Irving Penny and Jack McPhail, Port Stanley drowning victims. They are borne along Dundas Street to Woodland Cemetery on gun carriages, surrounded by representatives from the London garrison.

Sentry Duty at Wolseley Barracks, The Royal Canadian Regiment, circa 1922. Parade Square is in the background.

The Royal Canadian Regiment prepares for the Governor General's visit in the parade square at Wolseley Barracks, circa 1927.

Postcard view of Wolseley Barracks, circa 1933.

This temporary cenotaph on Dundas Street, just east of Wellington, was constructed by the military in London and used at services on Armistice Day, 1934.

Veterans march south on Waterloo Street between Princess and Dufferin avenues on November 11, 1936.

Mrs. Charlie Kerrigan pins a poppy on Bert Crocker, November 5, 1938, at the corner of Dundas and Richmond. The poppies commemorated the First World War, sometimes called the "war to end all wars." However, the headlines in the papers at the newsstand at right indicate the world was sliding into another devastating war.

The First Hussars, Western Ontario's only cavalry regiment, receive their annual inspection from Brigadier D.J. MacDonald at the Armouries on October 28, 1938.

On January 10, 1939, a special demonstration squad of The Royal Canadian Regiment showed the tear gas chamber in the Armouries to the public. Civilians were allowed to try out the chamber in groups of 25. Here, Lance Corporal T.M. McDonald instructs Bill Wenker (left) and John McNaughton as well as Edna Lindfield (left) and Marjorie Jones on how to properly wear a gas mask.

Major J.M. Dickinson of the First Hussars is sighting a new anti-tank rifle at the Armouries in January 1939. "It works fine," he commented to Cpl. O. White of The Royal Canadian Regiment demonstration squad who was displaying the rifle—the first weapon of its kind in Canada.

Twenty-four members of the London Naval Reserve posed for a photograph before leaving for Halifax on June 20, 1939. They were to spend two weeks training at the naval base.

Soldiers lined up for inspection at Wolseley Barracks, June 9, 1939. The Second World War was not declared until that fall.

Men marching into Wolseley Barracks, June 9, 1939.

The RCR are inspected at London Armouries on August 28, 1939.

The officer sporting a gas mask in this photo is likely Brig D.J. MacDonald CBE, DSO, MC, commander of Military District No. 1 from June 1938 to September 1944.

Scenes at the cenotaph service, Victoria Park, November 11, 1939. This service was particuarly sombre as Canada had just entered the Second World War one month previous.

On July 6, 1940, one of London's oldest landmarks was being demolished. Built by Dr. O'Flaherty at the corner of Richmond and Horton over 100 years earlier, the building was part of an area called "Officers' Row."

Dundas Street looking east from Richmond, November 1941. The Armistice Day banner is especially poignant considering another world war was taking place.

HMCS Prevost Armoury on the northwest corner of Richmond and Carling streets, July 2, 1948.

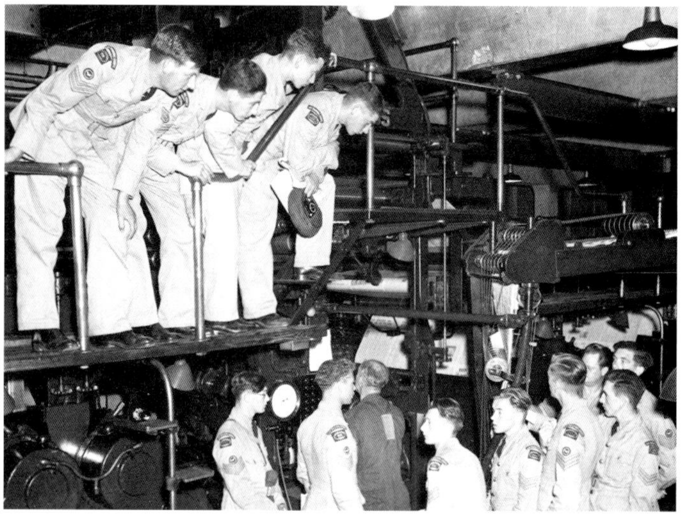

RAF cadets toured the press room at the *London Free Press* on August 10, 1948.

Twenty-one sea cadets were guests at Loew's Theatre on December 16, 1948, as a reward for capturing the efficiency award for November. The division, under the command of Sub-Lt. K. Lewis, won for their attendance, general seamanship, and dress. At centre are, left to right: E.H. DePotie, lieutenant-commander of the corps; Sub-Lt. Lewis; Campbell Calder, local president of the Navy League of Canada; Fred Jackson, manager of Loew's Theatre; and Bernard Murphy, ticket taker.

The Canadian Army was on display on Saturday, September 18, 1948, at the Armouries. A long armoured convoy—similar to those that rolled forward during the war—drove through the city and stopped to be placed on display in front of the Dundas Street building.

This weapon left London on October 18, 1948, to tour Western Ontario as a prime exhibit in Navy Week. Called the "hedgehog," it was an anti-submarine weapon just taken off the "secret list." Mounted on a vessel, the device shot a pattern of small depth charges over the bow. Other Navy Week events included a parade and an open house at HMCS Prevost.

Thousands of Londoners went to the cenotaph in Victoria Park on Armistice Day, November 11, 1948. A new inscription paying tribute to the veterans of World War II was unveiled on the occasion.

In May, 1949, Lt.-Gen. Charles Foulkes, chief of the general staff, graduate of Central Collegiate in 1921, returned to his alma mater to unveil a plaque in memory of students who died in the Second World War. Here, Gen. Foulkes (left) reads the honour roll with Wing Commander A.F. McKillop, Principal.

Army Week opened in London on May 15, 1949, with a Drumhead Service in Victoria Park, followed by a parade and march-past. Here, the pipe band of the Highland Light Infantry of Galt (Cambridge) leads the parade past the saluting base where Brigadier H.A. Sparling, area commandant, takes the salute.

On August 4, 1949, LAC W.T. Overton of London puts the final touches on the "Snowy Owl" crest on a Lancaster bomber, part of No. 420 City of London RCAF Fighter Squadron. The emblem was chosen because the bird of prey is only found in the Canadian northlands.

# PEOPLE & POLITICS

A host of colourful characters has called London home since its founding. Some were politicians exerting their influence, others figureheads representing the power of others, and some were private citizens working to make the city a better place. London has had its fair share of celebrities—men and women who shaped the city and live on in the pages of our history books.

Colonel Thomas Talbot arrived in Upper Canada long before there was a village called London. Born in Ireland, he first came to Canada in 1791 as private secretary to Lt.-Gov. John Graves Simcoe—and accompanied Simcoe on the first trip to the Forks of the Thames in 1793, soon to be declared "New London." Returning to Britain, Talbot convinced the British government to place him in charge of a land settlement scheme along the shore of Lake Erie. In this he was supremely successful. By 1836, Talbot had settled portions of 29 townships extending over a huge area of present-day southwestern Ontario. An eccentric loner, he died at the London home of a personal servant, George Macbeth, in 1853. By that time, he had given his name to St. Thomas, Talbotville, and streets named Talbot in London and elsewhere.

After pioneer days were over, Confederation laid the base for the political system we know today. Perhaps London's most famous nineteenth-century politician, beer magnate Sir John Carling represented the city in both provincial and federal governments at once until such a practice was disallowed in 1872. After losing the 1891 election to fellow businessman Charles Hyman, he was appointed to the Senate by Prime Minister John A. Macdonald. However, when the election results were disputed and declared void, Carling resigned from the Senate to run in an 1892 by-election—and this time, he won. He served in the House of Commons until just before the 1896 election, and then resigned, to be reappointed to the Senate.

Meanwhile, Carling remained active in London affairs, using his political positions to influence business. In 1875, he and his brother William built a new Carling Brewery, and built it again after it burned down in 1879. The brewery was one of the largest in Canada and rivalled Labatt. Carling was knighted in 1893 and served in the Senate until his death in London in 1911.

Another celebrity politician was Sir Adam Beck, the province's "king of hydroelectricity," who tirelessly advocated for the new, cheap form of power across Ontario in the early 1900s. He would go on to found the Hydro-Electric Power Commission of Ontario in 1906, which continues today as Ontario Hydro. Beck was knighted by King George V in 1914 for his promotion of electricity and the development of transmission lines. Sir Adam Beck Collegiate Institute, now the Thames Valley District School Board headquarters, was named after him. Beck also served as mayor of London from 1902 to 1904.

Londoners were proud of Ray Lawson—president of Lawson & Jones Ltd., a local printing firm—who became the 17$^{th}$ Lieutenant-Governor of Ontario from 1946 to 1952. Lawson had made a name for himself in the community as a philanthropist. He sponsored the building of a library at the University of Western Ontario in 1933, created various scholarships and trusts, and contributed to numerous charities.

Confined by traditional gender roles and the domestic sphere, nineteenth-century women were less often in the public eye—even more rarely for their own achievements instead of accompanying their husbands. However, there are a few notable elite women who were able to take advantage of their prominent positions and publicly contribute to society. One of particular note is Harriet Ann Boomer, who played a major role in establishing and administering a variety of women's societies, many of them associated with medical services. Boomer, known for her forceful personality, helped found the London Local Council of Women in 1893 and served as its president for twenty years.

London had its share of interesting mayors before 1950. Stove maker Murray Anderson was London's first mayor after it became a city in 1855. But the young city's most memorable mayor was Frank Evans Cornish, who served from 1861 to 1864. Cornish bribed the electorate with free beer, got into a fist fight with a British military officer, and assaulted the chief of police. His most memorable act came after he was arrested for driving his horse and carriage while inebriated. The next morning, in his capacity as Chief Magistrate, Cornish called out his own name in court, delivered a lecture on the evils of drink, and fined himself four dollars. He then removed four dollars from his right-hand pocket, placed it on the magistrate's desk, and then deposited it into his left-hand pocket. Finally, he remitted half of the fine in view of his previous good conduct and placed two dollars back in his right pocket. To the relief of many Londoners, Cornish eventually moved on to Manitoba where his shenanigans made him notorious as the first mayor of Winnipeg.

There was never a dull moment in the twentieth century either, at least not when the mayor was George A. Wenige. And Wenige was mayor quite often, from 1923–1925, 1928, 1934–1935, 1947–1948, and 1950. Altogether, he ran for mayor 20 times and won on nine occasions. Although a more law-abiding figure than Frank Cornish, Wenige did have a natural flair for attracting publicity. Whether he was firing department heads, establishing civic bingo games, advocating economy while being a big spender himself, teaching civic lessons to Grade 8 pupils, or wearing an inappropriate jaunty straw hat to Sir Adam Beck's funeral, there was no end to the ways Wenige could draw attention to himself.

London had its share of prominent visitors. Governors-General, Lieutenant-Governors, Prime Ministers, Premiers, and a host of other figures engaged with Londoners on political as well as ceremonial occasions. Frederick, Earl of Dufferin, Canada's third Governor-General, visited the city with Lady Dufferin in October 1872 while on an official tour of Canadian cities. The couple was greeted with a torchlight procession by London's firemen, illuminations and fireworks, and a levee and ball at City Hall. Dufferin's popularity even led to a street name change from Duke Street to Dufferin Avenue.

Political leaders from Sir John A. Macdonald to Louis St. Laurent visited London, before they took office, on the campaign trail, on official visits, and during retirement. Many less well-remembered personages, though important during their time, called on London as well—a sign of the growing prominence of the Forest City. As the twentieth century progressed, more and more VIPs were women, wielding influence over men and women alike. From aristocrats to commoners, from men of principle to men entirely lacking in them, these are the individuals who shaped London and the world.

Prime Minister Sir Wilfrid Laurier speaks to a crowd during a campaign stop in Strathroy September 19, 1908. Laurier was returned to power, with a majority government, for his fourth consecutive term.

A caricature of city aldermen playing baseball before the Crystal Palace on London's first fairgrounds, circa 1870s.

Settlement promoter Colonel Thomas Talbot. This portrait, attributed to J.B. Wandesford, is now in the collection of Western's McIntosh Gallery.

Charles Hyman, tannery owner, was elected MP for London in 1900 and 1904, holding the portfolio of Public Works from 1905 to 1907. He resigned due to ill health in 1907.

Ward 3 Liberal Association meeting held at Hyman Hall, February 5, 1941. The guest of honour was Mrs. Joseph Johnston, mother of Allan Johnston, MP, then in Britain with the Canadian Forces.

The widely travelled Governor-General, the Earl of Dufferin sought contact with as many Canadians as possible, making a tour of southern Ontario that included London in 1872.

Harriet Ann Boomer, social activist, was for many years President of the London Local Council of Women.

Sir John Carling, MP and brewery heir, poses here while he was Minister of Agriculture, December 1885.

On Sunday, November 20, 1938, citizens of various faiths and backgrounds gathered at the Grand Theatre to protest the persecution of Jews in Germany. The event was chaired by Col. the Rev. William Beattie and the first speaker was Mayor Thomas Kingsmill, Jr. Two hundred citizens were unable to get a seat in the filled theatre and are shown in this photo listening to the speakers on a public address system played onto the street.

Sir Adam Beck, hydroelectricity advocate, around the time he was elected mayor of London in 1902. Beck founded the Ontario Hydro-Electric Power Comission (Ontario Hydro) in 1906.

On October 15, 1938, Governor-General of Canada John Buchan, Lord Tweedsmuir, visited "Buchan House," headquarters of the Tweedsmuir Branch of the Canadian Legion, situated across the street from the Armouries. Here he autographs copies of his books for Legion members. Charles Smith, President of the Tweedsmuir Branch, stands at the right of the Governor-General.

Anti-fascist demonstrators greeted Italian Vice-Consul Guido Colonna di Paliano when he arrived at the CPR station in London February 8, 1939, to speak to the Canadian Club. Waiting for the Vice-Consul, from left to right, are Al Bernhardt, local Communist organizer, Verne Brimacombe, and Ray Noble.

Hon. Cairine R. Wilson of Ottawa, Canada's only female senator, spoke at the Kiwanis Club luncheon at Hotel London, on March 30, 1939. Sitting to the left is J.P. Nethercott, chairman of the London Committee on Foreign Refugees.

In January 1941, the London Women's Canadian Club welcomed guest speaker Thérèse Casgrain, right, a leader in the League for Women's Rights in Quebec seen here chatting with club president Mrs. H.B. MacMahon. Six hundred members crowded the Crystal Ballroom at Hotel London to hear her speak. One of her comments was: "I was told recently that woman is the queen of the home. It seemed so queer to hear that in 1941." She continued: "I am aghast at women in a democracy who say they are not interested in politics."

Dorise Nielson, Canada's only female MP, spoke to a crowd of 900 at the Palace Theatre on March 30, 1941, after being invited by the Canadian Hosiery Workers Union. Mrs. Nielson, left, who represented the Unity Party in Saskatchewan, is pictured here with Mary McCallum, national women's director of the union. Nielson's most controversial remark was that the War Measures Act meant Canadians were being ruled by "Hitlerism and dictatorship" in their own land while being asked to fight it in Europe.

Arthur Meighen, leader of the Conservative Party and twice Prime Minister of Canada, was in London on May 15, 1941, to attend the Directors' Meeting of London & Western Trusts, of which he was president. He also visited his daughter, Lillian Wright, wife of Donald Wright, assistant supervisor of music for the Board of Education.

On April 9, 1943, London lawyer W.B. Henderson (right) was elected President of the London Progressive Conservative Party at an annual meeting held in the Masonic Temple. John G. Diefenbaker, then PC MP for Lake Centre, was speaker at the meeting. Diefenbaker would go on to become Prime Minister in 1957.

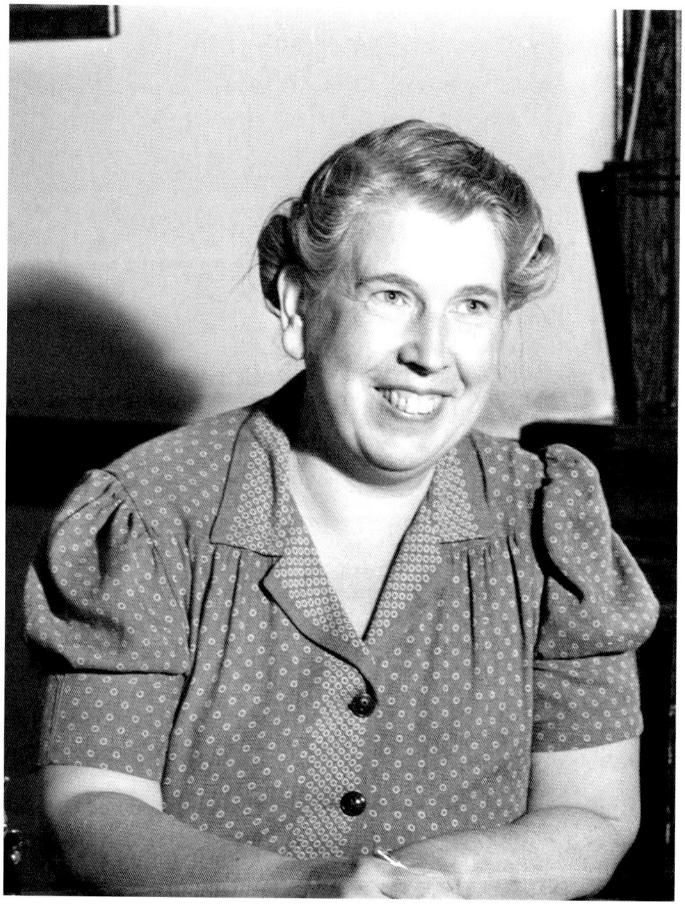

On September 8, 1943, Ida Jackson, city court clerk, sat on the city court bench as a Justice of the Peace in the absence of the magistrates.

On May 6, 1944, the Local Council of Women marked its 50th anniversary with a luncheon at Hotel London. About 160 women were present to hear guest speaker Dr. Mary Hall James of New Haven, Connecticut (left), chair of the Canadian-American Women's Committee on International Relations. At centre is Mrs. J.D. Detwiler, president of the local council and at right is Mrs. R.J. Marshall of Toronto, president of the provincial council.

Prime Minister Mackenzie King arrived in London for the first time in ten years to take part in a Liberal party rally at London Arena on May 29, 1945. Thousands were in attendance as King gave a radio address.

Prime Minister King signs autographs at the 1945 event.

City Clerk Sam Baker (centre) and staff circa 1920s. Baker was City Clerk from 1904 to 1934. The lady to Baker's left is Nora Toll, who served as City Clerk from 1944 to 1946.

A crowd gathers around the *Free Press* office on Richmond Street awaiting election results on June 27, 1949. Liberal Alex Jeffery won a seat in the House of Commons, defeating PC incumbent Park Manross and CCF candidate Everett Hall.

Londoner Ray Lawson, "one of Canada's most prominent industrialists," became Lieutenant Governor of Ontario on December 26, 1946.

Mayor George Wenige (left) sat on the chief magistrate's bench on April 29, 1947, and fined himself $1 for illegal parking next to City Hall. "Is this a good example for the public?" he reportedly asked. City Clerk Reg Cooper, acting as court clerk, recorded the proceedings.

On June 14, 1948, Dalton Higgs of St. Thomas pushed London Alderman Earl Nichols down Dundas Street in a wheelbarrow after losing a bet that Cam Calder would win London in the provincial election campaign. Calder, running for the Liberals, did indeed defeat PC incumbent Bill Webster. Higgs therefore had to push Nichols from the corner of Dundas and Richmond to City Hall at Dundas and Wellington in time for that night's council meeting.

## No Klansmen Need Apply, Says Wenige

Mayor Issues Statement Following Publication Locally of Propaganda of the Famous Hooded Order.

GEORGE A. WENIGE
Mayor

MAYOR'S OFFICE

CITY OF LONDON

London, March 15, 1923.

London needs no Ku Klux Klan or any other order that seeks to gain unjust ends by a cowardly parade of masks and mystery.

Gentlemen of foreign extraction in this municipality who may be planning local organization had first better give the matter serious thought. Canadians do not tolerate men with bloody hands walking unafraid in their midst. Justice in this Dominion is swift and sure.

As Mayor of London, I am glad to say that I will use every power of my office to rid this city of verminous missionaries of an order that seeks to terrify citizens who may differ from these so-called Knights of the Ku Klux Klan in race, color, religion or ability to succeed.

London, like the rest of the British Empire, has been safe for democracy for a long time. But London is not going to be safe for the Ku Klun Klan or any other hooded order. And any non-Canadian who may seek to establish it here will be deported as an undesirable alien so far as it lies in the hands of the mayor of this city to bring it about.

G. A. Wenige.

A statement from Mayor George Wenige March 15, 1923, asks for the deportation of KKK member Irwin R. Hignett, a southerner attempting to distribute Klan propaganda in London. The following day the Mayor received a death threat from the Klan via the *Free Press* office.

Sydney J. Gillet, former mayor of Gloucester, England, his son H. W. Gillett of London, and Mayor George Wenige, from left to right, pose with a Ting cartoon portraying Wenige as "His Majesty George the Eighth" in June, 1948. Gillet, who visited various city councils during his Canadian visit, sat in on a London council meeting and visited the mayor while in town.

When London voters went to the polls in December, 1948, they had new double booths instead of the old single style. Here, Alderman E.A. Bettam, chair of the city finance committee (left) and Mayor George Wenige cast mock votes at the new booth as a demonstration.

"Aunt Jemima" serves pancakes to Mayor Ray Dennis at City Hall on Shrove Tuesday, February 28, 1949. According to Jemima, "as good as they usually are, your Canadian maple syrup certainly does something for them." She later presided over a group of hungry university students, visited the Kiwanis Club, and donated gifts to the War Memorial Children's Hospital. Her visit was a joint effort of Mayor Dennis and Mayor H.D. Allison of her native St. Joseph, Missouri.

Future Prime Minister Lester J. "Mike" Pearson signs the visitors' book at City Hall, while Mayor Ray Dennis looks over his shoulder on March 9, 1949. Pearson, then Minister of International Affairs, was in London to speak to the Canadian Club.

Louis St. Laurent visited London on May 12, 1949, and is seen here waving to crowds at City Hall.

The Community Chest thermometer marking the city's progress in the United Way's Red Feather Campaign at the north-east corner of Dundas and Richmond, October 1948.

In January, 1948, Anne Bikow of the London Chamber of Commerce holds a model sign the Chamber hoped to place at three main entrances to the city on Highways 2 and 4. The signs were pricey, costing $750 each. The white circles on the signs are for the insignia of service clubs the Chamber hoped would contribute funds to the placement of the signs. While the population on the sign reads 88,330, it would soon be necessary to change it to 89,786.

# ROYAL VISIT

While there had been other Royal visits to the Canadian London—including the Prince of Wales (who became King Edward VII) in 1860 and the Prince of Wales (who became King Edward VIII) in 1919—when King George VI and Queen Elizabeth stepped off the train on June 7, 1939, it marked the first time that reigning British monarchs set foot in the Forest City. There were 300,000 people in the city to greet them, a remarkable number considering London's population was only 76,099.

Accompanied by Prime Minister Mackenzie King, the Royal couple arrived at the recently completed, patriotically decorated Canadian National Railway station on York Street. Police and military personnel positioned around the station stood at attention while His Majesty the King inspected The Royal Canadian Regiment.

The King and Queen then toured the city. The route had been described in the *Free Press* on June 3, well enough ahead of time so citizens could plan where to wait for the best view: "the four-mile tour of London streets starts at the CNR station, along York to Richmond, north to Dufferin, east to Wellington, north to Central Avenue, east to Waterloo, north to St. James, east to Maitland, south to Piccadilly, east to William, south to Queen's Avenue, west to Waterloo, south to Dundas, west to Wellington, south to York and west to the station." The Royal couple rode in a Detroit-built Ford Lincoln Model K Phaeton commissioned specifically for the visit. This four-door open convertible was accompanied by a police motorcycle escort, so most of the crowd could actually see Canada's head of state and his consort.

There were two stops during the visit. The King and Queen stepped out of their car on St. James Street for about 15 minutes to speak to a crowd that included patients from Westminster Hospital. Special stands had been set up on St. James to accommodate approximately 200 World War I veterans who were hospital residents. Later their Majesties stopped at City Hall to sign the city register before returning to the station. There was one more tour stop in Middlesex County, at the village of Glencoe later that same day. Despite its small size, Glencoe also produced an enthusiastic crowd and a pipe band to greet the King and Queen at the station.

The stakes for the Royals were particularly high, as the visit was a political maneuver, designed to quell isolationist movements in the Empire by raising patriotic sentiment. Moreover, it was an opportunity to introduce (and hopefully endear) Canadians to their new head of state, amid fears that the more reserved King George VI would be less popular than his older brother, Edward VIII, who had abdicated in 1936. Altogether, the tour was a resounding success, heightening loyalty to the Crown and affirming Canada's role in the Empire. The esteem in which the King and Queen were held came into play two months later when Londoners enlisted to fight Nazi Germany.

A family waits patiently to catch a glimpse of King George VI and Queen Elizabeth. They may have been visiting from Lambton County, as indicated by their pins.

A *Free Press* newsboy sells "extras" to the crowd.

Schoolboys demonstrate the use of the periscopes to catch a view of the Royal couple. The 'Dominion' periscopes read "Canada Welcomes Their Majesties," and the sticker on the car's front windshield boasts the same slogan.

King George VI and Queen Elizabeth set foot in London, arriving at the Canadian National Railway station on York Street.

The King and Queen before the CNR station on York Street, viewing The Royal Canadian Regiment Guard of Honour. In the background is the International Harvester Company building.

The Royal procession departs on their four-mile tour of London. The car carrying their Majesties was a Lincoln Phaeton V12, one of four specially commissioned vehicles for the visit by Ford, Chrysler, and General Motors.

King George VI and Queen Elizabeth drive north on Richmond Street, passing before the *London Free Press* building.

The Royal Motorcade pulls up in front of City Hall, one of two stops on the Royals' itinerary.

The Royal signatures in the city's commemorative book.

The Royal couple head south on Wellington Street, passing by Dundas Street and the Bank of Toronto building on the southwest corner.

King George VI and Queen Elizabeth stand on the rear platform of the train as it departs from London's CNR station on York Street.

Bagpipers greet the King and Queen at Glencoe Station.

Crowds in Glencoe, Middlesex County, greet the Royal Train.

King George and Queen Elizabeth "wave adieu" to the crowds at Glencoe, as they depart the station, on June 7, 1939.

# SCHOOL DAYS

Peter Van Every, jailor, opened the first school in London in the upper part of the settlement's first temporary courthouse in 1828. Van Every could hardly devote much time to his boy scholars, however, since he also had prisoners to look after. Miss Kezia Stinson's attempt to teach in a drafty log cabin in 1831 cannot have been much easier. Although her schoolroom had a fireplace, there were plenty of holes in the log walls to let the heat out. Her shivering pupils must have had difficulty concentrating during the colder months.

A decent education in London's earliest years was primarily for those who could afford it. Benjamin Cronyn, first Bishop of the Anglican Diocese of Huron, laid the foundation for what was first known as the Collegiate Institute on the northeast corner of Wellington and St. James streets in 1864. The school opened September 1, 1865, with over 70 rooms for its 150 pupils and masters. In 1868, it was renamed Hellmuth Boys' College after the second bishop, Isaac Hellmuth. The college's purpose was "to provide a Classical, Scientific and Commercial Education for the sons of gentlemen." Despite this admirable (albeit exclusionary) goal, however, the school collapsed due to lack of funds in 1877 and was sold to the new Western University as its first home.

Hellmuth Ladies' College was more successful. Opened by Queen Victoria's son, Prince Arthur, on

September 21, 1869, on a farm north of London, the school lasted until 1899. The college taught both arts and sciences, awarding medals to the girls for such subjects as divinity, mathematics, science, and languages. After closing, the building, located at on the southeast corner of Windermere Road and Richmond Street, became the site of Mount St. Joseph Orphanage.

The Catholic Ladies of the Sacred Heart opened Sacred Heart Academy for girls in downtown London in 1865. The building was the old 1854 home of Lawrence Lawrason, London's first police magistrate, but the Sisters expanded into a larger structure in 1867. They operated a school at this location until 1913, when the building was taken over by the Sisters of St. Joseph to teach commercial classes. It is now the site of Catholic Central High School.

London's first important common school was founded in 1849 as the Free School, and later renamed the Union School. The structure was built on the block bounded by King, Waterloo, York, and Colborne. Opening in 1850, the school replaced four ward schools. It had six rooms to house its three teachers and approximately 300 pupils. The first headmaster, Nicholas Wilson, taught for almost 60 years until his retirement in 1909 at age 76. The school was renamed the Central School in 1865 and placed under the direction of Principal Benjamin Bayly.

The forerunner of the School Board came into existence in 1848 when the Board of Trustees of Common Schools for what was then the Town of London held its first meeting. Originally elected by wards, in 1905, it was reorganized into a nine-person board elected at large.

As the city grew, so did the number of its children, leading to a need for more schools. By 1900, London had 17 public schools, as well as the Protestant Orphans' Home and a kindergarten. Separate schools were founded as well, the first adjoining St. Peter's Cathedral in 1857. By the turn of the century, the separate school board had been established and there were five separate elementary schools in London.

Not everyone in nineteenth-century London needed to, or could afford to, attend high school. But for those upper class families who could meet the expense, the London Collegiate Institute opened at the northwest corner of Dufferin and Waterloo in 1878. This building expanded over the years, adding laboratories in about 1888 and an auditorium in 1893. After a fire caused by a lightning strike burned the building in 1920, Central Secondary School was built on its site. Starting in 1921, all fees were abolished for pupils of any age who wished to attend high school.

In 1919, the new London Technical and Art School opened on the south side of Dundas between Maitland and William. This evolved into the London Technical and Commercial High School, H.B. Beal Technical and Commercial High School, and finally H.B. Beal Secondary School. The school is named after Herbert Benson Beal, its founder and first principal, who first recognized a need for technical education in London.

London had several specialized colleges for adult students, aside from Western University. An early example was the Jones Commercial College, operated by J.W. Jones starting in 1864. Jones taught commercial studies, telegraphing, drawing, and monochromatic painting as well as penmanship. James Westervelt and John York founded Forest City Business College in 1885, at first on the east side of Richmond south of King. Their college, renamed Westervelt Business School in 1913, had many locations throughout the city over the years, its most recent building on Wellington Road South in 2017.

The London Normal School, later London Teachers' College, was founded on Elmwood Avenue in London South for the training of elementary school teachers in 1899. Opened on February 1, 1900, the Normal School graduated over 12,000 teachers during its 60 years of service. Later, the building was the Monsignor Feeney Centre for Catholic Education and the building has recently been renovated for use by the YMCA.

Perhaps London's best-known educator was Dr. John Dearness, who began his teaching career in Middlesex County in 1869. Principal at schools in Lucan and Strathroy, he later became school inspector for East Middlesex before stepping up to teach biology at Western's Medical Faculty. Granted the freedom of the city on his 90$^{th}$ birthday in 1942, he was dubbed the "Dean of Ontario Education" at a banquet held in his honour in 1952.

Gradually, London's schools turned into the familiar educational facilities of today. The grade system was introduced in 1890 with a standardized curriculum in each of London's schools. Children could partake in a variety of subjects besides the "3 Rs," including music and sports. Special classes evolved for children with challenges such as visual or hearing impairments. After the Second World War, the beginning of the "baby boom" eventually led to increased class sizes and a need for more schools and expanded facilities. The new schools with their large windows, central heating, auditoriums, kindergartens, and staff lounges were a far cry from Peter Van Every's jail.

Hellmuth Boys' College, about the time of its opening in September 1865. It was named after Dean Isaac Hellmuth who later became the second bishop of the Diocese of Huron.

Students and staff pose at the front entrance of Hellmuth Boys' College in this undated early photograph.

Students gather for a photo outside Hellmuth Ladies' College about the time of its founding, 1869.

Hellmuth Ladies' College, also founded by Isaac Hellmuth, was opened by HRH Prince Arthur, Duke of Connaught. One of the best-known Canadian institutions for girls' education, this site was later occupied by the Mount St. Joseph Orphanage.

The Union School, circa 1875. The school was built on the block surrounded by King, Colborne, York, and Waterloo streets in 1849. It was torn down in 1890 and the block divided into building lots.

Classes at the Sacred Heart Academy, under the direction of Sacred Heart Convent, began for the first time in 1865 in the former residence of Lawrence Lawrason. This photograph of the school, located on the north side of Dundas between Colborne and Burwell streets, was taken circa 1875. In the 1950s, Catholic Central High School was built on this site.

The wedding portrait of John Dearness and his wife, taken by the Edy Brothers. One of London's most famous educators, Dearness became Inspector of Public Schools for East Middlesex in 1876.

Jones Commercial College on the west side of Colborne Street, north of Queens Avenue, circa 1876–81. Proprietors of the school were J.W. Jones and W.N. Yerex. The building had previously been a Methodist Episcopal Church.

Students gather in front of London Collegiate Institute, circa 1880.

The Kindergarten classroom at Lorne Avenue Public School, before 1901. Queen Victoria's portrait hangs on the wall.

Building Alexandra Public School, circa 1911. Originally known as Colborne Street Public School, it was located on the west side of Colborne between King and York.

The completed Alexandra Public School. Its principal was H.B. Beal and the building housed an industrial school which became the Technical High School, forerunner of H.B. Beal Secondary School.

One of London's most recognizable buildings, the Normal School, South London, pictured here in 1908.

Glencoe High School opened in 1889 with over 80 students. It was used for 63 years until Glencoe District High School opened in 1952.

Students and their teachers pose in front of Glencoe's first brick public school, 1914.

S.S. # 6, Shipley School, Lobo Township, circa 1915. The school was located at the corner of the 12th Concession of Lobo Township and the New Ontario Road. As with many rural schoolhouses, it was sold in 1965 to become a home.

Schoolchildren in the 1920s march to a picnic near the south end of Talbot Street, passing City Gas Company on their way.

The newly completed Central Collegiate in 1922, now Central Secondary School.

A class at the Forest City Business & Shorthand College, circa 1918. The school held its classes on the west side of Wellington north of Dundas Street. Its name later changed to Westervelt Business School and it moved to Richmond Street.

Teacher Jessie Eagan has 16 pupils in her Empress Avenue School "sight-saving" class in the fall of 1938. Students from all over London who had less than 3/10 of their sight when wearing glasses had access here to large print textbooks, special blackboards, and eye rest periods to prevent eye strain.

The first sod was turned for Sir Adam Beck Memorial High School on November 17, 1925. In this photo from the *London Advertiser*, S.F. Lawrason, chairman of the Board of Education, wields the shovel, surrounded by the principals of city secondary schools, officers on the board of education, trustees, and citizens. Fourth from the left is H.B. Beal, for whom Beal Secondary School is named. The 20-room school would cost $280,000 to build.

Mrs. Elliot's class at Ealing Public School, which opened its doors in 1912.

A Physical Culture exhibition at Alexandra Public School June 13, 1939. Thirty-five pupils in Grades 7 and 8 provided the show for the Alexandra Home and School Club. Here, W.D. Sutton's class gives a fencing demonstration.

Empire Day exercises were held in all city schools on May 23, 1940. Thousands of children took part in programs demonstrating their loyalty to the Royal Family and the British Empire.

The new $50,000 Mountsfield School opens just off of Ridout Street South on February 3, 1941. Many of the school's 155 pupils came from the historic Odell schoolhouse. The new school had such modern conveniences as 500-watt lighting units, a cloakroom for each classroom, library, lunchroom, and kitchenette. Four teachers were in charge of classes.

A class in lip reading is held under teacher Mr. Holmes in a class for the deaf at Lord Roberts Public School, November 1943.

A soundproof cubicle at Lord Roberts School helps deaf and partly deaf children learn to read lips. The class pictured here was conducted by teacher Anne Dunstan in May 1947.

In September 1945, a record 10,000 children jammed London's primary schools. Ealing School was forced to hold classes in the school auditorium and on the stage.

A crowded classroom in Ryerson School, April, 1947. Classrooms built to hold 35 pupils had as many as 40 or more. The *Free Press* stated the overcrowding was caused by the "rapid expansion of industry and in the increase of the city population."

Long-time resident of Kensal Park, Alfred Thompson, turns the sod at the future site of Kensal Park School on May 1, 1947. Looking on are Owen Foster, chairman of the school board, and numerous local children who would be attending the new school when it opened.

W.C. Walls, who had the bus contract for half of the East Middlesex High School area, demonstrates his ear-to-track method of determining whether a train is coming at the CPR level crossing on Adelaide Street in January 1948. Another bus driver had recently had a close call with a train on a foggy morning. School bus drivers brought 400 rural students to London's secondary schools daily.

A public school orchestra practises at Beal Technical School under the direction of Martin Boundy, April 13, 1948. In 1946, Boundy was named supervisor of instrumental music in London's schools. He directed the London Tech Concert Band and the Police Boys' Band.

S.S. No. 3, Westminster, Odell School, on Highland Road (Commissioners Road), was deserted in August 1948. The school was built in 1883 with additions made in 1899 and in 1920–21.

In August, 1948, 120 New Canadians took summer English courses at H.B. Beal Technical School. The students—from Poland, Romania, Lithuania, Greece, Estonia and Holland—were divided into classes of 20 students. Many of the students, aged 16 to 60, worked as nurses' aides at the Ontario Hospital, as well as domestics and farm workers.

On September 7, 1948, two identically designed separate schools opened: Blessed Sacrament School on Spittal Street and Holy Rosary School (pictured here) on Herkimer Street. Both were built for $80,000 and both schools are still standing, with additions, in 2017.

Pupils at city schools enjoyed Hallowe'en parties on Friday afternoon, October 29, 1948. Here, Grade 2 at Talbot Street School, taught by Miss Dolman, shows off their costumes for a visiting *Free Press* reporter.

A brand new school was being built next to the old Masonville schoolhouse in December, 1948, so it was decided to auction off the old school to the highest bidder. The old school bell was saved as a souvenir.

450 students moved into the "ultra-modern" Strathroy Public School in April 1949. The school had eleven classrooms, glass walls, "pint-sized" furnishings, a gymnatorium, comfortable staff lounge, wooden desks with non-spill inkwells, and a circular kindergarten classroom with the alphabet inlaid in its linoleum floor.

About 14,000 students in city schools marked Empire Day on May 23, 1949, with songs, flags, recitations, and plays to teach them awareness of Canada's place in the Commonwealth.

The Lucan school, pictured here in 1949, opened on January 5, 1890, operating as a high school until 1949 and then as a public school until it burned down in 1953. Beginning in the fall of 1949, the high school students were bused to the new Medway High School in Arva.

Celebrating his birthday, 97-year-old Dr. John Dearness, London educationist, planted a maple at the annual Arbor Day exercises at the London Normal School on May 14, 1949. Left to right: John Gregg, Dr. Dearness, Donald Irwin, and George Gall.

Four women master a phase of "craft study," their woodworking class at the Normal School, May 1949. From left to right: Suzanne Stacey, Katherine Stenton, Joan Wilson, and Eleanor Tomuick.

Sir Adam Beck Collegiate Institute, 1949. It was converted into the London Board of Education centre in 1985.

Beal Technical School, June 1949. Originally London Technical and Commercial High School, it was renamed H.B. Beal Technical and Commercial High School in 1935 after Herbert Benson Beal, founder and first principal of the school.

Knollwood Park School was built to relieve overcrowding in several nearby schools in north London. The situation was so critical that churches in the neighbourhood had been allowing Sunday School rooms for classes. The school opened in the fall of 1949 on the northeast corner of Grosvenor and Gammage streets in Bellwood Park.

Children walk along Thompson Road near the L. & P.S. crossing in June 1949. Many were concerned that when the new Princess Elizabeth School would open at Chelsea Green in the fall of that year, there would be many more children walking along the possibly dangerous road. However, the city planned to build a sidewalk to reduce the hazards.

Argyle Park School on Kathleen Street, north of Dundas, was expanded to six regular classrooms and two basement rooms in the fall of 1949. Renovations also included new furnishings, heating, and lighting. One of the teachers here at the time was Mildred Barons after whom the school was eventually renamed in the 1960s. The school closed in 1971 and was later demolished, leaving a park also named after Mildred Barons.

# SPORTS & LEISURE

In pioneer days, most Londoners had little time for sports or recreation. Many settlers worked all day on their farms or at their businesses just to survive. Leisure time was for those who could afford it. As a result, many of the earliest sporting activities—such as hunting, fishing, hiking, skating, swimming, snowshoeing and rowing on the Thames—developed out of practical skills, which slowly transformed from being performed out of necessity to being done for enjoyment.

Competitive races may have been the first spectator sports. On April 1, 1862, more than 2,000 people gathered on Waterloo Street to witness a 150-yard foot race between John McNamee, gunner in the Royal Artillery, and William Caldwell, Westminster Township resident. The stakes were high—$25 a side. Caldwell won by about a yard.

Golf was played in the London area from the 1870s onwards, Col. John Walker being credited with introducing the game to the city. It was generally played at the London Hunt and Country Club, where nine more holes were added to make eighteen in 1916. The Highland Golf Club opened in 1922, south of the city in Westminster Township, and the Thames Valley Golf Course opened in June, 1924, with membership fees of $10 a year. London's Charles Ross "Sandy" Somerville was a decorated Canadian golfer in the early twentieth century, eventually being inducted into the Canadian Sports Hall of Fame. When he won the Canadian amateur golf championship in Toronto on July 3, 1926, the city paid tribute by holding Somerville Day at the London Hunt and Country Club.

Tobogganing was all the rage in the 1880s. A toboggan slide was built in 1886 by William Tytler, located just west of the intersection of Ridout and Albert streets. With two chutes 480 feet long, the slide extended over the mill race leading to Blackfriars Mill and over "the flats" (Harris Park) to the river's edge. With London's notorious winters, snow sports were also popular, with hundreds of youth taking to the frozen Thames for skating, snowshoeing, or skiing.

Lawn tennis was played in London from about 1880, at first on the grounds of Huron College. One of the first exhibition matches was held in October, 1880, when Huron College played against a team from Kingston. Unfortunately for London players William Street, Gustavus Hellmuth, and Walter J. Blackburn, Queen's University emerged victorious.

In the mid-to-late nineteenth century, sports became increasingly organized into teams and leagues; in London, lacrosse was one of the first. The Victoria Lacrosse Club was organized as early as July, 1874, with Mayor Benjamin Cronyn as president of the 35-member group. However, despite lacrosse being regarded as Canada's national sport, it was soon overtaken by baseball as London's favourite summer game.

London's first organized baseball game was as early as 1855. The first known game on the present site of Labatt Park was in 1867, but it was likely used for baseball several years before that—which many historians claim makes Labatt the world's oldest continuously used baseball diamond. Originally Tecumseh Park, it was named Labatt Memorial Park in 1937 and formally reopened in 1940 by members of the Labatt family.

Two original baseball clubs—known as the Forest City and London baseball teams—amalgamated to form the famous Tecumseh Base Ball Club of London in 1868. Named after the sponsoring Tecumseh House hotel, the team became the international champions when they defeated the Pittsburgh Alleghenies to win the International Baseball Association championship on October 2, 1877. While the team disbanded fairly quickly afterwards, their name was rejuvenated for future London ball teams.

London produced at least two star ball players in the early twentieth century. George "Mooney" Gibson was a catcher for two different major league teams, starting in 1905 with the Pittsburgh Pirates and ending his career with the New York Giants in 1918. Frank Colman, also from the Forest City, played for the Pirates as well as the New York Yankees in the 1940s.

Other popular team sports included hockey and rugby football. A match on January 28, 1891, marked the beginning of organized hockey in London. The game was played between two groups of bank clerks, the Bank of Commerce defeating the Bank of Montreal 6–to–1. Football has been played in London since at least the 1870s, when games were played in Victoria Park.

Team sports created a need for sports facilities. Even the Armouries, built for military purposes in 1905, could be used for indoor sports—an attempt being made to play baseball indoors at the Armouries soon after the building opened. One of the earliest facilities was the London Skating Club that opened on Lake Horn, a man-made pond north of Pall Mall Street between Richmond and Waterloo. Opened in 1863, the club must have been a grand building for its time, designed by local architect William Robinson. Later rinks included the Westminster Skating Rink on the southeast corner of Wortley Road and Stanley Street and the Queen's Avenue Skating Rink, both active in the 1880s. However, the grandest sports building before mid-twentieth century was the London Arena that opened on the corner of Ridout and Bathurst streets in December, 1923.

In early days, women were excluded from organized sports for a variety of reasons. Whether they were thought to be too fragile to participate, whether their hoop skirts got in the way, or whether looking after their homes and families left them with little leisure time, women were generally spectators, not participants. But as emancipation progressed, women began to take part in physical recreation. A women's basketball club existed as early as 1900, playing at St. John's Athletic Club.

Women's softball gained popularity in the first half of the twentieth century. The London Ladies' Softball Association, organized by the city's Recreation Department in May 1942, is among the more memorable of women's athletic organizations. Divided into four teams called the Cardinals, Eagles, Royals, and Shamrocks, young women played at Labatt Park during the war years while male ball players were away on active duty. When this league ended in 1946, two teams called the Sapphires and Supremes were organized. As part of the Michigan-Ontario League, the ladies played against teams throughout the state and province. Few Londoners realize that, in the 1940s, they too had *A League of Their Own*.

Whether baseball or bicycles, early Londoners established a culture of sports and recreation that would only grow in the post-war decades, as leisure time increased for the working classes and the value of exercise was recognized by society.

Ida Gemley, who appears to be a member of the London Snowshoe Club, is believed to be a daughter of Rev. John Gemley, who lived with his family in London circa 1875–80. Snowshoeing would be one of the few activities women could partake in while wearing typical nineteenth-century dress.

Young girls enjoy a game of backyard croquet. The photographer, Cooper & Sanders, were in business from 1896 to 1909 at 403 Richmond Street, thus dating the photo to between those years.

Springbank was always a good place for an excursion—and a picnic—as far as back as 1895.

Springbank Park Pavilion, constructed by the London Street Railway in 1903, had a huge stage and seating for 1,200 as well as a dance floor. The structure was demolished in 1961.

Children's playground at Springbank, 1920.

Springbank Amusement Park, operated by the Victor Amusement Company, opened across the road from Springbank Park in 1914. It had closed by 1942. Note the popcorn vending cart at right.

Underprivileged city boys attend Silver Beach Camp on Lake Erie, August 18, 1939. Here the boys enjoy a "banquet" after returning to camp from an all-day hike.

John Wood, leader of Cabin 3, instructs the boys in folding blankets. From left to right are Ron Rogers, Harold Cake, Leader John Wood, Gerry Styles, Austin Wort, and John Doroskenko.

Alfred Pinnell (left) and Archie Horner enjoy a boxing bout at Silver Beach Camp, 1939.

McMahen Playground on Adelaide Street, a gift to the city from Archibald Thornton McMahen in 1926. McMahen, a partner in McMahen Granger & Co., was also a member of the London Railway Commission. The historic stone gate was knocked down by a motorist in 2016.

Silverwoods Pool officially opened on Friday, June 28, 1946, giving neighbourhood children their first chance to swim in the new facility. The 60' x 105' pool held 315,000 gallons of water and ranged from 2 ft to 8 ft in depth.

Mr. Silverwoods, sponsor of the new community pool, officially declares the pool open.

London Thistle Women's Lawn Bowling Club opened for the season on May 29, 1940.

Miss Kae Arnold and Mrs. W.J. McConaghy play a round of golf at Thames Valley Golf Course in July, 1940, just before the course was taken over to become a militia camp during the Second World War.

The Springbank Casino opened on May 20, 1946, with hundreds of couples in attendance. The evening was sponsored by members of the Service League of War Memorial Children's Hospital. In an evening filled with music, dancing, and contests, the biggest prize was a diamond ring, which went to the person who could give the closest estimate of the weight of a pile of coal.

Indoor roller skating rink, circa 1920s.

Members of the London Blind Bowling League in action in February, 1945. On the left is Doug Jackson, captain of the Streamliners, while on the right is Stan Hames of the Maple Leafs. Members of this bowling league were blind or nearly blind.

Tempo VI, Guy Lombardo's speedboat, broke many records at the 1946 Detroit River Classic, winning Lombardo the coveted Gold Cup. The speedboat was afterwards on display in downtown London before being transported to New York. Admiring crowds of home-bound workers and shoppers view the boat on Dundas Street on September 4, 1946.

Spectators at the racetrack at Queen's Park, the site of the modern Western Fairgrounds and racetrack, circa 1898. A racetrack had existed at Queen's Park since 1879. The occasion depicted on this postcard may have been an Old Boys' Reunion.

Action shot at the Strathroy races, 1949. The races were traditionally held on Dominion Day.

Thanksgiving Day meet of the London Hunt Club, Glenmore, 1929. Glenmore was the name given to an old farmhouse on the east side of Western Road, which became the club's first permanent residence in 1889.

Members of the London Hunt and Country Club, 1929. Early activities were fox hunting and trap shooting with golf added after more land was bought in 1915.

A three-day pheasant shoot was held in Westminster Township starting on Friday, October 21, 1938. From left to right are John Cook of Thorndale, Stuart Dunn of the Thamesford area, and Victor Pile of Thorndale. With the help of Brownie the dog, they bagged six birds in the first four hours.

The newly formed London Revolver Club practises at the Richmond Street pistol range in February, 1939. The club facility was described by the *Free Press* as "one of the finest revolver galleries in the Dominion."

Jack Carter (left) and Walter Smith examine a bull's eye at the London Revolver Club, 1939. Smith, a local bank employee, was among Canada's best revolver shots.

On January 19, 1948, members of the London Curling Club—from left to right, Skip A. R. Aylsworth, Don McCallum, J.M. Aikenhead, and Jack Wilkins—took part in the Western Ontario Colts Bonspiel.

Three young men ski in London Township, north of the city, on Easter weekend, March 22, 1940.

Two girls ski on the UWO campus in early January 1947.

Members of the London Ski Club cheer as "hangman" Ken Pringle pulls the death trap on an effigy of the weather man at the club's "No Snow Ball" held at the YMCA on January 26, 1949. The ski season had been delayed for two months due to a lack of snow. "Prosecuting attorney" was M.R. "Ting" Tingley, London cartoonist.

London Collegiate Institute hockey team, circa 1900. The seated teacher is Mr. McCutcheon.

The London Tecumsehs were "First Champions" in the Canadian Professional Hockey League, 1926–27. Back row left to right: Stan Jackson, "Speedy" Groh, "Babe" Morrison, John Duggan, William "Bill" Starkings, and "Goldie" Prodgers, Coach. Seated left to right: "Speedy" Oliver, Chris Speyer, Robert Boucher, "Dinny" Dinsmore, Larry Aurie, Jerry Lowery, and Hugh McCormick.

The Parkhill Creamery hockey team poses for a team photo on February 23, 1948.

Boys in Grades 2 and 3 at Chesley Avenue School play outdoor ice hockey in February, 1948. The final score was 1–1.

Skating in Victoria Park, February 1931.

The Coves were a natural winter playground with a smooth expanse of ice stretching for hundreds of yards nearly every winter. Several hundred skaters went to the Coves daily during the winter of 1939–40, including this group of south London girls.

Bette Shirley (left) and Margaret Knowles, students at South Collegiate, lace up their skates at the Coves on December 27, 1939.

In February, 1949, the annual Ilderton Ice Carnival became "Variety Fun Night." Here, members of the St. Thomas Ice Skating Club perform the "Dutch Waltz."

The London Skating Club held its 16th annual carnival on March 29, 1940.

Hundreds of schoolchildren jammed into the new Ontario Arena at Queen's Park on January 18, 1949. Here they sit on the boards, waiting for a signal to begin skating.

Both Seniors and Juniors are present for this photo of the London Collegiate Institute girls' basketball teams in 1902–03. Principal Radcliffe is the gentleman on the left.

National League Soccer, Hamilton & District Division, made its debut in London on May 1, 1948, when the Toronto Greenbacks defeated Labatts 4–1 at Labatt Park. This scene shows the opening Toronto goal being scored by player Bryans at the extreme left. Goalie Rodney of Labatt has just made a dive for the shot.

The RCASC (Royal Canadian Army Service Corps) Falcons Senior "B" ORFU (Ontario Rugby Football Union) team couldn't practise for their Monday, November 1, 1948, game versus the Sarnia Wanderers after the flood lights at Thames Park went out in a power shortage. Undaunted, they improvised by placing Jeeps and other army vehicles around a field at Wolseley Barracks.

Goderich cheerleaders show an original display at the Junior "B" WOSSA track meet held in London on October 16, 1948. Dressed in blue and white, the girls, directed by Maree Wall, demonstrated a lively cheer for the camera.

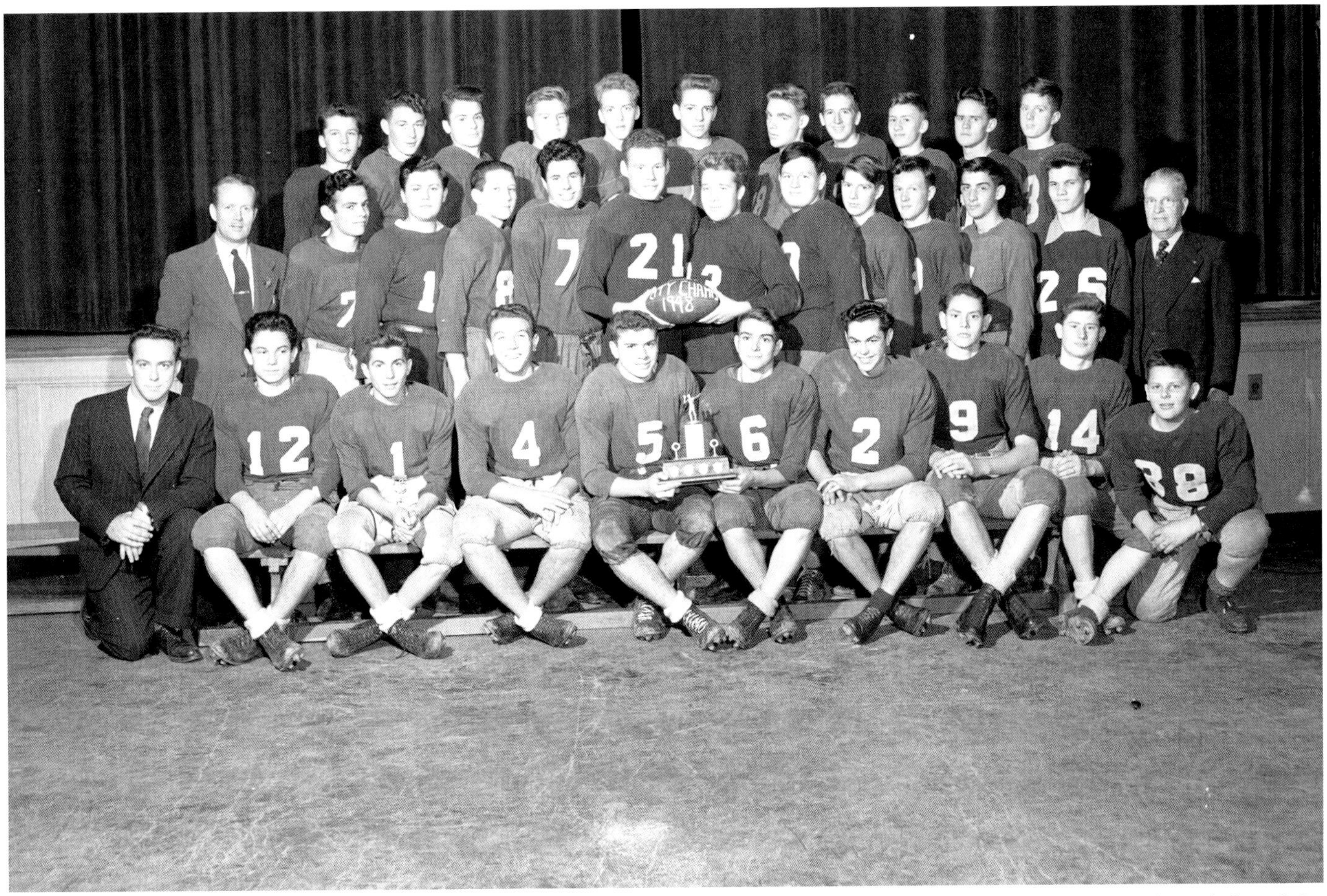

The Beck Collegiate Juniors were winners of the Junior City Football Championships two years in a row. They defeated St. Thomas Collegiate 23–3 in a game held at Beck in November, 1948.

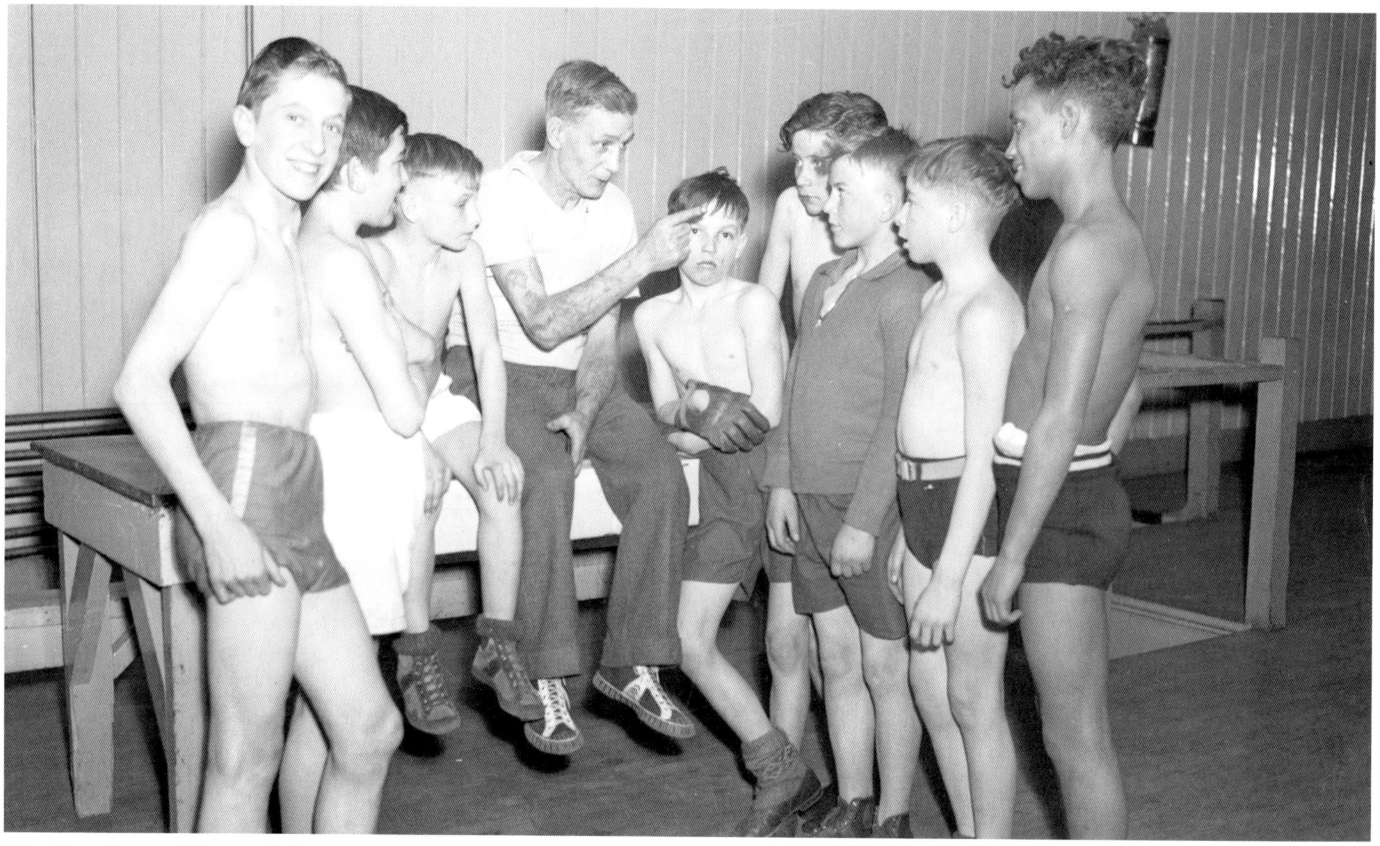

The London Athletic Club proposed to keep boys off the streets by offering boxing classes. Here, veteran trainer Tommy Wallace instructs juvenile pugilists in February 1939.

Heavyweight champion Joe Louis visited Labatt Park on September 3, 1947, bringing his fastball team, the Punchers, for a game against the London All-Stars. Here, young London boxer Frank Anderson has his fist in the grip of his idol. The Punchers won 4–0 and Frankie went on to have a boxing career of his own.

Blondy Simpson is at the punching bag while Ted Hefferman, Fankie Anderson, and Don Porter practise at the Chicken Coop Athletic Club on March 24, 1948.

Londoner George "Mooney" Gibson, at left, was star catcher for the Pittsburgh Pirates in the 1909 World Series. His MLB career lasted from 1905 to 1918, including stints with the Pirates and New York Giants, before becoming a manager.

George "Mooney" Gibson with his wife Margaret and children, circa 1905–07. The Gibson home, now demolished, was at 252 Central Avenue.

This baseball team posing in front of one of the Flint cottages in Springbank Park, circa 1912, is probably part of the Merchants League that played in Springbank that year. The league consisted of the teams: Moose, Bakers, Butchers, and Grocers. Judging by the shirts that read Comfort Soap and Red Rose Tea, these are likely the Grocers.

The London Tecumsehs baseball team posing in Tecumseh Park, now Labatt Park, circa 1924.

In September, 1938, the Queen's Park Bruins baseball team were winners of the city Bantam League championship.

A crowd of 4,000 watched London police and firemen play a baseball game August 16, 1939, at Labatt Park. The game, which the policemen won 20–5, was a benefit game for the City of London Fresh Air Fund, a charity that allowed underprivileged children to enjoy a camping holiday. On the left, Motorcycle Officer Glen Oliver scores on P.C. Sonley's double in the first inning. Fireman Ralph Leonard is about to catch the ball too late to tag the runner. In the right photo, Ralph Leonard scores for the Fire Department while "Lefty" Newman, police pitcher, is shown covering the base.

The annual Odell School picnic was held at Springbank Park on June 12, 1939, complete with a baseball game.

The first baseball game played on this site was held in at least 1867, making it the world's oldest continuously used baseball diamond. Previously known as Tecumseh Park, it became known as Labatt Park in spring 1937 when the Labatt family presented it to the city.

A great catch for the London Pirates, July 1941. The Pirates played in the "Pony" (Pennsylvania-Ontario-New York) League in 1940 and 1941 as a farm club of the National League's Pittsburgh Pirates. They were known locally as the Baby Bucs.

Reviving girls' softball, which had been dormant in London for about 10 years, the London Girls' Softball League started at Labatt Memorial Park in August 1942. There were four teams: the Cardinals, Eagles, Royals, and Shamrocks, representing the four wards in the city. In this photo is Mary Burr, "ace hurler of the Cardinals."

The flashy satin uniform of London's new girls' softball club, the Supremes, is displayed in May, 1946, by an unidentified model. The team was part of the Michigan-Ontario Ladies' Fastball League.

The Supremes featured pitcher Marion (Clarke) Knowles, in action in August 1946.

Members of the No. 6 Co. CWAC girls' softball team, August 27, 1943. Left to right, front row: S. Stephens; H. Meyer (captain); E.R. Berthlaume; E.K. Vance. Back row, left to right: Major Doris Weston; E. Reid; M. Gies; M.H. Thompson; V.M. Evans; J.F. Carder; H.M. Sault; Lt. M.G. King.

# THE THAMES RIVER

London was born at the Forks of the Thames River—first viewed by Lt.-Gov. John Graves Simcoe in March 1793, while he and his party travelled by foot from Detroit to Newark (Niagara-on-the-Lake). On his next journey to the spot a year later, in March 1794, Simcoe used the river for transportation. Taking advantage of high water and a swift current, he and his party were able to boat to Detroit. Other early travellers took river voyages before there were passable roads. The Moravian missionary Christian Dencke and his wife travelled by raft past the forks of the Thames on their way to their mission at Fairfield soon after the end of the War of 1812. For the settlers in "New London," as Simcoe first christened it, the Thames River was the centre of their lives, providing them with the very means of subsistence.

In 1821, 23-year-old Ira Schofield is said to have speared a sturgeon swimming upstream, sat astride it, and rode the fish, using his spear as a bridle rein, for nearly a mile downstream before it expired. Later fisherfolk had decidedly less dramatic experiences than Ira, but the Thames remained a source of lore, food, and recreation throughout the nineteenth century and beyond.

Bridges have always been a necessary part of London's transportation grid since residents have always needed to cross the Thames at one point or another. The first may have been Westminster Bridge, built in 1826 to join present-day York and Stanley streets, linking the new village of London with Westminster Township. Soon bridges were built in other locations, such as on Wellington Street into Westminster or on the Proof Line (Richmond Street) over the north branch of the Thames. London's first iron bridge is now its oldest bridge. Blackfriars was built over the north branch in 1875, connecting the main portion of the city with London West at Ridout and Blackfriars streets. Built by the Wrought Iron Bridge Company of Canton, Ohio, it is now recognized as one of the few remaining bow-type bridges in North America.

Early Londoners had a close relationship with the river, using it as a playground for fishing, boating, swimming, picnicking, and strolling. On July 8, 1880, the Grand Thames Regatta—likely the biggest sporting event held in the London area up to that date—was held near Byron. Large crowds flocked to the site to see Ned Hanlan, Canada's famous sculler, who was in attendance.

In 1878, the City of London purchased property near Byron from the Coombs brothers to build a water-pumping station and dam. In 1879, the dam and first hydraulic pumphouse were completed and the waterworks officially turned on. At first called Waterworks Park, more and more land was attached to this area until, by 1911, the Water Commission owned 546 acres of land forming Springbank Park.

Springbank became a popular day trip from the city, usually accessed by riverboat. Captain Joseph Andrews offered a pleasure cruise to the public on his steamboat, the *City of London* in July 1876, at a cost of 25 cents for adults and 10 cents for children. But it was the Thames Navigation Company's steamer, the Forest City, which first ran a regular ferry between the Forks and Springbank during the summer months, starting in 1878. The following year, there were moonlight river cruises with an Italian band on board to entertain patrons.

London's most famous steamboat, however, was the *Victoria*, launched by the Thames Navigation Company in April 1880. Unfortunately, the steamer is not remembered for its quaint appearance or travel speed, but for the tragic way it met its end. The city's worst disaster struck on May 24, 1881, when the overloaded Victoria capsized, drowning some 200 people. While not the end of river transportation, the disaster certainly made travel by steamboat less popular, and the extension of the London Street Railway to Springbank in 1896 meant city dwellers had an alternate route to the park.

Other early bridges have unfortunately been destroyed, often swept away in floods, replaced due to wear and tear, or widened into two lanes as traffic increased.

While London reaped the benefits of life along the river's edge, the young city also faced the reality of its positioning on a floodplain. Floods could be devastating to communities, easily wiping out infrastructure, destroying crops, or even claiming lives. On July 11, 1883, after a five-inch rainfall, the Thames took the lives of 18 victims, making this the city's worst flood for loss of life. However, for many Londoners, the Flood of 1937 was *the* flood, remembered as London's worst-ever natural disaster. Swollen by snowmelt and torrential rain, the Thames rose 23 feet above its normal levels on April 26 and 27 of that year. Both the north and south branches of the river flooded, inundating all of London West and other low-lying areas. About 500 acres were under water for four days during which thousands were driven from their homes. About 1,100 houses were damaged with repair costs estimated as high as $3,000,000. Five deaths were attributed to the flood, including one in London when a strong current swamped the boat of rescue worker Joseph L. Britton, forcing him to step into an open manhole beneath.

As the years went by, the Thames was brought under control by modern engineering. Without the ever-present threat of flooding and the lack of reliance on the river for their livelihoods (or even recreation), the Thames seems less and less like a river to present-day Londoners. Indeed, water levels are low, the Springbank Dam dysfunctional, and there has been a general paradigm shift away from the city's roots at the river forks. It begs the question: what purpose will future Londoners have for their Thames?

A nineteenth-century view of the Thames River with Eldon House visible on the hill at right.

"Canada's London on the Canadian Thames," circa 1874, by London photographer John Cooper for *Canada's Illustrated News*. The fencing is to keep livestock out of the river at a time of low water. The tallest structures at this time were factory chimneys and church spires, but very few buildings in this photograph have survived to 2017.

Official opening of the waterworks at Springbank, 1879.

Victoria riverboat anchored at the forks of the Thames, circa 1880. The words "Victoria Port Stanley" are painted on the stern, since all of London's riverboats were registered at the nearest port of open water. In the background, at right, is the Princess Louise, while the steam tower of the Sulphur Springs can be seen on the left.

Waterworks dam and the pumphouse, looking south from the north side of the river, circa 1880. On the left is the Northern Hotel and its dock.

This composite photograph shows the last trip of the *Victoria* on May 24, 1881. The boat image has been superimposed on an original photograph that shows another glimpse of the *Victoria* at far left. Even the smoke is painted on. During this voyage, the overcrowded boat capsized, killing 200 of 650 passengers on board.

The aftermath of the great flood of July 1883, in the working-class district of London West.

Flood damage around Jerry McDonald's Riverside Hotel, July 1883.

Dundas Street looking west from the bridge after the flood of 1883. The damaged cottage at right belonged to John B. Allenby, while the Kensington Hotel was kept by John Horseman.

A picture taken by London photographer John Cooper portrays the significant damage to the Springbank Pumphouse after the flood of 1883. After the flood, the City of London started to erect a system of dykes to circumvent future disasters.

The *Thames* steamboat, last of the nineteenth-century riverboats, was built by Capt. David Foster in 1888, but scuttled near the original Waterworks Dam in Springbank in 1899. After the *Victoria* disaster and the building of a streetcar line, river travel to Springbank was less popular.

Blackfriar's Bridge with Carling Brewery in the distance. The wrought-iron bridge, London's oldest in 2017, was constructed in 1875 to span the north branch of the Thames.

A lady, identified only as Aunt Daisy, fishes in the Thames near Byron, circa 1900.

The old wooden Centre Street Bridge across the Thames at Byron, circa 1900. Built in 1895 to replace a previous wooden bridge lost to flood damage, it lasted until June 1904 when it too fell in a spring flood.

The waterworks and pumphouse complex with a streetcar loaded with passengers.

A view of the Thames from Reservoir Hill. The village of Byron can be seen in the distance on the left. The large house on the far side of the river is probably J.W. Little's estate, "Hazelden."

View of the river at Byron looking west from the north bank of the Thames. The wooden mill at left is likely the Ross Grist Mill, which was swept away in the Flood of 1937. The river is very shallow in this photograph.

The grist and sawmill at Byron and the Byron bridge are visible in this circa 1930 photograph.

Boys swimming in Gibbons Park, circa 1930. Originally known as the Flats, and sometimes Becher's Island, this swampy area was at one time completely contained by the North Branch of the Thames and a mill stream. In 1926, Mrs. Ronald Harris purchased 64 acres of the Thornwood Estate from the Becher family and donated the land to the city to be used as a park in memory of her late father, Sir George Gibbons.

Looking east along Mount Pleasant Avenue during the flood of 1937. London's worst natural disaster, the Thames rose 23 feet, leading to five fatalities, the destruction of more than 1100 homes, and three million in property damage across southwestern Ontario.

A Labatt Brewery truck is capsized before a Supertest station during the flood of 1937.

Webb Furniture, at the corner of Wharncliffe Road and Mt. Pleasant Avenue, is partially submerged, 1937.

Flooding near London Soap Works on Ottaway Avenue (South Street), 1937.

An aerial view of the flooding on Josephine Street in Chelsea Green, 1937.

Looking north at the Hydro Substation, City Gas Company tank skeleton, and London Arena, 1937. With the substation flooded, power was shut down in south London.

Water is up to the level of the Wellington Street Bridge, 1937. The catastrophic flood would lead to the creation of the Upper Thames River Conservation Authority (UTRCA) eleven years later.

Pleasure boating on the Thames, summer of 1939. The *Free Press* photographed sailboats from the newly formed Thames Valley Boat Club on the river between the CNR and Golf Club bridges. Hundreds of spectators watched the graceful sailboats, along with power boats, canoes, and rowing skiffs.

Sailboats from the Thames Valley Boat Club held their weekly race on Sunday, September 24, 1939. The race that day was won by George Couper, skipper of a boat called the Wren.

Krikor Hekimian stretches nonchalantly on the frozen Thames River to lick an ice cream cone before undertaking a Polar Bear swim in January, 1939. The Armenian-Canadian known as the "Human Polar Bear" and the "Human Icicle" attracted a crowd of 5,000 people who watched him spend four minutes swimming in the icy river.

Krikor Hekimian meets London Street Railway ticket man Henry Kew at the corner of Dundas and Richmond, 1939. The difference in costume indicates just how cold the weather—and the river—was that day. Hekimian travelled across Canada performing his winter stunt.

The one-car-wide Adelaide Street Bridge, pictured here, had outlived its usefulness by August 1, 1939. Built in 1904 by the county, it was given to the city when Chelsea Green was annexed by London in 1912. As the population of the suburb increased, a new wider bridge became necessary.

A scene on the Thames between London and Springbank in May, 1941. Fleets of small boats are tied up at wharves along the shoreline, and the river is used by roaring motorboats and sails.

The city engineer's department tries to reduce the danger of flood damage on Front Street, August 1941. Places on the Thames where the bank jutted out into the river were being removed. The earth was used to make a 7-foot breakwater along the riverbank.

# TRANSPORTATION

Getting around early London usually meant "hoofing it," either on one's own two feet or a horse—although, well-to-do residents might have had a carriage. Then along came the steam locomotive or "iron horse," ushering in a whole new era of faster, more convenient travel. The Great Western Railway's first train passed through London on January 17, 1854, providing the impetus for London to become a city on January 1, 1855. More railway building followed, so much so that the Canadian Pacific, Michigan Central, London & Port Stanley, and London, Huron & Bruce railways all operated in London in the nineteenth century. The Great Western, meanwhile, was taken over by the Grand Trunk in 1882.

With the advent of the railways, it was easier to transport freight as well as passengers, which not only increased trade and commerce, but also lured business and manufacturing heavyweights to set up in the city. The railway allowed the development of oil refining in London—the oil being brought in from Petrolia and later shipped to Toronto for export. Tourism became another offshoot industry, as the train allowed Londoners to travel farther faster. The L. & P.S. offered the possibility of jaunts out to nearby Port Stanley. Soon, everyone travelled by railway, whether visiting friends, working as travelling salesmen, or troops departing for the front. Even the King and Queen arrived in London's new art deco train station when they visited in 1939.

Within the city, there was public transportation. The London Street Railway, incorporated in 1873, made its first trip in a horse-drawn car along Dundas Street that year. An electric tram system was inaugurated in London West in 1893 and throughout the city in 1895. One year later, the streetcars ran all the way into Springbank Park, allowing Londoners to take day trips to this riverside resort outside the city limits. That May, the street railway carried 15,000 Londoners to Springbank to celebrate Victoria Day.

In its heyday in 1922, the Street Railway tallied 13,413,945 passengers—a remarkable number for a city with a population of about 61,000. With the increased popularity of the automobile, however, ridership on the streetcar declined, and Londoners suddenly viewed the aging cars as an inconvenience, holding up traffic and making street surfaces uneven. The streetcars ran in

London for the last time in November 1940 and the tracks were ripped up in 1941. The LSR still existed, running buses only, until January 1, 1951, when the city purchased the company and London Transit Commission was born.

When Londoners viewed their first "horseless carriage" in 1899 at the Western Fair, they couldn't imagine the changes the automobile would make to their city. London's first automobile owner was likely Verschoyle Cronyn, son of Bishop Benjamin Cronyn, in approximately 1901, when he purchased a steamer operated by a tiller. In a few short years, cars would be manufactured in the Forest City. The Harding Twenty was built by Fred C. Harding at his Harding Motor Car Co., the London Six was founded by William R. Stansell of London Motors, and a Ford plant opened in 1913 on the east side of Waterloo Street, just north of the CPR tracks. Early car dealerships were the McLaughlin Motor Car Company on Richmond, Gallagher Motor Sales on Wellington and King, and Durant Motor Sales on King.

Soon companies were buying motorized vehicles, such as the one bought by Bell Telephone in 1909. Bell's first vehicle never arrived, breaking down in Hamilton. Sent back to its manufacturer, the Tudhope Carriage Company of Orillia, for repairs, it was soon destroyed there in a fire, forcing Bell to start again. Many companies would have trucks for deliveries of all sorts, including ice, furniture, and food. Bakeries and dairies, however, continued to use horses for home delivery well into the 1940s and beyond.

Driving did cause a few problems. London's first speeding ticket went to Fred Mitchell in 1903, when he was fined five dollars for driving his Geneva Steam Machine at more than 10 miles an hour on Richmond Street. Eventually, there were traffic jams, forcing the city to widen its streets and provide more lanes for traffic and parking. To alleviate downtown traffic woes, King Street and Queens Avenue became London's first one-way streets in April 1950.

Like automobiles, flying machines started as luxury playthings for those who could afford them. The first Londoner to own an airplane was Arthur B. Jones, a former RAF pilot who bought a plane in June 1919. The city's first airfield (and one of Canada's earliest airports) was at Lambeth, just northwest of what is now Wharncliffe and Wonderland. The site had soft soil, an advantage when airplanes had hard-pressure tires prone to breaking on hard-surface runways.

London's current airport opened in July 1940, east of the city in the hamlet of Crumlin. On August 1, 1940, Trans-Canada Airlines (later Air Canada) began its first scheduled airline passenger service to London. The airport—more than the train, streetcar, automobile, or any other transportation marvel—broadened Londoners' horizons, linking the Forest City to the world.

Horses pulling telephone poles near O.W. Cambridge grocery store, corner of Rectory and Lovett, East London.

Looking east along King Street with a Spramotor Co. sprayer in the foreground. The company made whitewashing and spraying equipment. Note the horse and buggies that line the unpaved street.

The John Campbell and Son Carriage Factory showroom was located at 77-85 King Street, south side, between Talbot and Ridout.

An ornate wrought-iron horse trough, pictured here in November 1948, stood on King Street by Covent Garden Market. Installed by the London Humane Society at an unknown date, horses drank from one side, while humans could drink from the other. Although restored in 1948, cars continually knocked it off its base, and the city decided to remove it. It is now housed at Museum London.

The Grand Trunk Car Works on Egerton Street, circa 1883. Note saddle tank locomotive to right.

Grand Trunk platform, 1910. Several G.T. officers stand beside their official inspection train carrying G.T. Chairman Rivers-Wilson on an annual inspection of stations. The Tecumseh House hotel at Richmond and York streets is visible in the background.

The Grand Trunk Railway Depot, south side of York Street between Richmond and Clarence, circa 1890. Originally built as the Great Western Railway station in 1854, it became the property of the Grand Trunk when the two railways merged in 1882. The station was demolished in 1935 to make way for a new CNR station.

A CPR engine at the CPR roundhouse just east of Adelaide Street along with a work crew, circa 1890.

CPR Engine 305 on the roundhouse turntable. The engine is a 4-4-0 American-type locomotive, typical of those made before 1890.

Michigan Central Railway Station, 1890. The station was constructed in 1886–87 on the southeast corner of Clarence and Bathurst in time for the first Michigan Central passenger train to pull into the station September 12, 1887. The last train departed June 30, 1915, and the station was demolished 1937.

A train crosses the Grand Trunk Railway Bridge, circa 1900. The London Street Railway Powerhouse blows smoke from its chimney at centre.

In this photo by London photographer John Cooper, May 30, 1887, CPR locomotive 192 becomes the first Canadian Pacific passenger train in London. The "track gang" has not yet finished its work.

The first London & Port Stanley railway electric locomotive was photographed at St. Thomas in June 1915.

GTR coal chutes at Glencoe.

The GTR Station was draped in black to mourn GTR President Charles M. Hays, who drowned on the Titanic on April 15, 1912.

A summer outing from the city to Port Stanley on board the L. & P.S. Railway The motorman can be seen at the controls up front, while the passengers have lifted their windows to poke their heads out into the breeze.

Train derailment at York and Clarence streets, circa 1930. The westbound freight train has suffered little damage, but a crane was needed to haul the engine back on the tracks. Although marked GTR, the company had become CNR in 1923.

Pile-driver equipment being used in the first phase of construction building "subways" at Wellington and Richmond streets in 1931. A subway refers to a city street passing beneath a railway right-of-way.

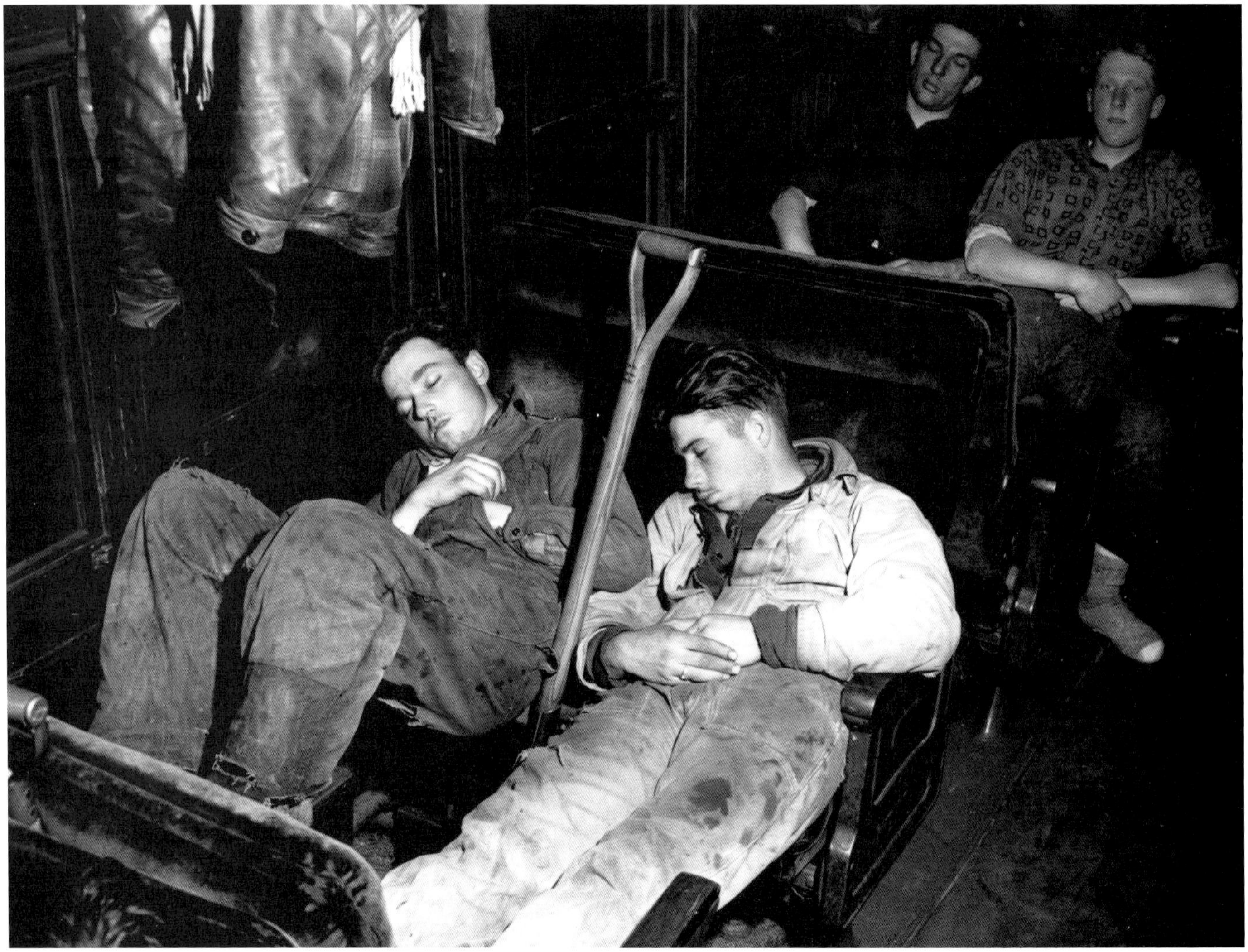

Russ Fagan (left) and Bill Fisher collapsed into an exhausted sleep after digging through mammoth snowdrifts blocking the Huron and Bruce Railroad line. They were on board a work train that pushed through the drifts from London to Clinton and back, struggling to keep the line clear during one of the worst blizzards in the area's history, March 6, 1947.

The London and Port Stanley Railroad Coal Yard on Bathurst Street, circa 1920s.

Rectory Street CNR depot, built in 1875, was demolished in December, 1948, as personnel moved into a new building at the Egerton Street crossing. The depot was built by the Great Western Railway to serve east London, but trains had not stopped there since the turn of the century.

In June, 1949, steam was being replaced by Diesel in the CPR yards. Here city council members and CPR officials pose on a new diesel locomotive.

The CPR roundhouse, pictured here in August 1949, closed after diesel power supplanted "smoke-belching" locomotives. S.M. Taggart, divisional master mechanic, told City Council that month, "The roundhouse will be just a hole in the ground in a few years' time."

The southeast corner of Dundas and Richmond is seen through a web of overhead wires, circa 1883. A horse-drawn streetcar turns south onto Richmond Street.

The first electric streetcar in London, No. 52, was photographed as the London Street Railway expanded to London West on October 25, 1893. This view looks east along Oxford Street with the CPR railway bridge in the background. Large crowds await the free trip offered on car 52.

No. 52 streetcar at Kensington Bridge, built in 1897, at the west end of Dundas Street to connect the city with London West. The bridge itself had no tracks and passengers walked across. The Courthouse and Sulphur Springs may be seen in the background on the other side of the river.

On February 22, 1914, streetcars ran on a Sunday for the first time. This photo—looking at the northwest corner of Dundas and Richmond—includes three streetcars and a number of people posing for the historic occasion. Superintendent Henry H. Hummeston stands at left.

London Street Railway streetcar No. 120, West London, circa 1920. The motorman and conductor pose by the car door.

Young passengers cram onto a London Street Railway car in an undated photograph.

A variety of transport shared the road near Dundas and Richmond in the early twentieth century, including the Ridout streetcar (106), an early automobile, and horse and buggy as pictured here.

Streetcar 170 turns south off Oxford Street onto Richmond Street on one of its last runs, November 1, 1940. This intersection was one of the corners where London motorists were "most bothered by the slowness of the cars."

Workmen remove the trolley rails at the CPR crossing on Richmond Street, November 1940. The tracks were laid 60 years earlier for horse-pulled streetcars. Note the CPR station in the background, later The Keg restaurant. The former Ford factory (Siskinds in 2017) can be seen in the background at left.

The last London streetcar is removed from the city by transport trailer in late January 1941, to be used as a summer house on a farm east of the city. Other streetcars were sold to tobacco farmers to be used as bunkhouses or chicken coops. One or two likely became highway lunch counters. The wheels were usually sold as scrap iron to be used in war industries.

London Street Railway bus no. 41, circa 1940. In 1933 and 1934, the London Street Railway saved money by buying seven bus chassis from General Motors in Walkerville and building the bodies of wood and metal in their own shops in London. Bus no. 41 was one of these, built in 1933.

By August 1946, Motorman Winfield Armstrong had worked for the London Street Railway for 56 years, ever since he was age 14 in 1890. He began in the horse era, worked through the electric era, and began driving a bus at an age when most men were contemplating retirement.

A city bus stuck in a snowdrift at the corner of Wellington and Dufferin in late 1944.

London Bicycle Club in Victoria Park by the bandstand, circa 1900. A first request to use the park was turned down by the city. The cyclists were eventually allowed, provided they didn't ride too quickly.

F. Benson & Co. Bicycle Shop, 260 Dundas Street, circa 1915. The Indian Motorcycle out front, made in Springfield, Massachusetts, was on a cross-country promotional tour.

George Wenige's Bicycle & Motor Sales Co. at 425-427 Wellington Street, west side, just north of Dundas Street. Wenige, elected mayor of London nine times, was known as "the man who made walking expensive." The group may be the London Bicycle Club.

A horse-drawn delivery wagon passes an early automobile mired in mud on Richmond Street north of Oxford.

Motoring in Victoria Park, circa 1905. C. Ed Bernard and his wife sit in the car while Senator Thomas Coffey stands to the right. The park was closed to vehicular traffic in 1951.

125 motorcyclists attend a one-hour "conference" in Springbank Park on August 13, 1948, with city officials including Mayor George Wenige and Police Chief Earl Knight. The meeting's purpose was to discuss ways to eliminate complaints about noisy and careless driving by bikers.

Crystal Lake Ice Co. was one of several ice dealers in the city who supplied ice to downtown hotels such as the Brunswick, pictured here at Talbot and York streets. The solid rubber tires, right hand drive, and crank start date the truck to circa 1912.

Bell Telephone car, April 1909.

Automobile show in the Armouries on Dundas Street, March 1913.

J.W. McLaughlin, Ford dealer, store, and service station, was located on the south side of Dundas just east of Wellington Street, pictured here circa 1920.

Supertest Gasoline vehicle, 1924.

Ruggles Motor Truck Factory, 1924. The building was later used by Kelvinator, Firestone, and House of German Furniture. It is Dundas Auto Sales in 2017.

The Winter Gardens dance hall, circa 1929. A Hudson-Essex car dealership by day, in the evening, cars were rolled to a nearby parking lot so the site could be used for dancing. The site was later occupied by the Elsie Perrin Williams Memorial Library.

The *Free Press* reported that March 1947 "went out like a whole pack of lions," as a late winter storm stalled traffic and made walking hazardous. Here, city workers clear the intersection of Richmond and Queens in front of the old post office building.

Few pedestrians ventured outside after the worst storm of the winter hit London on March 20, 1940, but city workmen shovelled snow into a truck in an attempt to keep the streets clear in London's business section.

After being a blacksmith shop for over 50 years, this Richmond Street smithy was sold in April 1947 to become a lunch shop called the Toddle Inn. By this date, there were only five smithies left in London, automobiles having almost entirely taken over from horse-drawn vehicles.

Aboutown Taxi line-up at 426 Clarence Street, 1948.

On June 30, 1947, Theresa Wallach pulled into London on her way to Chicago. In 1935, when only 17, this famous adventurer and a friend completed an eight-month motorcycle trip down the length of Africa from the Sahara to Cape Town. Later, during the war, she rode thousands of kilometres as a dispatch rider during air raids and blackouts. Here, she poses in front of HMCS Prevost, Richmond Street, on her English Norton motorbike.

A thunderstorm hit London with sudden fury on July 11, 1948, causing minor street flooding. When sewers couldn't drain the water fast enough, a pool formed where the CPR tracks cross Waterloo at Pall Mall Street. Here, children enjoy the "swimming hole;" for the motorist, however, a flooded street was less agreeable.

Rush-hour traffic on September 4, 1948, blocks the doors of the Central Fire Hall on King Street. Fire equipment could not leave the station on weekdays after 5:00 p.m. and Saturdays from 11:00 to 1:00 p.m. In response, Fire Chief R.C. McRonald said, "We hold our breath and hope there will not be a fire."

The London Junior Chamber of Commerce opened its safety campaign on January 19, 1949, with a parade of wrecked automobiles through downtown. The cars, often towed by wreckers, bore posters describing the death and injury to the drivers.

A "traffic jam" on King Street, looking toward Richmond, July 2, 1949. The street would not become one way eastbound until April 17, 1950.

London's first parking metre made its appearance on August 12, 1948, on Dundas near Ridout. It was made from a cigar box covered with paper, bearing the words "Parking Meter Inc. Reserved." The joke was a response to the ongoing city council debate. Mayor George Wenige opposed parking metres, but downtown merchants supported the measure, claiming the devices would reduce illegal parking and ease London's downtown traffic problems.

James Medcalf and Terrence Tully pose with the Sir John Carling, a Stinson-Detroiter monoplane they would attempt to fly from London, Ontario, to London, England, in 1927.

The Sir John Carling takes off from its special two-mile runway on its ill-fated London-to-London flight. The runway was south of the Governor's Road (Dundas Street) at the hamlet of Crumlin. The flyers and their plane went down in the Atlantic.

The official opening of the new London Airport on July 27, 1940. From left to right are: C. D. Howe, Federal Minister of Munitions, Supply, & Transport; Mayor Allan Johnston, MP; Squadron Leader F.R. West, in charge of the wartime flying school at the airport; and Brigadier D.J. MacDonald, officer commanding Military District No. 1.

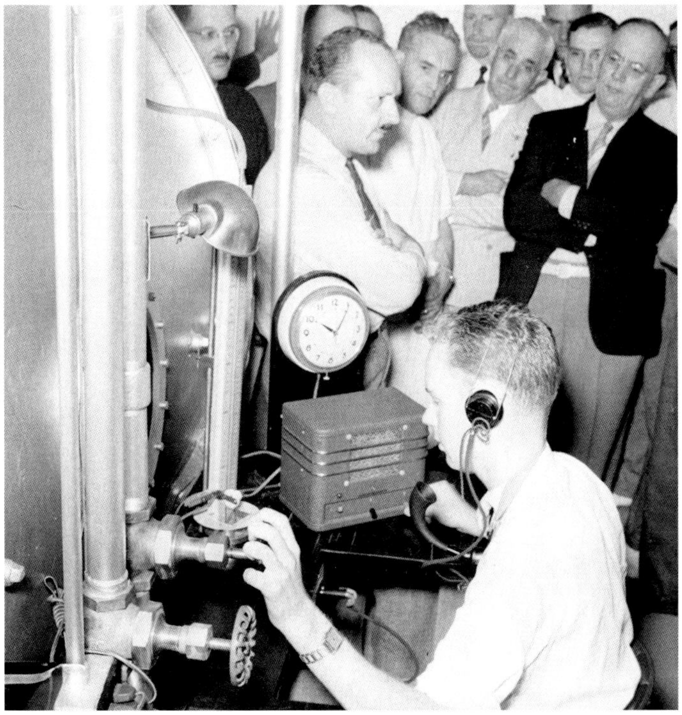

Crowds watch the radio operator at work at the official opening of London Airport, 1940.

A Trans-Canada Airlines flight is the first to arrive at the new London Airport, July 1940.

On June 22, 1945, Isabel Pearson became the first woman to fly solo from London Airport, making a 15-minute circuit and landing perfectly. A radio operator at Trans Canada Airlines, Isabel had been taking flying lessons since March 1944. She hoped to gain a pilot's licence and fly commercially.

American investigators look at the scene of the plane crash that took the lives of Dr. Willard H. Dow, his wife, and three others. Dr. Dow was one of the best-known chemists in the United States and head of Dow Chemical Company. Their plane went down four miles north of London Airport on April 1, 1949. The only survivor was Calvin Campbell, head of the legal department at Dow, who crawled from the wreckage. From left to right are: D.A. Brown, Chief of Police; R.W. Rogers of Midland, Michigan; Sherriff Ira Smith of Midland County; and Constable Ray Rowe of Midland.

# WESTERN FAIR

On March 21, 1868, two organizations—the Horticultural and Mechanical Association of London and the East Middlesex Agricultural Society—held a joint meeting to amalgamate for the creation of a London fall fair. Their new name was the Western Fair Association. That September, the first Western Fair was held on a site north of Great Market Street (Central Avenue) between Richmond and Waterloo. The site was the upper portion of the old British Garrison land, north of today's Victoria Park. An impressive octagonal exhibition building known as the Crystal Palace was built for the event, taking its name from the famed Crystal Palace designed for the Great Exhibition in London, England, in 1851. While nowhere near as grand as the English exhibition hall, it did boast a staggering 48 windows on its second floor.

In 1885, Londoners voted to hold their annual fair at Queen's Park in East London instead. The downtown location took up space needed for residential development and there would be more room for an exhibition on the open lands to the east. Accordingly, on September 20-23, 1887, the fair was held for the first time at its current location, in the park formerly known as Salter's Grove. The main building, London's second Crystal Palace, was designed by local architect George Durand in time for opening day. The four-day fair attracted 75,000 spectators. A fair has been held there every year since then, except during the Second World War, when the military commandeered the park as a barracks and training ground from 1939 to 1947.

When the second Crystal Palace burned down in January 1927, it was replaced by the red-brick Confederation Building. It was not the first time fire had struck the fairgrounds, however. On September 12, 1895, the poultry shed and the Carriage Hall were destroyed by fire on the evening of the opening day of the fair. Fortunately, fair staff saved all the display and exhibition articles. The next day, work crews cleared the rubble and erected tents to house the displaced exhibits.

Since the fair was founded for agricultural purposes, it's not surprising that its displays included livestock, vegetable harvests, and farm implements such as tractors and combines. Over the years, however, Western Fair became one of London's main attractions by including thrill rides and commercial exhibits to appeal to city folk as well as visiting farmers. At the 1911 fair, visitors had a chance to see a London-built automobile when five Harding Twenty cars were exhibited on the opening day. The cars were designed by Fred C. Harding and built by his Harding Motor Car Co. at the corner of King and Glebe streets. In 1949, Londoners could view Marconi television receivers displayed by the Benson-Wilcox Electric Company. It was likely the first time most Londoners had seen television.

Not all past exhibits would appeal to the sensibilities of today's fairgoers. A 1911 midway performer was one "Prince Nicholi, the Russian Prince," said to be the smallest man in the world at 16 ½ lbs and a height of only 27 inches. Sadly, "Nicholi" died at London's Grand Trunk Railway Station on September 16, 1911, aged 36. In 1921, the "Siamese Twins" Josefa and Rosa Blazek were displayed at the fair. Such sideshows became less prevalent as Londoners, like people elsewhere, changed their attitudes towards the treatment of those with physical differences.

The Western Fair marks the end of summer in London and Middlesex. A reminder of the region's agricultural roots, it has also provided entertainment that reflects changes in London and the world.

The Crystal Palace at the original fairgrounds built for the 1861 fall fair. Designed by architect William Robinson in octagonal layers, it was constructed just north of Great Market Street (Central Avenue) between Richmond and Waterloo streets. It was demolished in 1888 when the fairgrounds were moved to Queen's Park in East London.

Crystal Palace, early 1900s. Constructed in 1887, after the Western Fair moved to Queen's Park in East London, it was designed by London architect George Durand. It burned in 1927.

An early view of the park and pond in front of the Crystal Palace, 1900s.

The Wall of Death carnival game, 1928. First appearing at New York's Coney Island in 1911, stunt drivers, like the men pictured here, ride along the vertical walls of the silodrome.

Crystal Palace, the "Main Building" at the Western Fair, 1908.

Officials judge corn as well as other vegetables at the 1938 Western Fair.

Crowds at the 1927 Western Fair.

Ladies judge needlework at the 1938 fair.

A shovel plow used by pioneers in 1830 is held by A.H. Jury in a 1938 fair display. His son Wilfrid, a well-known archeologist in his later years, kneels by his side.

A trainer gives children "a little ride on a little elephant" in 1938.

The Western Fairgrounds are jammed with huge crowds on September 14, 1939. Whether attracted by the ideal late summer weather or looking for a distraction from the declaration of war the previous week, Londoners and residents of western Ontario's counties went to the fair in droves. It would be the last fair until 1947, as the fair was placed on hiatus for the war's duration.

The 1938 fair included an astronomy exhibit from Western University. Alex Groshak, left, a student at Aberdeen School, and Ronald Stone of Lord Roberts School, are trying a refracting telescope.

A "jalopy race" at the grandstand on September 18, 1939. The show was put on by Flash Williams Thrill Drivers.

Bob North scrutinizes "a pigmy pouter" while judging pigeons in the poultry building at the fair in September, 1948. The bird was owned by Mrs. E. Taylor of 162 Mt. Pleasant Avenue. Looking on in the background is Cecil Snelling.

Children lost at the Western Fair on September 13, 1948, grin as they are packed into a police cruiser waiting to be restored to their parents.

Attendance at the 1949 fair broke attendance records at 200,000 visitors. The *Free Press* aerial camera recorded this view of Queen's Park from the *Free Press* News Hawk. In the foreground is the midway with rides and shows while the new stock building is at the left. At centre right is the covered grandstand with the Manufacturers' Building just to the left. The parking area in front of the racetrack is full.

For children attending the fair, the chief attraction was the midway. Children could enter for free on Children's Day, September 12, 1949, and made a beeline for tickets to the games and rides.

Elsie the Cow and her son Beauregard appeared at the fair all week in 1949. Proceeds from their visit went to the Kinsmen's Club fund for the Hugh A. Stevenson camp and playground for underprivileged children. Here Elsie meets Ontario Premier Leslie Frost (left) and London Mayor Ray Dennis.

Lloyd Wright of CFPL Radio interviews Elsie the Cow, September 14, 1949.

# WESTERN UNIVERSITY

Established in 1878, Western University—now an internationally recognized institution with nearly 30,000 full-time students—developed over many decades as society's educational needs advanced. In the mid-nineteenth century, a university degree was a privilege of the elite, reserved for upper-class males. When Huron College, the predecessor of Western, officially opened in December 1863, there was no need for a large campus. A theological college founded by Bishop Benjamin Cronyn, Huron was located in "Rough Park," the former home of Lionel Ridout on the property bounded by Grosvenor, St. George, St. James, and the Thames River.

The staff and alumni at Huron College had a bigger dream: they wanted to build a university. On March 7, 1878, royal assent was given to the bill incorporating Western University of London, Ontario, as it was first known. Huron College became affiliated as the Faculty of Divinity. The new university moved into the old Hellmuth Boys' College (renamed Dufferin College), where lectures officially began in October 1881. Less than two years later, on April 27, 1883, Western held its first convocation and awarded two degrees—a Bachelor of Arts to Robert Franklin Sutherland and a Bachelor of Medicine to William James Roche.

Western University began with four faculties: art, divinity, medicine, and law. In 1882, Dr. William Waugh delivered the first medical lecture for London Medical College—the forerunner of the Medical School of Western University. Waugh would also give the inaugural lecture at the new London Medical College building, erected at the northeast corner of York and Waterloo in 1888.

The Faculty of Arts, however, quickly devolved into financial crisis and was shuttered in 1885. Huron College returned to Rough Park, and ended its affiliation, albeit temporarily. Ten years later, Western's Arts program was revived; it would share space with Huron College until the 1920s. From there, the university stabilized and grew, becoming a secular institution in 1908, which opened it up to government funding.

In 1908, the library at Western consisted of only 200 books. Ten years later, librarian Fred Landon would famously negotiate the acquisition of the private collection of curator-librarian John Davis Barnett of Stratford—a staggering 40,000 volumes, including many rare editions and Canadiana. The agreement was signed August 10, 1918—the cost, one dollar. His remarkable bargaining skills were likely part of the reason that Landon became chief librarian at Western from 1923 to 1947.

At the end of the First World War, Western University was still sharing facilities with Huron College. Despite the pressures of low enrollment during the war, it was obvious that the university needed more space. In fact, the site for a new campus was purchased in 1916—the former "Bellevue Farm," owned by the Kingsmill family north of the city in London Township. The site was expanded by purchasing adjacent lands, with financial assistance from the city, the province, and the County of Middlesex.

Not all Londoners approved of the choice of location. Humorous comments such as "the college in Kingsmill's cow pasture" and "halfway to Lucan" were overhead in those days. But the University Board of Governors showed much foresight in choosing a large, self-contained site near the river for the developing university. Western grew into one of the most attractive campuses in the province, if not in all of Canada.

On April 15, 1922, Governor-General Lord Byng participated in the official sod-turning for the new buildings. The occasion was deemed so important that a half-holiday was declared. A little over a year later, the university was renamed The University of Western Ontario and, on June 18, 1923, Premier Ernest Charles Drury laid the cornerstone of the Arts Building (University College) and the Natural Sciences Building (Physics and Astronomy Building). In his speech, Drury affirmed his belief in the value of smaller regional universities.

With blessing—and financial support—from the provincial government, the building of Western's new campus was underway. The iconic bridge over the Thames from Richmond Street was completed in November 1923. Regular classes began in the Arts and Natural Sciences buildings in September 1924. On October 16 and 17, Dr. William J. Roche, Western's first medical graduate, officially opened the two buildings in a public ceremony. At last, Western had its own 225-acre campus with two Collegiate Gothic-style structures.

The campus grew quickly. Fred Landon received his first separate library building when the Lawson Memorial Library, named after benefactors Frank and Lorena Lawson, opened in 1934. In 1940, the Hume Cronyn Memorial Observatory opened, a gift of Frances (Labatt) Cronyn in memory of her late husband.

Women's involvement at Western developed gradually. Mary L. Cowan, the first female student admitted in 1895, was also the first woman to graduate in 1898. The first female faculty member was Hilda Baynes, hired in 1914 to teach French. In 1919, a Women's Faculty Club was organized by Mrs. W. Sherwood Fox and a year later, the University Women's Club was formed. Lectures for female students began at Brescia Hall, originally known as Ursuline College in 1920, but a new building was built on Western Road in 1925 that has since been renamed Brescia College.

In the fall of 1920, Kathleen Braithwaite became the first female student to enroll in medicine at Western, graduating in 1924. In 1921, Dr. Madge Thurlow Macklin, formerly of Johns Hopkins, became the first female member of the medical faculty. In 1947, UWO's School of Nursing came into existence, in those days exclusively for women.

It was after the Second World War that Western really expanded. The Department of Veterans Affairs paid the tuition of any returned soldier who wished to enter university—the result being a flood of applications. In 1945, Western accepted 700 first-year students, compared to only 297 the year before, many of them veterans. The university didn't have the space, but managed by holding classes at night and at other locations within the city. The expansion also forced the creation of new professional schools and programmes. In 1948, 27 students graduated with a BA in Journalism, the first such graduating class in Canada.

As the university expanded academically, its athletic program kept pace. However, in its early days, sports were not considered an important part of university life—just as there was not always opportunity for recreation in daily life elsewhere. But as campus living developed, sports programmes were recognized as another way for students to develop their bodies as well as their minds, and to blow off steam. As early as 1915, the University Senate adopted purple and white as the official university colours. The first use of the moniker "Mustangs" in reference to sports teams was in 1926.

When one thinks of university athletics, football is often the first sport that comes to mind. On September 28, 1929, senior rugby was inaugurated at Western with an exhibition game against the Sarnia Imperials of the Ontario Rugby Football Union at the new J.W. Little Memorial Stadium. Unfortunately for the Mustangs, Sarnia won 10 to 4 before a crowd of 3,200. The team's luck only worsened on October 9, 1929, the date the stadium officially opened with some 4,000 spectators. Queens University won that game 25 to 2. Nevertheless, coached by Joe Breen, the team did go on to make a good showing in its first season. The Mustangs won their first Senior Intercollegiate football championship in 1931. Johnny "the bull" Metras was football coach from 1940 to 1969, leading them to seven Yates Cups and one Vanier cup.

Over the years, sports at Western included basketball, swimming, hockey, wrestling, boxing, and track and field, as well as less typical activities such as fencing and archery. Women took part in athletics as well as men, Mary Manly being appointed the first director of women's athletics in 1916. After 1945, with the huge increase in student enrollment, the sports program benefited with expanded facilities and activities.

Whether it was academics or athletics, Western had grown into one of Ontario's leading universities—a reputation that would continue to grow into the post-war decades and beyond.

An early view of Huron College, the founding institution that led to the incorporation of Western University in 1878. Huron College affiliated with the new university, becoming its Faculty of Divinity. For much of the university's early history, it shared facilities with Huron here at "Rough Park."

London Medical College, circa 1890. At first, Western's Medical School was housed in a small cottage next to Hellmuth College, until this building was constructed at the corner of York and Waterloo streets in 1888.

Western University moved into Hellmuth Boys' College, pictured here circa 1875, in time to hold the university's first lectures in October 1881. However, Western only occupied this building for a short time, and it was demolished in 1895.

An anatomy lesson in progress at Western's Medical School, circa 1900.

Volunteers from Western's Medical School, led by faculty chair Dr. Edwin Seaborn, formed the majority of the No. 10 Stationary Hospital in the First World War, first located in England, then on to Calais, France, in 1917.

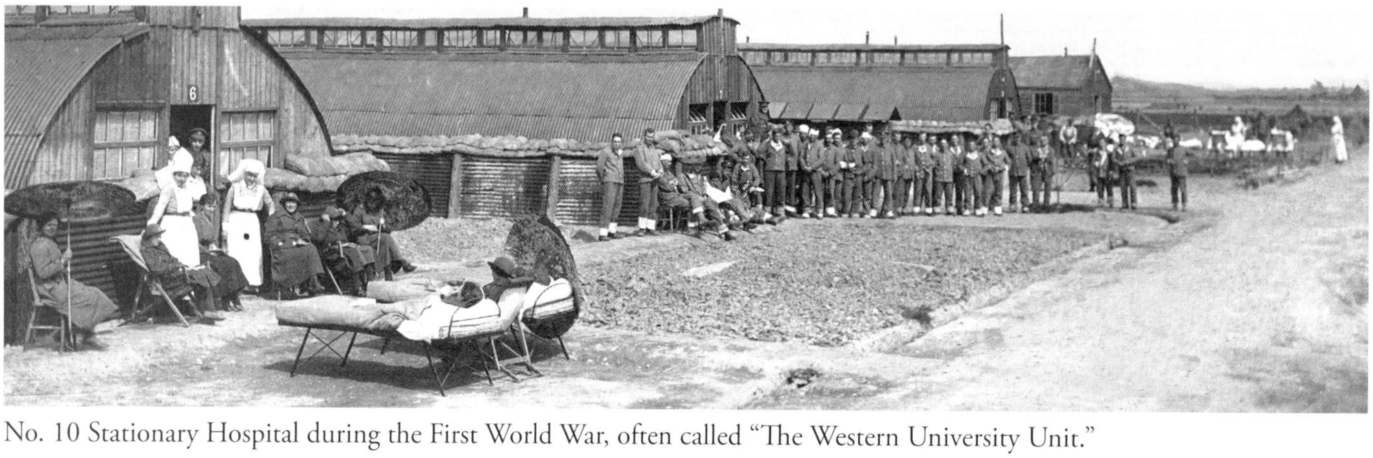

No. 10 Stationary Hospital during the First World War, often called "The Western University Unit."

The old Kingsmill Farm, just north of the city proper, was purchased by the Board of Governors in 1916 as the location for Western's new campus. This panoramic view shows off the 150 acres, from a vantage point on the riverbank near the present-day Delaware Hall.

Construction was underway on both the new Natural Sciences Building (just visible in the background, to the left) and the Arts Building (foreground, to the right) in September 1922.

The construction of University Bridge by the Puterbough Construction Company, seen here looking east toward Richmond Street, 1922.

Premier Ernest Drury laid the cornerstones for the Arts Building and the Natural Sciences Building on June 19, 1923.

The first students cross University Bridge from Richmond Street for summer school classes in 1924.

The official opening of the new campus was marked by a special convocation on October 16 and 17, 1924. Here, a procession of graduates and dignitaries make their way from the Natural Sciences building to Convocation Hall.

When the Natural Sciences Building opened its doors in 1924, it was considered state of the art. The modern design included fireproof tiles on interior walls, two electrical systems, and exposed pipes (to facilitate quick repair).

A laboratory and classroom amphitheatre in the Natural Sciences Building, circa 1925. The building was designed to allow for abundant natural light, leading it to be nicknamed "the sunshine building."

Pictured here in 1925, students could take a streetcar from Richmond Street to campus from 1924 to 1940.

The Arts Building, now University College, looking from University Bridge, c. 1930. It was built in 1924 in the Collegiate Gothic style.

An aerial view of London from the tower of the Arts Building, November 1930. As the Board of Governors' chairman Charles Somerville predicted in 1917, the city was growing around the campus.

In the 1920s, initiation traditions for freshmen included an annual "tug of war" contest across the Thames River, pictured here in 1934.

The exterior of Western's new Hume Cronyn Memorial Observatory, opened October 25, 1940.

University telescopes in Victoria Park allow children to look at Mars in July 1939. Behind the tripod is Dr. G.R. Magee and in the background are some of the thousands of spectators who showed up to peep into the four-inch refracting telescope.

On April 3, 1939, Western students held a mass meeting at H.B. Beal Technical School auditorium to protest cuts in government grants to the university. The provincial government planned to reduce its annual grant to Western by $25,000. Here students, parents, and friends listen as Don Wright leads the Western band in the school's "victory" song.

Western students check mid-year exam results February 1, 1939. Only 12 of approximately 2,000 undergraduates "flunked" that year and only 40 were put on "good behaviour" for the rest of the year. Girls did better than boys, being only 4 out of the 12 failures and 6 of the 40 probationers.

UWO costume party held February 17, 1939, at Convocation Hall. The theme was "Hard Times" and students turned out in odd, worn-out attire—a nod to the financial difficulties faced by many during the Great Depression.

Archeologists from UWO excavate the scene of an "Indian massacre" in Kent County, June 1939. The skeletons of an Aboriginal man and girl were found three feet below the surface on a farm two miles south of the village of Duart. The find was considered evidence of a 1656 massacre in which an invading band of Iroquois murdered the Attawandarons who occupied the area. Here, Wilfrid Jury (left) and Donald MacPherson remove dirt from the remains.

Bill Wood, chair of the petition committee, shows a placard to C.C. Carrothers, Western graduate and chairman of the Board of Education. The government's planned funding cuts did not occur due to the start of the Second World War.

On September 25, 1939, more than 300 "freshies" signed up for the 1939–40 term at Western. Here they wait in line to pay their tuition fees to the cashier.

Two "freshies," Lloyd McAninch of Guelph (left) and Bruce King of Chesley, have their registration cards checked by Dorothy Phillips of the university staff.

Western's medical school at Waterloo Street and Ottaway Avenue (now South Street) in January 1948. The University wished to build a medical school on campus and convert this building into a hospital for incurables, chronically ill, and convalescent patients. The Faculty of Medicine moved into the new Medical Sciences Building on campus in 1965.

An aerial shot of the University of Western Ontario campus in June, 1946. On the left is the Arts and Administration Building, on the right is the Science building. The proposed site of the new medical school building was in the centre of the two.

An aerial view of the Arts building and Lawson Library, circa 1940, looking east towards the university entrance. The library was built in 1934, designed by London architect John M. Moore.

Connie Laidlaw, aged 19, walked a narrow bridge stretched across the Thames as part of a UWO initiation September 1948. Connie had won the "health, beauty, talent and personality" section of the Miss Canada beauty contest earlier that year. She used her $500 prize money to attend UWO, intending to study journalism.

In December 1948, Scottish stonemasons were at work on Thames Hall, the new cut-stone athletic building. Masons were in short supply in Canada, so William Cowie, George King, Sid Hurd, and Norman Murray were flown in to assist.

Members of the graduating class wind their way across campus to the J.W. Little Memorial Stadium, 1947.

Graduates of the UWO nursing class of 1949—two years after the School of Nursing opened its doors.

The Huron College soccer team, 1898. Back row: T.B. Howard, Fred Waide, Professor Sykes, Provost B. Watkins, H. Sutton, and Professor Fred Hall. Middle Row: D.W. Collins, T.B.R. Westgate, and R. Herbert. Front Row: W.E.V. McMillan, S.P. Irwin, Ernie Smith, and C. Purton.

Western Arts Tug of War champion team 1903–04. Back row: F.K. Hughes, T.J. Hamilton, H.P. Westgate, and C.A. Scheaf. Front row: F.E Powell, Dr. W.F. Tamblyn, and J.M. Horton.

Western Medical College basketball team members sport skull and crossbones shirts, 1905–06. Back row: J. Watson, J. Folinsbee, and R. McAlpine. Middle: F. Moore, P. Poisson, J. Wood, and A. Ross. Front: W. Crawford.

Western's intermediate football team in 1928. Left to right: Dr. Pritchett, P. Waugh Wilson, P. Mountain, P. Stull, S. Ward, S. Valeriate, S. Kress, C. McGinnig, E. Horton, M. Valeriate, V. Diamond, C. Hauch, A. Dobie, S. Morton, M. Little, P. Huach, R. Brown, M. Jewel, C. Thompson, B. McLachlin, K. Kennedy, and E. Letts.

The University winter sports club poses for a group photograph, circa 1919.

Ladies' Basketball Team, 1920–21. Back row: Jean Javis, G. Met Brock (coach), and Helen Baker. Front row: Katherine White, Jean Walker, Edith Anderson, Gwen Williams, and Rhea Peever.

1926–27 hockey team. Back row: Harry Whitefield (trainer), Dick Kidd, S. Morrin (manager), S. Tieman, W. Marsden (coach), and A. Mowry. Middle: J. Bowen, C. Procunier, Mel. Walkem (captain), R. Lanoue, and A.E. Kregg. Front: Adam Dobie (mascot).

In the first decades of Western Athletics, cheerleading was a males-only sport. Western's 1933 squad, from left to right: D. Harcourt, M.M. Manus, F. Sanders, N. Richmond.

1933 hockey team. Seated: D. Steadman, G. Paterson, A. Vogelsang, J. Schnarr, and J.M. Janes. Standing: D. Lofft, H. Clarke, J. Rankin, D. Knight, P. Pigeon, F. Marsden, and W. Meacitem.

1933 wrestling team. Seated: O. Scott, W.G. Duncan, B. Higgins, C. McEachren, and P. Elson. Standing: P. Acres, L. Forman, F. Schram, W. Sharpe, V. Lafontaine (coach), S. Sharpe, W. Baines, T. Borderick, and W.S. Duncan.

Women's badminton, 1934. Left to right: M. Kirkpatrick, M. Dampier, O. Thompson, and O. Miller.

1935 harrier (track and field) team. Back row: McPherson, Ramrie, and Johnson. Front: Huiser and McCubbin.

Men's boxing class, 1934. Left to right: P. Hunt, D.M. McLeod, G. Freebord, J. McCubbin, J. Griffiths, P. Millar, G. Ponsford, J. Woodhouse, and W.M. Manus.

1935 tennis team. Left to right: Bob Rider, G. Matheson, H. Clarke, K. Hodson, K. Roth, and D. Goodge

Women's senior basketball, 1935. Standing: Plumptre (coach), Cherry, Davis, Wallace, Timpany, Rintoul, and Bendle (manager). Seated: H. Timpany, Wong, and Blackall.

1935 golf team. Left to right: B. Cameron, G. Wilson, J. McHale, and P. Bernhardt.

Men's basketball team in action, 1936.

Senior soccer team in action, 1936. D. Trumper was in goal for Western.

Western's first female cheerleader, Doris Eagles, in October 1938.

1938 women's hockey. Back row: Bette Heuston, E. Young, L. Aiscott, and L. Graham. Middle row: A. Wray, R. McLaughlin, D. Brickenden, D. Golding, and Miss Weston. Front row: M. Snell, K. Rex, K. Veitch, D. Johns, M. Webster, and E. Cram.

An action shot from October 15, 1938, as the Mustangs take on Queens. Western made a comeback to win the game 10 to 7 before a record-breaking crowd of 6,000 at J.W. Little Stadium.

On November 12, 1939, 3,500 Londoners and students greeted Western's "conquering heroes" at the CNR station after the team returned from Kingston where they had defeated Queen's Tricolors 13 to 8. The Mustangs had won the Senior Intercollegiate Football Championship for the first time in 8 years. At right, team captain Alf Hurley is carried by his supporters.

Western defeated U of T February 25, 1939, in what the *Free Press* described as "the most exciting senior intercollegiate basketball game ever played in London." Western staged a last-minute rally to defeat Varsity 42-41 at Beal Technical School on a Saturday night. "Red" Cahill, Varsity forward, unleashes a one-hand shot in this photo.

Some claimed the game had been improperly lengthened by "time-outs" in the last minute of play, leading to a near riot after the final whistle. In this photo the crowd and players mill around the referee when the argument is at its height.

McGill versus Western, 1939. Left to right: M. Thomas (14), G. Oliphant (15), A. Hurley (1), W. Wong (25), and B. Benson (10).

Robert Greenway, Captain of the basketball team, 1943–44.

In the autumn of 1941, for the first time in UWO history, women could take fencing classes. Their coach was M.B. Sandor.

Miriam Morrow (left) and Phyllis Godwin practise archery.

Ladies' senior archery, 1940s. Back row: G. Logan, E. Harrison, I. Wheeler, C. Tucker, E. Schendel, and M. Hughes. Front row: J. Dobson, and B. Andrews.

An undated photo of Western girls swimming in formation. The swimmers are June Taylor, Jane Hicks, Helen German, Beverly Brough, Dodie Flavelle, and Margaret Kerte.

The 1944–45 men's swimming team prepare to take the plunge. Left to right: T. Nishio, A. Galbraith, V. Traynor, and N. Cuthbertson.

Ski Club at Chicopee, Kitchener circa 1940–44. Back row: V. Ross, D. Willson, J. Evans, M. Vickers, P. McKendry, J. Cooper, J. Draper, F. Mark, and E. Tamblyn. Front row: J. Burrows, R. Smith, M. MacKenzie, and J. Liddy.

Western's 1945 marching band featured leader Max Magee and Drum Majorette Kaarina Ronni.

Intermediate Intercollegiate Rugby Champions for 1946. Back row: B. Trumper (manager), V. Brown, J. Koskie, D. Scott, B. Pillsworth, G. Wearring, B. Downe, B. Purdom, D. McKinley, J. Reynolds, H. Douglas. Middle row: L. Mellor, B. Krol, D. Hutchinson, R. Winter, H. Lawler, A. Wiley, D. DeMarco, J. Parry, J. Stephens. Front row: T. Hodgins, S. Carson, M. Yuhasz, J. Whitton, J. Sullivan.

Intercollegiate men's swimming team, 1947–48. Back row: A. Galbraith, G. Gill, N. Wolf, J. Augustien, Cody Moffat (coach) R. Wilkins, C. Work, Wm. Foote, and W. Burnes (manager). Front row: H. Johnson, R. Whitside, T. Stewart, G. Bending, J. Walker, S. Sandborn, W. Hannah, and H. Lowther.

On March 5, 1948, announcers Cornell and Filman broadcast live on CFPL radio a basketball game between Western and the University of Detroit Titans.

Students shake their fists at an effigy representing the University of Toronto hanging in front of the Arts building, November 17, 1948. "Trample Toronto" was the rallying cry for the football game coming up on November 20.

During the football pep rally on November 17, 1948, the U of T effigy is burned at the CNR station while the UWO band plays funeral music and clowns do a slow march around the burning figure. Despite their efforts to rally the team, U of T won 18 to 7.

A snake dance at a UWO pep rally outside University College, on November 17, 1948.

# WORLD WAR I

When Archduke Franz Ferdinand, heir to the throne of Austria-Hungary, was assassinated by a Serbian nationalist on June 28, 1914, not many residents of London, Ontario, would have believed that it could affect the Forest City. Within weeks, however, the major European powers were at war and much of the developed world was entangled in the conflict. Germany invaded neutral Belgium before moving towards France from the north, causing Britain to give Germany an ultimatum: either remove its troops from Belgium or face a declaration of war.

On August 4, crowds began gathering in front of the newspaper offices in London, reading the news bulletins placed on the boards. The last bulletin of the night read "GREAT BRITAIN DECLARES WAR," and the next day, the *London Free Press* reported the city's reaction:

> Wild cheers went up when the declaration of war was announced and, gathering at Richmond and Carling streets, the crowd lustily sang "God Save the King," "Britannia Rules the Waves," "The Maple Leaf

Forever," "O Canada" and other national and patriotic airs. There was no thought save that of victory…

Perhaps this enthusiasm was what made London one of the largest recruiting centres in Canada. By 1916, more than 16,000 troops were being trained at Carling Heights in a giant tent city consisting of numerous battalions. Buildings at Queens Park (Western Fair) were also taken over to house troops in training. In 1914, Wolseley Barracks was quickly remodelled for the headquarters staff of the 1st Divisional Area, later Military District No. 1. Altogether, about 45,000 troops were raised in the military district and many of them received at least part of their training in London.

On June 9, 1916, nearly 10,000 uniformed soldiers from the nine infantry battalions and field ambulance and hospital units training in the city marched through London in the greatest procession of troops the city had ever seen. Thousands lined the streets that afternoon to watch the men in khaki march from Carling Heights through the downtown core.

Women's organizations were active throughout the war in London. The IODE, for example, ran a service club with a recreation room on the south side of Dundas Street near the Armouries. The London Red Cross, which had been created during the Boer War, was revived in September 1914, with Lady Lilian Beck as president. Lady Beck herself worked for the Canadian Red Cross in England for most of the war.

At first, Londoners were excitedly confident about the outcome of the conflict. It would be over by Christmas, they were told, and "the Hun" would be taught a lesson! When, on November 22, 1915, the first war loan went on sale, Londoners raised half a million dollars for the Allied cause in just 24 hours.

As time wore on, however, passion waned as the possibility of a quick, decisive victory faded and the brutality of the conflict became apparent. Private Clarence H. Smith became the first London man to be killed in action in France. He was followed by many more—so many that, during the war years, the *Free Press* printed a record of the latest casualties on the front page. As the list of dead and "missing" grew longer, Londoners became less eager to join or support the ongoing conflict. Rationing of such commodities as coal also dampened enthusiasm on the home front.

One might suppose Londoners had no heart to celebrate the fiftieth anniversary of Confederation on July 1, 1917. In fact, however, the city celebrated Canada's golden jubilee in the war-like spirit of the time with another grand parade on Monday, July 2. About a mile and a half in length, the parade again began at Carling Heights and ended at Victoria Park where the South African War soldiers' monument was decorated in honour of London men who had fallen. Two of London's great men, Sir George Gibbons and Sir Adam Beck, delivered addresses about Confederation, Sir George speaking about the first Dominion Day that was celebrated on that very spot when it was still the military barracks.

At last, Germany agreed to an armistice on November 11, 1918. The celebration in London was the greatest in the history of the city thus far, including a parade through the streets with a Victoria Park gathering of some 20,000 people. Many in the crowd verged on hysterical as an effigy of Kaiser Wilhelm was burned. Afterwards, men and women returned from overseas and life returned to normal. But, neither London nor the world would ever be the same after the war to end all wars.

Tent city at Carling Heights on Oxford Street East, circa 1914. A barracks could not be built in time to house the thousands of recruits training to be sent overseas.

The military campgrounds in London, from a postcard marked August 29, 1914.

Men from the 6th Field Battery pose for a photo while training in Queen's Park, August, 1914.

6th Field Battery training at Queen's Park for overseas service, August, 1914.

Recruits in London being outfitted with their uniforms, 1914.

Training at Carling Heights with Wolseley Barracks in the background, 1914.

135th (Middlesex) Battalion at Carling Heights, circa 1915–16. The battalion began recruiting in November 1915 and sailed to England in August 1916 where they were absorbed into other battalions.

An aerial view of the great crowd seeing the 7th Regiment (Fusiliers) depart from the GTR station on August 22, 1914.

These Guelph "boys" enlisting in London would be going to the front with Lt.-Col. Brown's artillery. They were recruited by Captain Sampson.

Colour-Sergeant Holmes and three privates escort two Germans and an Austrian, reservists in the armies of the Kaiser and the Emperor Franz Joseph, respectively on August 27, 1914. All three Europeans were arrested just as they were about to depart for the then-neutral United States. As prisoners of war, they were taken to the GTR Depot to be confined at Old Fort Henry in Kingston. One of the Germans is said to have shown little concern at his arrest, stating that the Germans would "soon be running things here anyway."

Seven Hungarian POWs, all reservists in the Austrian army, were arrested by detectives on a Grand Trunk train at London station. Here, Detectives Robert Egelton and Harry Down escort the men into the police station on August 28, 1914. The men would be sent to Fort Henry in Kingston.

First Nations recuits from Moraviantown join the 33rd Battalion, CEF, 1914.

Men from the Canadian Expeditionary Force at Wolseley Barracks, 1915, with military transport trucks.

Men lean out of the windows of a Canadian Pacific train to say goodbye in this undated photograph.

Military wedding on Carling Heights, circa 1915.

33rd Infantry Battalion, CEF marching before Wolseley Barracks. The 33rd was authorized on November 7, 1914, and left for Britain on April 1, 1916.

Panorama view of a Sunday field service before Wolseley Barracks.

September 1915 military scene at Western Fair Race Track, which was occupied by the Department of National Defence for the war's duration.

These three brothers joined the 33rd Battalion for service with the 3rd contingent: George, Charles, and Alfred Gleed of West London.

A truck with military blankets, circa 1918. The vehicle, with solid rubber tires, was made by the Kelly-Springfield Motor Truck Co. of Ohio.

Col. Sir John Hendrie, Lt.-Gov. of Ontario, presenting colours to the 33rd Battalion, CEF, at Carling Heights on June 21, 1915.

Officers from the 1st Canadian Infantry Battalion (Ontario Regiment) pose for a photo at Bustard Camp, Salisbury Plain, England. The battalion was created September 2, 1914, with recruits from Military District No. 1.

The 142nd Battalion, known as "London's Own," had a soccer team in 1916. The 142nd began recruiting in London in late 1915, sailed to England in November 1916, and was absorbed into the 23rd Reserve Battalion.

A winter colours ceremony with the 33rd Battalion in Victoria Park.

Knights of Columbus took over St. Peter's Parish Hall as the Catholic Army Hut on Richmond Street, circa 1917. The army huts were recreation/community centres for soldiers, located both at the front and at home (for veterans), like the one pictured here.

During the First World War, Spramotor—which manufactured spraying equipment in peacetime—became a munitions factory for the war's duration. Note the sign at top right in the bottom image that boldly declares: "To Kaiser Bill, with Compliments, the Spramotor Co." The five scenes are from 1916.

## The Boys of 110th Battalion

The war still on, it's summer time,
We await our turn to strengthen the line,
Doing our duty as our boys can do,
For King and Country, and for you.
We pack up our troubles in our kit bags
And always try and smile;
So long as we have tobacco or fags,
To worry is not worth while.
So we are ready to go to the Motherland,
Where they have wet canteens, I understand,
And the Canadian boys command respect
For the way they fought and are fighting yet.
So Cheer Up is our motto; Downhearted, No!
And we will soon be on our way.
We live in hopes to lick them soon
And be home again next May.

**From** H. J. Knipe............

**Reg. No**...................... **Company**..D...........

THE

**110th Canadian Battalion**

**Carling Heights Camp,**
**LONDON - CANADA**

A.M. Reg. No. 57,231

## "I'm Thinking of YOU Everyday."

A Soldier's Letter

I haven't had time to sit down and write,
And thought perhaps you might pine;
So I send you this card just to say I'm alright,
And getting along "real fine."
When the Empire's Call for more men to fight
For her Honour—in me caused a thrill;
I felt I must or else I should "bust,"
So I'm around about London hard at drill
The work it is stiff, we're "at it" all day,
And sometimes half of the night;
But we're hardening to it and getting quite fit,
And thank goodness for "Boots" we're alright.
My duty calls me as you very well know,
To the Front where the fightin' is done;
And when our bunch get a grip on the foe
There's no letting go till they've won.
So cheer up, my dear friend, tho' parted we are,
And though I'm not far away,
My loved ones are ever FIRST in my thoughts,
*I'm thinking of YOU everyday.*

Postcards from the 110th Canadian Battalion, Carling Heights, featuring war poetry. The 110th recruited in Perth County.

135th Overseas Battalion standing at attention in front of the Carling Heights tent city on June 29, 1916.

Soldiers depart from the GTR station in east London. Belton Lumber is visible in the background, while Gorman, Eckert & Co. stands at far right.

The Carling Heights Military Camp housed the 110th, 111th, 118th Overseas Battalions, CEF Engineers, and YMCA. By 1916, there were more than 16,000 troops stationed here—a significant influx, considering that London's population in 1911 was less than 50,000.

The Daughters of the Empire Soldier's Club, south side of Dundas, near the Armouries.

Soldiers halt their training for a midday meal, circa 1916.

Members of the Red Cross Society headed by Lady Beck march along Dundas, November 11, 1918. Thousands took part in the parade celebrating the end of the war, then went to a Thanksgiving service held in Victoria Park.

Victory Bond headquarters and sales team photographed November 14, 1918. The building at 361 ½ Richmond, west side, south of King, has since been demolished.

Return of the 18th Battalion, May 24, 1919. Their commanding officer was Lt.-Col. L.E. Jones.

A warm welcome greets the Canadian Expeditionary Force at Dundas and Richmond on May 24, 1919, as they return from overseas duty.

The triumphal arch welcoming troops home on Richmond Street looking south from Dundas.

The Simcoe School War Memorial commemorated those from the school who died in the First World War. The memorial still stands on Simcoe Street where the school used to stand.

# WORLD WAR II

On Sunday, September 3, 1939, the *London Free Press* published a four-page extra with the dramatic banner headline: "CANADA IS NOW AT WAR. FRANCE JUMPS IN, TOO." This marked the beginning of nearly six years of newspaper coverage of the war abroad, as well as on the home front. Ironically, Canada was not technically at war yet. Britain declared war on September 3, but unlike World War I, this did not mean that Canada was automatically entered into the conflict. However, as indicated by the *Free Press*'s premature headline, there was little doubt that Canada would follow suit. Nevertheless, Prime Minister Mackenzie King held an emergency session of Parliament and King George VI officially announced Canada's declaration of war on September 10.

London was the headquarters for Military District No. 1, which stretched across Western Ontario from Essex County to Bruce County. Recruiting stations were quickly established and London's regiments—the First Hussars and The Royal Canadian Regiment—were mobilized. According to the *Windsor Daily Star*, London factories were also "combed for [German] aliens," who "will bear watching as hostilities proceed." By 1942, the Canadian Fusiliers, City of London Regiment, were also called to action. Troops were originally housed in tents at Carling Heights, but were moved by November 1939 to winter quarters at Queen's Park or the Western Fairgrounds. Buildings were remodelled for the use of soldiers and the Western Fair was placed on hiatus for the duration of the war.

Similarly, the new London Airport—located east of the city near the hamlet of Crumlin and under construction at the beginning of the war—was leased to the federal government for military use in January 1940. By July, runways were paved and C.D. Howe, federal Minister of Munitions and Supply, officially opened the new airport. While civilian flights still occurred during the war years, the Royal Canadian Air Force established RCAF Station Crumlin there in 1940. The station hosted the No. 3 Elementary Flying School and No. 4 Air Observer School, both part of the British Commonwealth Training.

More than 4,000 airmen graduated from London's air program by December 1944.

Considering London's stature as a military centre, it is not surprising that the city voted for conscription by a majority of 24,050 in the April 1942 plebiscite. By the war's end, more than 30,000 men had been recruited from Military District No. 1, with over 500 fatalities.

Life on the home front—while decidedly less harrowing without the bombing campaigns endured by European civilians—was still affected by the war effort and Londoners rallied to support King and country. Over 1,000 citizens joined the Civil Defence Committee, or CDC, which provided civilian training in firefighting, policing, and first aid. Beginning on May 31, 1943, the CDC held a number of mandatory blackouts and air warning tests.

London was also an ideal audience for the government's Victory Loan campaigns, purchasing an impressive $273,383,050 in Victory Bonds over nine sales. On one notable occasion in April 1944, over 6,000 members of the armed services and cadets paraded to support the sixth sales campaign, on what was known as Victory Loan Sunday. Moreover, Londoners regularly organized rallies and concerts to support Britian and its allies. On January 18, 1942, Loew's Theatre on Dundas Street was packed for a concert to raise funds for medical supplies to be sent to the Soviet Union.

Women led the charge on the home front, allowed greater social mobility in reaction to the pressures of warfare and the gap left by men fighting overseas. They organized into military units to perform support services such as clerical work, food services, technical assistance, and driving ambulances and supply vehicles. London's first office for the Canadian Women's Army Corps (CWAC) opened on September 2, 1941, with Helen Brownlee and Dorothy Hansen being first to enlist. However, military service was not the only way for women to be active in the war effort. The Local Council of Women coordinated much of the women's work by setting up the Central Volunteer Bureau, which matched volunteers with appropriate organizations. Many women worked with the Red Cross & St. John's Ambulance, providing food, medical supplies, clothing and bedding for overseas, knitting socks and sweaters, rolling strips of bandages, and putting together bags filled with soap, socks, combs, and razors. Among the women's groups that assisted were the IODE, Hadassah, Catholic Women's League, YWCA, and church groups.

This was also the era of 'Rosie the Riveter'—or in Canada, 'Ronnie, the Bren Gun Girl.' As male factory workers enlisted, their places were taken by hundreds of women who quickly learned to put together airplane parts and other war materials. Local factories employing large numbers of women included General Steel Wares, Webster Air Equipment, and Sparton of Canada.

After a long, bloody conflict, the war in Europe would finally come to an end. On May 7, 1945, as reports came in of Germany's probable surrender, schools emptied, stores closed, people took to the streets, and parishioners filled their churches to give thanks. May 8 became V-E or Victory in Europe day. Servicemen began to return to the city, and, on June 22, cheering crowds of Londoners greeted more than 300 returning servicemen at the train station. But this was nothing compared to August 15, when over 200,000 people—the largest crowd in London since the royal visit of 1939—celebrated V-J Day. With Victory over Japan, the war was finally history.

After Canada's declaration of war—one week after Britain—recruiting began, and London men were urged to do their part in defeating Hitler's tyranny. This sign appeared on the Richmond Street recruiting centre.

On September 4, 1939, men who volunteered for service with local units of the Canadian Active Field Force were brought to the Carling Block on Richmond Street for examination by medical boards. Here, a group of volunteers for the Royal Canadian Army Service Corps arrive downtown by truck. Note the *Free Press* building in the background.

A parade sign urges Londoners to enlist—warning of the consequences if Canadians did not fight.

On September 7, 1939, a military parade marched through downtown London to inspire recruitment. Here, the men march west on Dundas and turn north onto Richmond.

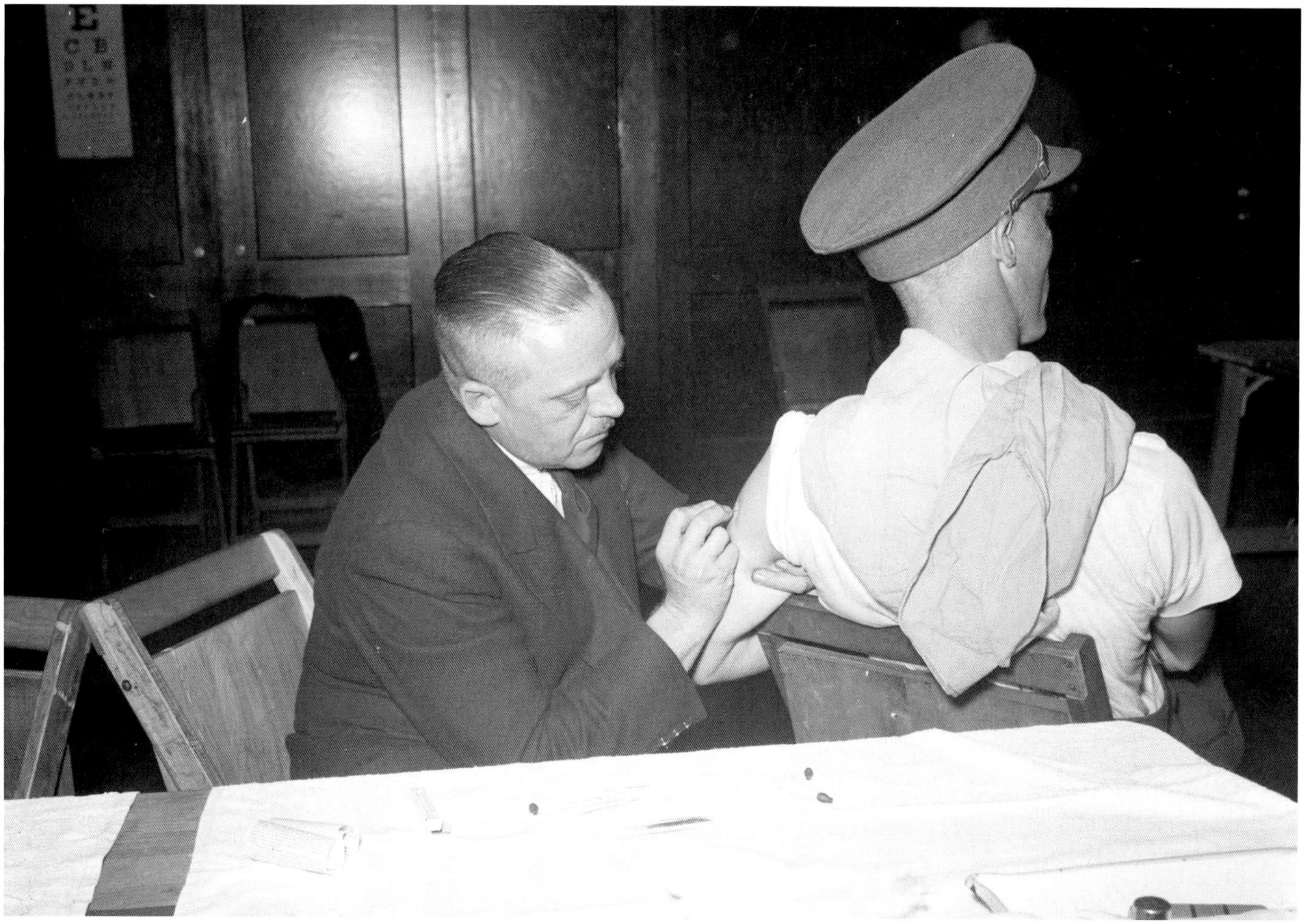

Troops camped at Carling Heights are vaccinated against smallpox in September 1939.

Soldiers of the First Hussars regiment line up for their army pay at Carling Heights training camp.

On October 16, 1939, London's First Hussars paraded from Carling Heights to their new quarters at Queen's Park. Eventually, more than 2,000 troops in the Canadian Active Service Force would be stationed at the fairgrounds for training.

The First District Signal Corps depart London in October 1939, headed for Barriefield (near Kingston) for specialized training before moving overseas with the 1st Canadian division. They were the first unit of the Canadian Active Service Force to leave the city after the declaration of war.

On October 17, 1939, the 114th Bomber Squadron marched along Queens Avenue, then formed a square for an outdoor divine service led by Rev. Charles E. Jeakins, Rector of St. Paul's Cathedral. The 181 officers and men of the 114th then departed London for training.

The Royal Canadian Regiment C-Company leaves London on November 17, 1939, from the CPR station on Quebec Street. According to the *Free Press*, censorship regulations prevented them from reporting details on the troops and their movements, save that they arrived at their destination safely.

The Hon. Albert E. Matthews, Lieutenant-Governor of Ontario, formally inspects the Canadian Army Special Forces (CASF) units training on November 3, 1939, in London at Wolseley Barracks.

In November, London women volunteered for war service in a number of capacities at over 20 offices, as part of the Dominion-wide voluntary registration of Canadian women.

Sappers of the 7th Field Company, Royal Canadian Engineers, dig model trenches in November 1939, for instruction of CASF troops. Inspecting the trenches are Major G.H. McTavish, commander of the 7th Field Company (right) and Regimental Sergeant Major H. Nichols.

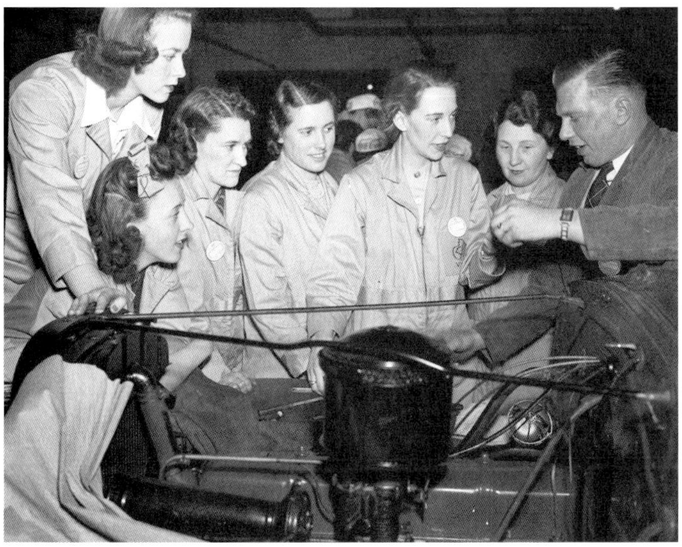

In April, 1940, more than 40 London women underwent 10 weeks of instruction in elementary motor mechanics and roadside repairs as part of their training to become drivers in the Auxiliary Driver Corps.

Mrs. Jack Lavis at the wheel of the kind of truck she might be asked to drive if called to active service.

A group of women prepares to change a tire. Frances Hart is jacking up the front end of the vehicle, surrounded by her class members.

Mrs. Douglas Switzer removing radiator support bolts.

Catherine Hargan lubricates a spring.

On June 3, 1940, Violet and Edward Cooper, aged 13 and 9, arrived in London, Ontario, having crossed the Atlantic to live with their aunt and uncle, Mr. and Mrs. Alexander Ross of 58 Albion Street, for the duration of the war. Both children were Canadian—Violet was born on Walnut Street in London, while Edward was born in New Brunswick. Their parents moved to Welwyn Garden City, south of London, England, three years earlier. Here, Mrs. Ross serves them their first home-cooked dinner since leaving Britain.

Workmen transform Thames Valley Golf Course into a military camp in July 1940. Beginning in August, hundreds of soldiers from NPAM (non-permanent active militia) from throughout Western Ontario would be camping there.

Londoners attend an outdoor worship service in Victoria Park on Sunday, September 8, 1940, after King George VI requested an Empire Day of Prayer. Clergymen and laymen of various London churches cooperated to lead the service.

On May 7, 1941, Londoners lined downtown streets to greet the 12th Battery, Royal Canadian Artillery, as it displayed a variety of mechanized equipment such as artillery pieces, ammunition carriers, transport trucks, and motorcycles. The 12th paraded to City Hall, on the northwest corner of Dundas and Wellington streets, where commanding district officer Brigadier D.J. MacDonald took the salute. The display, part of a recruiting campaign, moved on to Windsor for a similar parade the next day. This photo appears to have been taken from a window at Hotel London.

The symbolic golden Victory Loan Torch arrives at London Airport by bomber on June 5, 1941. Hundreds of Londoners greeted the four-foot-high carved and gold-painted wooden "torch." Here Mayor William Heaman (right) accepts the torch from three guards.

The "King's Own Rifles" pose on Southgate Street in London South. According to the *Free Press* on July 8, 1941: "The unit is composed of youngsters who hope that by the time they are old enough to become soldiers they will have mastered all the rudiments of army life." Organized by Captain Chuck Pinches (left), the boys held mock battles and war games on south London streets.

W.E. Handley of Byron, Westminster Township, has a large clump of firebush trimmed into a V for Victory symbol in July 1941.

Major Arthur Calvert, head of the Salvation Army's London Citadel, rides his bicycle in September 1941 to save on rationed gasoline.

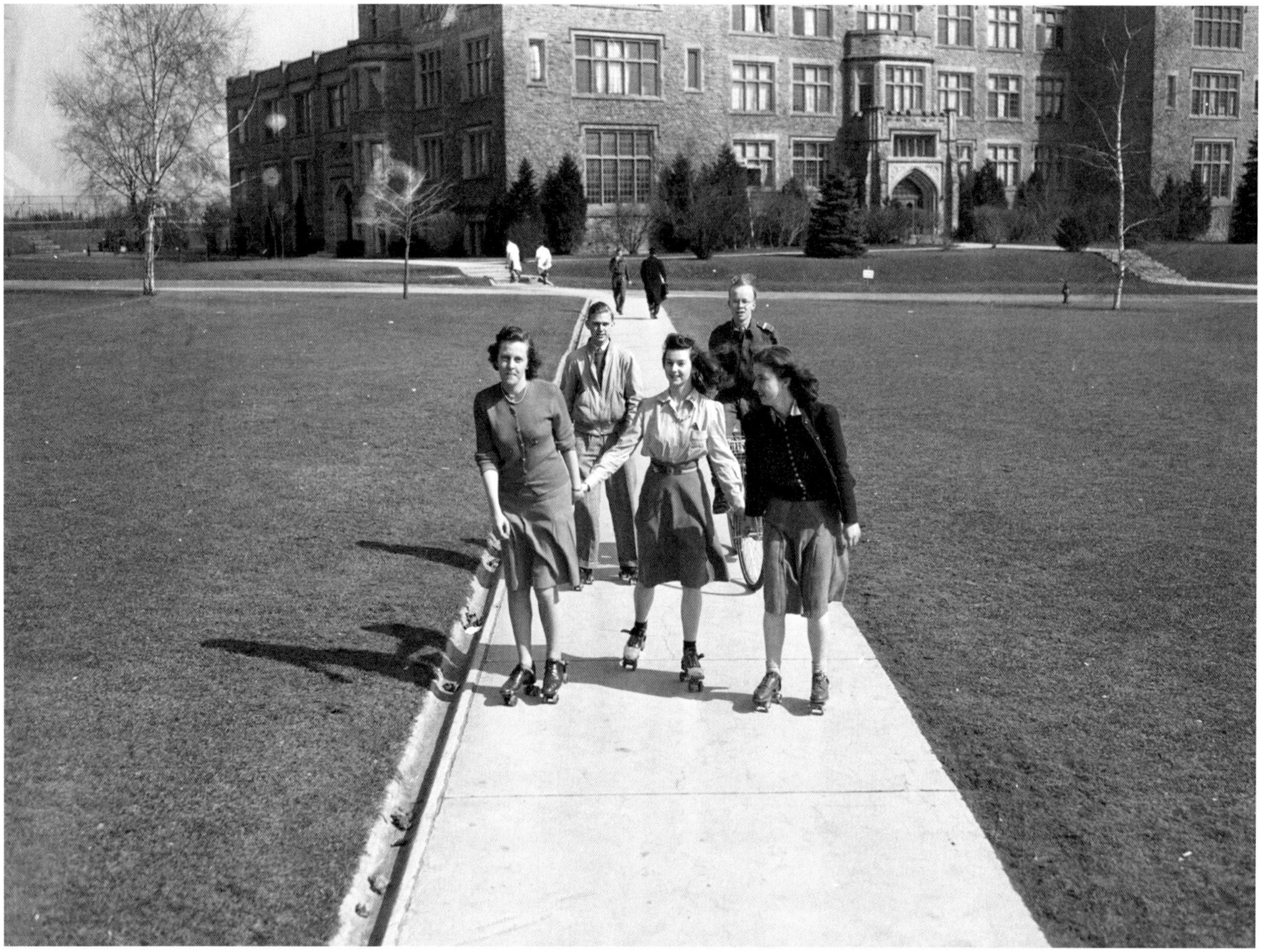

By April 1942, gas rationing meant Western students were bicycling and roller skating to the campus north of the city, leaving cars at home in garages. At front, from left to right, are Ruth Johnson, Peggy Lang, and Mary Scott, who skated from St. James Street to UWO in about 20 minutes. At rear is Leo LaFontaine on roller skates and Kenrick Gunn with a bicycle.

Sparton was one of many London factories that transitioned from peacetime manufacturing to all-out war effort. Hundreds of female staff, pictured here in September 1943, operated the machines.

At last, on May 7, 1945, the war was over in Europe. As soon as the first papers of the *Free Press* Extra Edition were off the press, sailors at HMCS Prevost posted a page on the wall of their building.

Girls at London's Bell Telephone switchboards, May 7, 1945. News of German surrender kept the girls busy as Londoners called their friends and neighbours to tell them the news. Some citizens even called the *Free Press* to learn if the rumours of the war ending in Europe were true.

Sailors fly streamers from windows at HMCS Prevost as news of Nazi surrender reaches London on May 7,1945.

The scene at Richmond and King on V-E Day as victory in Europe is celebrated.

Hundreds of Londoners mob Dundas Street newsboys selling the Extra Edition. The boys ran out of papers only one block away from the *Free Press* office.

Hon. C.D. Howe (left), Minister of Reconstruction, visits a London war plant May 12, 1945. The Ministry of reconstruction was established in June 1944 to ensure a smooth transition (with maximum industrial output) from wartime to peace.

On Saturday, June 23, 1945, hundreds of Londoners turned out at 7:00 a.m. to welcome more than 300 returning veterans arriving at the CNR station on a special troop train from Halifax. The returning soldiers included 50 paratroopers from the First Canadian Parachute Battalion. According to the *Free Press*, "fifty tough-sinewed war-hardened Western Ontario paratroopers, the eldest of them only 27, captured and held the spotlight at the station."

Bulletins on the *Free Press* building announce the news of Japanese surrender August 15.

A group of boys hang the Japanese emperor in effigy in front of a crowd gathered at the *Free Press* building to read the bulletins announcing Japan's surrender.

The V for Victory sign on City Hall on V-J Day, 1945. An estimated 10,000 people jammed the block between Wellington and Waterloo on August 15 for the greatest mass celebration in the city's history.

V-J Day was a wild victory celebration as thousands swarmed the downtown streets. Dundas became a huge dance floor as the bands of the RCAF and army played. All stores, offices, and factories closed and only essential services such as buses were operational.

A victory parade of over 200 Chinese Londoners with decorated floats marched through London, afterwards holding a special ceremony on the Market Square. It was the Chinese community's response to the formal surrender of Japan to China, signed September 9 at Nanking. Over 20,000 people lined the streets and a "dragon" danced before 4,000 spectators in Market Square.

On September 13, 1945, Mrs. George R. Kerr signs a petition to end meat rationing handed to her by her butcher, John Marshall. The petition was organized by the Retail Food Merchants Association. Rationing did not formally conclude until 1947.

# BIBLIOGRAPHY

Adams, Bill, *The History of the London Fire Department: Of Heroes, Helmets, and Hoses*. London, ON: The London Fire Department, 2002.

Addington, Charles; Phillips, Glen C. (ed.), *A History of the London Police Force: 125 Years of Police Service, 1855-1980*; with an update to 1991. Phelps Publishing Co., 1991.

Armstrong, F. H., *The Forest City: An Illustrated History of London, Canada*. Windsor Publications, 1986.

Baker, Michael (ed.), *Downtown London: Layers of Time*. London, ON: London Advisory Committee on Heritage/London Regional Art and Historical Museums, 1998.

Baker, Michael & Hilary Bates Neary (eds.), *100 Fascinating Londoners*. J. Lorimer, 2005.

Baker, Victoria, *Paul Peel: A Retrospective, 1860-1892*. London, ON: London Regional Art Gallery, 1986.

Bremner, Archibald, *City of London, Ontario, Canada: The Pioneer Period and the London of Today*. London, Ontario, London Public Library Board, 1967.

Brock, Daniel J., "The Pioneer Phase of Automobiles in London and Area." London & Middlesex Historian Vol. 23, 2014. pp. 6-21.

Brock, Daniel J.; McEwen, Catherine B. (ed.), *Fragments From The Forks*. London, ON: London & Middlesex Historical Society, 2011.

Brock, Daniel J., *Best Wishes From London, Canada: Our Golden Age of Postcards: 1903-1914*. Gatherick Press, 1992.

Conron, Brandon, et al, *A History of the First Hussars Regiment 1856-1980*. 1981.

Curnoe, Glen, *The London & Port Stanley Railway, 1915-1965: A Picture History*. 1974.

Gibb, Alice (ed.), *London Township: A Rich Heritage, 1796-1997*. Arva, ON: London Township History Book Committee, 2001.

Grainger, Jennifer (ed.), *Delaware and Westminster Townships: Honouring Our Roots*. Westminster Township Historical Society, 2006.

Grainger, Jennifer, *Early London 1826-1914: A Photographic History from the Orr Collection*. Windsor, ON: Biblioasis, 2016.

Kapelos, George Thomas, *Course Studies – Tracking Ontario's Thames: An Exploration of the River*. London, ON: Museum London, 2001.

London Public Library Image Gallery. http://images.ourontario.ca/london/search

McTaggart, Ken & Paul Merrifield, *The History of the Pumphouse and Springbank Park*. 2010.

McTaggart, Kenneth D., *London's Darkest Hours*. 1999.

McTaggart, Kenneth D., *The Victoria Day Disaster*. 1978.

Miller, Orlo, *Gargoyles and Gentlemen: A History of St. Paul's Cathedral, London, Ontario, 1834-1964*. Ryerson Press, 1966.

Miller, Orlo, et al, *London 200: An Illustrated History*. London, ON: London Chamber of Commerce, 1992.

Noon, Alan, *East of Adelaide: Photographs of Commercial, Industrial and Working-Class Urban Ontario 1905-1930*. London, ON: The London Regional Art and Historical Museums, 1989.

Paddon, Wayne, *Steam and Petticoats: The Early Railway Era in Southwestern Ontario*. 1977.

Phelps, Edward, et al (eds.), *Middlesex: Two Centuries*. Frontline Publications, 1989.

Phillips, Glen C. *On-Tap: The Odyssey of Beer and Brewing in Victorian London-Middlesex*. Sarnia, ON: Cheshire Cat Press, 2000.

Richardson, Mark & John Lisowski, *On The Beat: 150 years of Policing in London, Ontario*. London, ON: Museum London, 2005.

The Royal Canadian Regiment Museum. http://www.thercrmuseum.ca/

Sanmiya, Inge V., *A Celebration of Excellence: The History of the Western Fair Association, 1867-2000*. London, ON: Western Fair Association, 2000.

Shawyer, A. J., Broughdale: *Looking For Its past: A History of a Residential Neighbourhood Within the City of London, Ontario*. London, ON: Broughdale Community Association, 1994.

Simner, Marvin, "London's First Summer Resort: The Waterways Region in Springbank Park." *London & Middlesex Historian Vol. 25*, 2016, pp. 5-24.

Smith, Douglas N. W., *Canadian Rail Passenger Review.* Trackside Canada, 1999, pp. 52-95.

Sullivan, John R., *Growing To Serve: A History of Victoria Hospital, London, Ontario*. London, ON: Victoria Hospital Corp., 1985.

Talman, James John, *Huron College, 1863-1963*. 1963.

Torrens, Les, *The London and Port Stanley Railway*. 1984.

Vintage London. www.facebook.com/vintagelondon/

# PHOTO CREDITS

Archives Collection, The Royal Canadian Regiment Museum at Wolseley Barracks, London, ON: 229, 230, 232, 233, 376, 379
Attic Books: 66
First Hussars Museum: 231, 234, 237
Library and Archives Canada: 30, 31, 56, 84, 97, 99–101,133, 145, 149, 160, 162, 179, 229, 230, 245, 267–269, 281, 286, 316, 326, 328–330, 381, 385, 386
*London Free Press* Archives: 207–210
*London Free Press,* courtesy of Stephen Harding: 36, 59, 65, 103, 140, 149, 284, 298, 300, 320, 331
*London Free Press* Employee Association: 14, 201–206
London Life Corporate Archives: 76–78
London Police Archives: 189, 190, 195
London Public Library: 17–22, 24, 27–29, 35, 45–47, 49, 52, 53, 58, 61, 83, 84, 87, 93, 99, 100, 105, 109, 118, 119, 131, 132, 134, 135, 145, 150, 151, 155, 156, 158, 162–165, 179, 201, 213, 214, 230, 238, 245, 246, 257, 258, 260, 264, 265, 276, 281, 284, 291, 297, 298, 303, 304, 306, 307, 309, 318, 322, 323, 325, 347, 357
Museum London: 12, 56, 155, 177, 178, 347, 348
Ontario Jewish Archives: 90
Toronto Reference Library: 135
Western Archives, Western University (Albert A. Phipps Photo Album): 82, 227, 338
Western Archives, Western University (Glen Curnoe): 352
Western Archives, Western University (J. Malcolm Smith Postcard & Ephemera Collection): 26, 27, 28, 30, 51, 53, 56, 58, 85–87, 111, 120, 124, 131, 134, 215, 217, 218, 231, 252, 269, 287, 382, 384–386
Western Archives, Western University (Kingsmill Family Fonds): 72–75
Western Archives, Western University (Labatt Brewery Company Collection): 171–174, 308
Western Archives, Western University (Leonard Family Fonds): 17, 24, 45, 49, 82, 146, 148, 176, 213, 228, 302, 317, 326, 338
Western Archives, Western University (O'Connor and Lancaster Album): 47, 51, 52, 187, 306
Western Archives, Western University (Public Utilities Commission Collection): 268
Western Archives, Western University (Regional Collection): 18, 19, 21–23, 25, 26, 28–31, 33, 48, 51, 54, 55, 57, 76, 81–83, 86, 104, 109, 117–120, 121–125, 130, 132, 133, 136, 139, 146–148, 150, 156–161, 165, 172, 179, 186–190, 216–218, 226, 228, 229, 231–233, 243, 244, 250, 263–267, 281, 288, 292, 294, 297, 303–308, 314–323, 326–329, 334, 339, 340, 347–352, 374–382, 385, 387, 388
Western Archives, Western University (Ronald Harris Album): 24, 281
Western Archives, Western University (Shaw-Wood Family Photos): 133, 387, 388
Western Archives, Western University (Smallman Family Photo Album): 49
Western Archives, Western University (Spramotor Company Fonds): 159, 315, 383
Western Archives, Western University (University Athletics Scrapbook): 359–365, 367–370
Western Archives, Western University (Un-catalogued): 83, 121, 214, 265, 268, 269, 281, 306, 308, 309, 318, 322

All other photographs courtesy of the *London Free Press* Collection of Photographic Negatives, Western Archives, Western University.

# INDEX

# ACKNOWLEDGEMENTS

The author wishes to thank the staff at Western Archives, particularly Theresa Regnier and Barry Arnott, for their assistance in choosing illustrations for this photo history. Other city archives also provided interesting pictures, however, and the author also wishes to thank Georgiana Stanciu (The Royal Canadian Regiment Museum), Steve Liggett and staff (First Hussars Museum), and Don Spanner (London Life Corporate Archives) for their assistance in identifying appropriate photos. The following London historians have provided information according to their individual specialties: Glen Curnoe; retired Fire Chief James F. Fitzgerald of London Fire Department; Paul Grabowski; Cindy Hartman; Genet Hodder; John Lisowski; Brian Logie; John Lutman; Catherine McEwen; Mike Rice; and Marvin Simner. A special word of thanks goes to Stephen Harding, London photo historian extraordinaire, for assistance in identifying baseball teams, steam locomotives, concrete sewers, and other subjects outside the author's expertise. Lastly, my thanks also belongs with the *London Free Press* and Western Archives for partnering with us on this book, particularly to Editor-in-Chief Joe Ruscitti and University Archivist Robin Keirstead for their help in making this project a reality.